KU-430-170

Spurgeon's Daily Treasures in the Psalms

Spurgeon's Daily Treasures *in the* Psalms

Selections from the Classic
Treasury of David

UPDATED AND EDITED BY
Roger Campbell

Kregel
Publications

Spurgeon's Daily Treasures in the Psalms: Selections from the Classic Treasury of David
© 2013 by Roger Campbell

Published by Kregel Publications, a division of Kregel, Inc., P.O. Box 2607, Grand Rapids, MI 49501.

Previously published by Thomas Nelson © 1997.

All rights reserved. No part of this book may be reproduced, stored in a retrieval system, or transmitted in any form or by any means—electronic, mechanical, photocopy, recording, or otherwise—without written permission of the publisher, except for brief quotations in printed reviews.

Scripture quotations are from the New King James Version®. Copyright © 1982 by Thomas Nelson, Inc. Used by permission. All rights reserved.

Library of Congress Cataloging-in-Publication Data
Campbell, Roger F., 1930-
Spurgeon's daily treasures in the Psalms : selections from the classic Treasury of David / updated & edited by Roger Campbell.
    pages cm
1. Bible. O.T. Psalms—Meditations. 2. Devotional calendars. I. Spurgeon, C. H. (Charles Haddon), 1834-1892. Treasury of David. II. Title. II. Title: Daily treasures in the Psalms.

BS1430.54.C35 2013   242'.2—dc23   2012044166

ISBN 978-0-8254-4320-6

Printed in the United States of America
13 14 15 16 17 / 5 4 3 2 1

Dedicated to
Andy and Sylvia Rivers
who introduced me to
The Treasury of David

Preface

Charles Haddon (C.H.) Spurgeon took nearly twenty years to write his rich commentary on the Psalms, titled *The Treasury of David*. His biographer, W. Y. Fullerton, calls it his greatest work. The first volume was published in 1869 and the last in 1885. In his introduction to volume 1, Spurgeon wrote: "The delightful study of the Psalms has yielded me boundless profit and ever-growing pleasure; common gratitude constrains me to communicate to others a portion of the benefit, with the prayer that it may induce them to search further for themselves." Spurgeon's prayer has been answered. As a result of his labor, thousands have studied the Psalms with boundless profit and ever-growing pleasure for more than a hundred years. The length and cost of this great commentary have, however, kept it largely confined to the libraries of pastors and other students of theology. As a result, many have missed out on Spurgeon's practical insights and life-changing observations on the Psalms. I have attempted to enlarge the circulation of this helpful material by making it easier to read and obtain.

Spurgeon's Daily Treasures in the Psalms has been hidden in *The Treasury of David* for more than a century. I have only liberated these treasures by lifting them out of their exhaustive setting and placing them in this daily devotional form. Updating has been done carefully to keep from losing Spurgeon in the process. If you are enriched by spending a year in the Psalms with C. H. Spurgeon, consider your daily delight an answer to his prayers . . . and mine.

ROGER CAMPBELL

Multiplied Blessings

> *Today's Faith Builder:*
> Blessed is the man
> Who walks not in the counsel of the ungodly,
> Nor stands in the path of sinners,
> Nor sits in the seat of the scornful. (Psalm 1:1)

See how this book of Psalms opens with a benediction. The word translated "blessed" is plural ("blessednesses"). May this blessed benediction rest on us.

Here the blessed man is described both negatively (v. 1) and positively (v. 2). He is a man who does not walk in the counsel of the ungodly. His footsteps are ordered by the Word of God, not by the advice of deceitful and wicked men.

And now note his positive character: His delight is in the law of the Lord. He takes a text and carries it with him all day long; and at night, when he cannot sleep, he meditates on it. When trouble comes, he comforts himself with the promises of the Bible.

"He shall be like a tree planted": not a wild tree, but "a tree planted," chosen, considered as property, cultivated and secured from the last terrible uprooting. He is planted by the rivers of water so that even if one river should fail, he has another. The rivers of pardon and the rivers of grace, the rivers of promise and the rivers of communion with Christ are never-failing sources of supply.

He brings forth fruit in his season. The man who delights in God's Word, being taught by it, brings forth patience in the time of suffering, faith in the day of trial, and holy joy in the hour of prosperity. Even the trials of a believer are part of God's plan by which He grows and brings forth abundant fruit.

Psalm 1

The Pleasant Yoke

❯ *Today's Faith Builder:*
He who sits in the heavens shall laugh;
The LORD shall hold them in derision. (Psalm 2:4)

We might call this psalm The Psalm of Messiah the Prince. Let us read it with the eye of faith, seeing the final triumph of our Lord Jesus Christ over all His enemies.

The psalm begins abruptly with an angry question; and well it may; it is no wonder that the sight of men in arms against their God should amaze the psalmist. We see the nations raging, roaring like the sea, tossed to and fro with restless waves, as the ocean in a storm. Where there is much rage there is generally some folly, and in this case there is plenty of it.

But what are they saying? What is the meaning of this commotion? "Let us break their bonds in pieces. Let us rid ourselves of all restraint. Let us be free to commit all manner of sin. Let us be our own gods."

However mad the resolution to revolt from God, it is one which people have pursued ever since Creation, and they continue to revolt to this very day. The glorious reign of Jesus in the latter day will not come until a terrible struggle takes place among the nations. The conflicts of the last days will illustrate both the world's love of sin and Jehovah's power to give the kingdom to His Son.

To a graceless neck the yoke of Christ is a burden, but to the saved sinner it is easy and light. We may judge ourselves by this: Do we love that yoke, or do we wish to cast it from us?

Psalm 2:1–6

God Reigns

> *Today's Faith Builder:*
> I will declare the decree:
> The LORD has said to Me,
> "You are My Son,
> Today I have begotten You." (Psalm 2:7)

The first psalm was a contrast between the righteous man and the sinner; the second psalm is a contrast between the disobedient, ungodly world and the righteous Son of God. In the first psalm, we saw the wicked driven away like chaff; here we see them broken in pieces like a potter's vessel.

God's anointed is appointed and shall not be disappointed. Look back through all the ages of unbelief, hearken to the high and hard things which men have spoken against the Most High, listen to the rolling thunder of earth's volleys against the majesty of heaven, and then think that God is saying all the while, "Yet have I set My King on My holy hill of Zion. Yet Jesus reigns!"

God has reigned at the counsel and ravings of the wicked, and now Christ the Anointed Himself comes forward as the Risen Redeemer, "declared to be the Son of God with power according to the Spirit of holiness, by the resurrection from the dead" (Rom. 1:4).

Here is positive proof of the deity of our Immanuel, What a mercy to have a Divine Redeemer in whom to rest our confidence! Oh, how wise, how infinitely wise is obedience to Jesus, and how dreadful is the folly of those who continue to be His enemies!

Note the benediction with which the psalm closes: "Blessed are all those who put their trust in Him." The more we trust, the more fully shall we share in His blessing.

Psalm 2:7–12

Times of Trouble

⟩ *Today's Faith Builder:*
But You, O LORD, are a shield for me,
My glory and the One who lifts up my head. (Psalm 3:3)

This is a psalm of David when he fled from Absalom, his son. You will remember the sad story of David's flight from his own palace, when in the dead of night he forded the brook Kedron and went with a few faithful followers to hide from the fury of his rebellious son.

Remember that David in this was a type of the Lord Jesus Christ. He too fled; He too passed over the brook Kedron when His own people were in rebellion against Him, and with a feeble band of followers He went to the Garden of Gethsemane. The poor brokenhearted father complains of the multitude of his enemies. The conspiracy was strong, for the number of people with Absalom increased continually while the troops of David constantly declined. Troubles always come in flocks. Sorrow has a large family. Let us recall the opponents of our Redeemer. The legions of our sins, the crowd of bodily pains, the host of spiritual sorrows, and all the allies of death and hell are themselves against the Son of Man. How precious to know that He has overcome all His foes!

David complains before his loving God of the worst weapon of his enemies. "Oh!" says David, "Many are they who say of me, 'There is no help for him in God.'"

It is the most bitter of all afflictions to fear that there is no help for us in God. And yet remember our blessed Savior had to endure this when He cried, "My God, my God, why have You forsaken me?" Surely we should love Him who suffered this bitterest of trials for us.

Psalm 3:1–3

Rest Well

❭ *Today's Faith Builder:*
I lay down and slept;
I awoke, for the LORD sustained me. (Psalm 3:5)

We need not fear a frowning world while we rejoice in a prayer-hearing God. David's faith enabled him to lie down; anxiety would certainly have kept him on tiptoe, watching for an enemy. He was able to sleep in the midst of trouble, surrounded by foes. "So He gives His beloved sleep" (Ps. 127:2). There is a sleep of holy confidence; God help us to close our eyes!

But David says he awakened also. Some sleep the sleep of death, but he, though exposed to many enemies, reclined his head on the bosom of his God, slept happily beneath the wing of Providence in sweet security, and then awoke in safety.

Buckling on his harness for the day's battle, our hero sings, "I will not be afraid of ten thousands of people who have set themselves against me all around." Observe that he does not underestimate the number or wisdom of his enemies. Yet he trembles not, but looking his enemy in the face, he is ready for battle.

David is too wise to venture into battle without prayer. His only hope is in his God, but that is so strong a confidence that he feels the Lord has but to arise and he is saved. It is enough for the Lord to stand up, and all is well. He compares his enemies to wild beasts and declares that God has broken their jaws so that they cannot injure him.

Rejoice, believer! Your adversary is a dragon whose head is broken and the teeth of your enemies are dashed from their jaws.

Psalm 3:4–8

God Answers Prayer

> *Today's Faith Builder:*
> Hear me when I call, O God of my righteousness!
> You have relieved me in my distress;
> Have mercy on me, and hear my prayer. (Psalm 4:1)

This is another example of David's common habit of pleading past mercies as a reason for present favor. Surely He who has helped us in six troubles will not leave us in the seventh. God does nothing by halves, and He will never cease to help us until we cease to need. The manna shall fall every morning until we cross the Jordan.

Observe that David speaks first to God and then to men. Surely we would all speak more boldly to others if we had more constant conversation with God. He who dares face his Maker will not tremble before people.

The name by which the Lord is here addressed, "God of my righteousness," deserves special attention since it is not used in any other part of Scripture. It means, "You are the author, the witness, the maintainer, the judge, and the rewarder of my righteousness." Here is wisdom; let us imitate it and always present our case, not to the petty courts of human opinion, but to the superior court, the King's Bench of heaven.

God is a never-failing comforter. All the deliverances of believers and the pardon of sinners are the free gifts of His grace.

He who chose us for Himself will hear our prayers. When you are on your knees, the fact of your being set apart as God's own peculiar treasure should give you courage and inspire you with fervency and faith.

Psalm 4:1–3

God's Pillow

❭ *Today's Faith Builder:*
   I will both lie down in peace, and sleep;
   For You alone, O LORD, make me dwell in safety. (Psalm 4:8)

Oh, that all would take the advice of David and commune with their own hearts. Surely a lack of thought must be one reason why people are foolish enough to reject Christ and hate His mercy. A thinking person should have enough sense to discover the vanity of sin and the worthlessness of the world.

Ask advice of your pillow, and let the silence of the night instruct you! Let reason speak! Let the noisy world be still.

"It is better," said one, "to feel God's favor one hour in our repenting souls than to sit whole ages under the warmest sunshine that this world affords." Christ in the heart is better than corn in the barn or wine in the vat. Corn and wine are but fruits of the world, but the light of God's face is the ripe fruit of heaven. "You are with me" is a far more blessed cry than "Harvest home." Let my storehouse be empty, I am yet full of blessings if Jesus Christ smiles upon me. If I have all the world, I am poor without Him.

I will lay down in peace and sleep for You make me dwell safely. I will not sit up to watch through fear, but I will lie down; and then I will not lie awake listening to every rustling sound, but I will lie down in peace and sleep, for I have nothing to fear. The Lord's protection is better than bolts or bars. Armed men kept the bed of Solomon, but he was no safer than David, who slept on the ground.

They slumber sweetly whom faith rocks to sleep. No pillow is as soft as a promise; no cover is as warm as faith in Christ.

Psalm 4:4–8

Starting the Day Right

> *Today's Faith Builder:*
> My voice You shall hear in the morning, O LORD;
> In the morning I will direct it to You,
> And I will look up. (Psalm 5:3)

There are two kinds of prayers: those expressed in words, and silent meditations. Words are not the essence but the garment of prayer. Yet the use of words may prevent distraction, assist the powers of the soul, and excite devotion.

There may be prevailing prayer without words and, sadly, there may be words where there is no true prayer.

Let us cultivate the *spirit* of prayer, which is even better than the habit of prayer. We should begin to pray before we kneel down, and we should not cease to pray when we rise up.

An hour in the morning is worth two in the evening. While the dew is on the grass, let grace drop on the soul. Let us give God the mornings of our days and of our lives. Prayer should be the key of the day and the lock of the night. Devotion should be both the morning and evening stars.

Do we not miss much of the sweetness and power of prayer because we do not prepare our hearts to pray and then expect answers after praying? We should be careful to keep the stream of meditation running. Let our prayers and praises be like the steady burning of a well-kindled fire.

And we must not forget to watch for the results of our praying. Let holy preparation link hands with patient expectation, and we shall have far greater answers to our prayers.

Psalm 5:1–4

Worship During Difficulty

> Today's Faith Builder:
> But as for me, I will come into Your house in the multitude of
>   Your mercy;
> In fear of You I will worship toward Your holy temple. (Psalm 5:7)

Having expressed his resolution to pray, the psalmist pleads against his wicked and cruel enemies. He begs God to put them away from him because they are displeasing to God Himself.

Let us learn here that our righteous God hates sin. Its glitter has no charm for Him. Neither on earth nor in heaven shall evil share the favor of God.

Oh, how foolish we are if we attempt to entertain two guests so hostile to one another as Christ Jesus and the devil! Rest assured, Christ will not be at home in the living room of our hearts if we entertain the devil in the basement of our thoughts.

The psalmist has bent his knee in prayer; he has described before God, as an argument for his deliverance, the character and fate of the wicked, and now he contrasts this with the condition of the righteous.

"But as for me, I will come into Your house," I will not stand at a distance, I will come into Your sanctuary, just as a child comes into his father's house. But I will not come there by my own merits. No, I have a multitude of sins, and therefore I will come in the multitude of Your mercies. I will approach You with confidence because of Your immeasurable grace.

God's judgments are all numbered, but His mercies are innumerable; He gives His wrath by weight, but without weight His mercy.

Psalm 5:5–7

Rejoice!

> *Today's Faith Builder:*
> But let all those rejoice who put their trust in You;
> Let them ever shout for joy, because You defend them;
> Let those also who love Your name be joyful in You. (Psalm 5:11)

"Lead me, O Lord," as a little child is led by his father, as a blind man is guided by his friend. It is safe and pleasant when God leads the way.

"Make Your way," not my way, "straight before my face." When we have learned to give up our own way and long to walk in God's way, it is a happy sign of grace and a great blessing to see the way of God with clear vision.

But beware of the wicked man, for there is nothing that he will not say to ruin you. He will long to destroy your character and bury you in the grave of his own wicked throat.

A smooth tongue is a great evil; many have been deceived by it. There are many human anteaters that, with their long tongues covered with oily words, entice and entrap the unwary. When the wolf licks the lamb, he is preparing to wet his teeth in its blood.

Joy is the privilege of the believer. The eternal God is the source of our peace. We love God, and therefore we delight in Him.

Our heart is at ease in our God. We feast every day because we feed on Him. We have music in the house, music in the heart, and music in heaven, for the Lord is our strength and our song; He has also become our salvation. Nothing shall rob us of our inheritance of joy.

Psalm 5:8–12

Weak Days

> *Today's Faith Builder:*
> Have mercy on me, O LORD, for I am weak;
> O LORD, heal me, for my bones are troubled. (Psalm 6:2)

This psalm is commonly known as the first of the Penitential Psalms, and certainly its language is consistent with penitence. It expresses the sorrow, the humiliation, and the hatred of sin, which are unfailing marks of the contrite spirit when it turns to God.

The psalmist is very conscious that he deserves to be rebuked, not for condemnation, but for conviction and sanctification. He does not ask that rebuke be totally withheld, for then he might lose a blessing in disguise. So we may pray that the chastisements of our gracious God, if they are not entirely removed, may at least be sweetened by an awareness that they are not in anger but in love.

A sense of sin had so ended the psalmist's pride and taken away his strength that he found himself too weak to obey the law, weak through his sorrow, too weak, perhaps, even to lay hold of a promise.

When the soul has a sense of sin, it is enough to make the bones shake. Lest, however, we should think this was merely bodily sickness, the psalmist says, "My soul also is greatly troubled."

Soul trouble is the soul of trouble. It matters not that the bones shake if the soul is firm, but when the soul itself is also greatly troubled, this is agony indeed.

But this weak one knows where to look and what arm to lay hold of. He knew his own sins too well to think of merit or appeal to anything but the grace of God.

Psalm 6:1–7

Confidence

> *Today's Faith Builder:*
>   The LORD has heard my supplication;
>   The LORD will receive my prayer. (Psalm 6:9)

You may have times of weeping, but let them be short. Get up! Cast aside your sackcloth and ashes! Weeping may endure for a night but joy comes in the morning.

David has found peace, and rising from his knees he begins to separate himself from the wicked. The best way for us to avoid trouble with an evil man is to have a long distance between us.

It is not enough to complain about the desecration of the temple of the heart, we must drive out the buyers and sellers, and overturn the tables of the money changers. A pardoned sinner will hate the sins which cost the Savior His blood. Grace and sin are quarrelsome neighbors and one or the other must be put away.

Is there a voice in weeping? In what language does it speak? Why in that universal tongue which is known and understood in all the earth, and even in heaven above. Weeping is the eloquence of sorrow. It is an unstammering orator, needing no interpreter, but understood of all.

Let us learn to think of tears as liquid prayers. My God, I will weep when I cannot plead, for You hear the voice of my weeping.

The Holy Spirit had given the psalmist confidence that his prayer was heard. This is frequently the privilege of believers. Praying the prayer of faith, they are often assured that God will answer.

"The LORD will receive my prayer." Here is past experience used for future encouragement. *He has, He will.* All believers can have this same confidence in God's faithfulness.

Psalm 6:8–10

Under Attack

❭ *Today's Faith Builder:*
O LORD my God, in You I put my trust;
Save me from all those who persecute me;
And deliver me. (Psalm 7:1)

This psalm may be called the Song of the Slandered Saint. What a blessing it would be if we could turn the most disastrous event into a theme for a song and so turn the tables on our great enemy! Let us learn a lesson from Luther, who once said: "David made the Psalms; we also will make Psalms, and sing them as well as we can to the honor of our Lord and to spite and mock the devil."

David appears before God to plead with Him against the accuser, who had charged him with treason and treachery. He begins by stating his confidence in God. Whatever our problems may be it will always be right to affirm our reliance on our God. I shake, but my rock moves not. It is never right to distrust God and never vain to trust Him.

And now, with both his relationship to God and his holy faith to strengthen him, David expresses the burden of his heart: "Save me from all who persecute me." We should never consider our prayers complete until we ask for deliverance from all sin and all enemies.

No innocence can shield us from the slander of the wicked. David had been scrupulously careful to avoid any appearance of rebellion against Saul, whom he always called "the Lord's anointed," but all this could not protect him from lying tongues.

Let us be very careful not to believe rumors about good people. If there are no believers in lies, there will be a poor market for falsehood and good men's characters will be safe.

Psalm 7:1–9

Praise the Lord Anyhow!

> *Today's Faith Builder:*
> I will praise the LORD according to His righteousness,
> And will sing praise to the name of the LORD Most High.
> (Psalm 7:17)

The Judge has heard the case, has cleared the guiltless, and has raised His voice against the persecutors. Now the slandered one, with his harp in hand, sings of the justice of his Lord and rejoices in his own deliverance.

God defends the right. Filth will not stay long on the pure white garments of the saints but will be brushed off by the Lord to the anger of the one by whose wicked hands it was thrown upon the godly.

Believer, fear not all that your foes can do or say against you, for no winds can hurt the tree which God plants. He has not given you up to be condemned by the lips of persecutors. Your enemies cannot sit on God's throne, nor blot your name out of His book. Let them alone, then, for God will make all things right. Judgment may tarry, but it will not come too late.

Let us look to the end of the scene. The persecutor has fallen into the ditch he made. He cast forth evil from his mouth, and it has fallen into his bosom. He has set his own house on fire with the torch which he lit to burn out a neighbor. He sent forth a foul bird, and it has come back to its nest.

Praise is the occupation of the godly, their eternal work and their present pleasure. Singing is a fitting way to praise, and therefore the saints make melody before the Lord Most High.

Psalm 7:10–17

Seeing the Glory of God

❯ *Today's Faith Builder:*
O Lord, our Lord,
How excellent is Your name in all the earth,
Who have set Your glory above the heavens! (Psalm 8:1)

No heart can measure, no tongue can describe half the greatness of God. The whole creation is full of His glory and radiant with the excellency of His power; His goodness and His wisdom are manifested on every hand.

God works ever and everywhere. There is no place where God is not. Ascend to the highest heaven, and God is praised in everlasting song; dive into the deepest hell, and God is justified in terrible vengeance. Everywhere and in every place, God dwells and is at work.

In the sky, the massive orbs, rolling in their stupendous grandeur, are witnesses of His power in great things while here below, the lisping words of babes show His strength in little ones.

How often will children tell us of God, whom we have forgotten! Their simple expressions refute those learned fools who deny the existence of God. Many older ones have had to hold their tongues while children have given witness to the glory of God.

Did not the children cry "Hosanna!" in the temple when proud Pharisees were silent and surly? And did not the Savior quote these very verses as a justification of their cries?

He who delights in the songs of angels is pleased to honor Himself in the eyes of His enemies by the praises of little children. What a contrast between the glory above the heavens and the mouths of babes and nursing infants! Yet by both the name of God is praised!

Psalm 8:1–2

Singing Under the Stars

> *Today's Faith Builder:*
> O LORD, our Lord,
> How excellent is Your name in all the earth! (Psalm 8:9)

We may call this psalm, The Song of the Astronomer. Let us sing it beneath the starry heavens at night, for it is very likely that this was the setting when it first occurred to the poet's mind.

The first and last verses are a sweet song of admiration in which the excellence of the name of God is praised. The intermediate verses are made up of holy wonder at the Lord's greatness in creation and at His love for all people.

A look at the solar system has a tendency to reduce pride and promote humility. Well might the psalmist wonder at the exaltation of man in relation to the rest of creation, when compared to the beauty of the starry universe.

Not only is the Lord seen in the heavens above, but the earth beneath tells of His majesty. The countless earthly creatures, from man the head to the creeping worm at the foot, are sustained by the Lord's provision. The fabric of the universe leans on His eternal arm.

Everywhere and in every situation, God is at work. His glory exceeds the glory of the stars. The believing heart is thrilled with what it sees and gives glory to God, but only God knows the extent of His glory.

What a sweetness lies in the little word *our*! How much is God's glory made precious to us when we consider that He is our Lord! Remember that even the heavens cannot contain His glory—it is set "above the heavens" since it is too great to be expressed.

Psalm 8:3–9

Good Resolutions

❯ *Today's Faith Builder:*
I will praise You, O LORD, with my whole heart;
I will tell of all Your marvelous works. (Psalm 9:1)

We have before us a song of triumph; may it strengthen the faith of the bold and stimulate the courage of the timid among us as we see here the conqueror, on whose robe and thigh the name is written, "King of kings and Lord of lords."

With a holy resolution, the songster begins his hymn: "I will praise You, O LORD." Sometimes it requires all our determination to face the foe and bless the Lord, vowing that whoever else may be silent we will bless His name. Here, however, the overthrow of the foe is seen as complete, and the song flows with fullness of delight.

David's praise is all given to the Lord. Praise is to be offered to God alone; we may be grateful for servants of the Lord who help us, but our thanks must have long wings and mount to heaven above.

Half heart is no heart. There is true praise in the thankful telling to others of our Heavenly Father's work in our lives. This is one of the themes on which the godly should speak often to one another, and it will not be casting our pearls before swine if we make even the ungodly hear of the lovingkindness of the Lord to us.

Gratitude for one blessing enables us to remember a thousand others. One silver link in the chain draws up a long series of tender memories. There can be no end to telling of all His deeds of love.

Daily rejoicing is an ornament of Christian character. God loves a cheerful giver, whether it be the gold of his purse or the gold of his mouth which he presents on the altar.

Psalm 9:1–2

A Shelter in Our Storms

❯ *Today's Faith Builder:*
The Lord also will be a refuge for the oppressed,
A refuge in times of trouble. (Psalm 9:9)

God's presence is always sufficient for the defeat of our enemies, and their ruin is so complete when the Lord takes over that even flight cannot save them. They fall to rise no more. We must be careful, like David, to give all the glory to Him who gives the victory. Let us make the triumphs of our Redeemer the triumphs of the redeemed and rejoice with Him at the defeat of His foes.

If we seek to maintain the cause and honor of our Lord we may suffer reproach and misrepresentation, but it is comforting to remember that He who sits on the throne knows our hearts and will not leave us to the ignorant and selfish judgment of unjust people.

In the light of the past, the future is not doubtful. Since the same Almighty God fills the throne of power, we can with full confidence rejoice in our security for all time to come. The enemy and his violence will come to an end, but God and His throne will endure forever.

Whatever earthly courts may do, heaven's throne ministers honest judgment. The prospect of appearing before our impartial Great King should act as a restraint to us when we are tempted to sin and as a comfort when we are slandered or oppressed.

There are many forms of oppression both from man and from Satan, but a refuge is provided for us in the Lord Jehovah. God is a high tower so strong that the hosts of hell cannot take it by storm. From its lofty heights faith looks down with scorn upon her enemies.

Psalm 9:3–10

Singing Through Suffering

> *Today's Faith Builder:*
>   Sing praises to the LORD, who dwells in Zion!
>   Declare His deeds among the people. (Psalm 9:11)

The heavenly spirit of praise is gloriously contagious, and he who has it is not content unless he can excite others to join him in praising his Lord. Singing and preaching as means of glorifying God are here joined together, and in all the revivals of history there has been a sudden outburst of gospel songs. The singing of the birds of praise fitly accompanies the return of the gracious spring of spiritual awakening through the preaching of the gospel.

Memories of the past and confidences concerning the future moved the man of God to pray for all the needs of the present. He gave all of his time to praising and praying. How could he have spent it more profitably?

His first prayer is one suitable for all people and occasions. It breathes a humble spirit, indicates self-knowledge, and appeals to proper attributes and to the fitting Person: "Have mercy on me, O LORD." The ladder seems short, but it reaches from earth to heaven.

What a noble title is here given to the Most High: "You who lift me up from the gates of death"! What a glorious lift! In sickness, in sin, in despair, in temptation, we have been brought very low, and the dark door has seemed as if it would open to imprison us, but underneath were the everlasting arms and therefore, we have been uplifted even to the gates of heaven.

When David speaks of his showing forth all God's praise, he means that in his deliverance grace in all its heights and depths would be magnified.

Psalm 9:11–20

When God Seems Far Away

❯ *Today's Faith Builder:*
    Arise, O Lord!
    O God, lift up Your hand!
    Do not forget the humble. (Psalm 10:12)

To the tearful eye of the suffering psalmist the Lord seemed to stand still, as if He calmly looked on and did not sympathize with His afflicted one. The Lord appeared to be afar off, no longer "a very present help in trouble" (Ps. 46:1).

The presence of God is the joy of His people, but any suspicion of His absence is distracting beyond measure. Let us, then, ever remember that the Lord is near us. The refiner is never far from the mouth of the furnace when His gold is in the fire, and the Son of God is always walking in the midst of the flames when His children are cast into them.

The proud boastings and perverted blessings of the wicked have been received in evidence against him and now his own face confirms the accusation. Proud hearts breed proud looks and stiff knees. Honesty shines in the face, but villainy peers out the eyes.

This cruel man comforts himself with the idea that God is blind or at least forgetful—a foolish idea indeed. If we had a sense of God's presence with us, we would be careful not to wound other believers. In fact, there can scarcely be a greater preservation from sin than the constant thought that God continually sees us.

With what bold language faith addresses God! And yet what unbelief is mingled with our strongest confidence. Fearlessly the Lord is asked to arise and lift up His hand, yet timidly He is begged not to forget the humble—as if God would ever be forgetful of His own.

Psalm 10:1–12

The Lord Hears the Humble

> *Today's Faith Builder:*
>
> LORD, You have heard the desire of the humble;
> You will prepare their heart;
> You will cause Your ear to hear. (Psalm 10:17)

Here the description of the wicked man is presented and the evil of his character traced to its source: atheistic ideas with regard to who is in charge of the world. We can see at once that this is intended to be another plea with the Lord to show His power and reveal His justice.

There is no hiding from divine sight and no fleeing from divine justice. Nor are these the only proofs of the presence of God in the world, for while He punishes the oppressor, He befriends the oppressed.

The poor give themselves up entirely into the Lord's hands. Resigning their judgment to His enlightenment and their wills to His sovereign will, they rest assured that He will order all things for the best and He does not disappoint them. He preserves them in times of need and causes them to rejoice in His goodness.

The psalm ends with a song of thanksgiving to the great and everlasting King, because He has granted the desire of His humble and oppressed people, has defended the fatherless, and has punished the unbelievers who trampled on His poor and afflicted children.

Let us learn that we are sure to come out well if we carry our complaint to the King of kings. Rights will be vindicated and wrongs redressed at His throne. His government never neglects the interests of the needy, nor does it tolerate the oppression of the mighty.

Great God, we leave ourselves in Your hand.

Psalm 10:13–18

When Tempted to Doubt

❭ *Today's Faith Builder:*
In the LORD I put my trust;
How can you say to my soul,
"Flee as a bird to your mountain"? (Psalm 11:1)

When Satan cannot overthrow us by pride, he will seek to ruin us by distrust! He will use our dearest friends to argue us out of our faith, and he will use such persuasive logic that unless we assert our immovable trust in Jehovah he will make us like a timid bird which flies to the mountain at every sign of danger.

How forcibly the case is presented! The bow is bent, the arrow fitted to the string: "Flee, flee, you defenseless bird, your safety lies in flight; fly away, for your enemies will send their arrows into your heart; hurry, hurry, for soon you will be destroyed!"

David seems to have been strongly affected by this advice for it came home to his soul. Still he would not yield but would rather face danger than distrust the Lord his God.

Doubtless, the perils which encircled David were great and imminent; it was quite true that his enemies were ready to shoot at him. But what were all these things to the man whose trust was in God alone?

He could brave the dangers, escape his enemies, and defy the injustice which surrounded him. His answer to the question "What can the righteous do?" would be "What cannot they do?" When prayer places God on our side and when faith secures the fulfilling of the promise, what cause can there be for flight, however cruel and mighty our enemies? There is no such word as "impossibility" in the language of faith; that martial grace knows not how to flee.

Psalm 11:1–3

God's Gracious Gaze

> *Today's Faith Builder:*
> The LORD is in His holy temple,
> The LORD's throne is in heaven;
> His eyes behold,
> His eyelids test the sons of men. (Psalm 11:4)

David here declares the source of his unflinching courage. He borrows his light from heaven. The God of the believer is never far from him; He is not merely the God of the mountain fortresses but of the dangerous valleys and battle plains.

The heavens are above our heads in all regions of the earth, and so is the Lord ever near to us in every state and condition. There is One who pleads His precious blood on our behalf in the temple above, and there is One upon the throne who is never deaf to the intercession of His Son. Why then should we fear? What plots can men devise which Jesus will not discover?

Satan has doubtless desired to have us that he may sift us as wheat, but Jesus is in the temple praying for us, so how can our faith fail? What attempts can the wicked make which Jehovah will not see? And since He is in His holy temple, delighting in the sacrifice of His Son, will He not defeat every foe and send us sure deliverance?

The eternal Watcher never slumbers; His eyes never know sleep. He carefully inspects our actions, words, and thoughts.

God sees each person as much and as perfectly as if there were no other creature in the universe. He sees us always; He never removes His eyes from us. Is not this a sufficient ground for confidence? My danger is not hidden from Him; He knows my limits, and I can rest assured that He will not allow me to perish while I rely on Him alone.

Psalm 11:4–7

A Cry for Help

❭ *Today's Faith Builder:*
Help, LORD, for the godly man ceases!
For the faithful disappear from among the sons of men.

(Psalm 12:1)

Help, Lord!" is a short, sweet, suggestive, seasonable, and serviceable prayer; a kind of angel's sword to be turned every way and to be used on all occasions. The psalmist sees the extreme danger of his position and turns to his all-sufficient Helper, who never denies His servants and whose aid is enough for all their needs.

"Help, Lord!" is a very useful cry which we may send up to heaven on occasions of emergency, whether in labor, learning, suffering, fighting, living, or dying. As small ships can sail into harbors which larger vessels cannot enter, so our brief cries and short petitions may trade with heaven when our soul is too wind-bound and business-bound for longer prayers, and when the stream of grace seems too low to float a longer prayer.

The death, departure, or decline of godly men should be a trumpet call for more prayer. We must not, however, be rash in our judgment on this point, for Elijah was wrong in counting himself the only servant of God alive when there were thousands whom the Lord held in reserve. The present times always appear to be especially dangerous because they are nearest to our anxious gaze and whatever evils are near are sure to be seen, while the faults of past ages are far off and more easily overlooked.

The glory and triumph of our Lord Jesus should encourage us in our life and labor. Made bold by His power we can meet the evils of the times with holy resolution and hopefully pray, "Help, Lord!"

Psalm 12:1–2

Pure Words

> *Today's Faith Builder:*
> The words of the LORD are pure words,
> Like silver tried in a furnace of earth,
> Purified seven times. (Psalm 12:6)

In His time, the Lord will hear His elect ones, who cry day and night to Him and will avenge them of their oppressors. The mere oppression of saints, however silently they bear it, is in itself a cry to God: Moses was heard at the Red Sea, though he said nothing, and Hagar's affliction was heard despite her silence.

Jesus feels with His people, and their pains are mighty orators with Him. Nothing moves a father like the cries of his children; he stirs himself, rises like a man, overthrows the enemy, and brings his loved ones to safety. Man's extremity is God's opportunity. Jesus will come to deliver just when His needy ones shall sigh as if all hope had gone forever.

What a contrast between the vain words of man and the pure words of Jehovah. The words of the Lord are true, certain, holy, faithful, and pure as well-refined silver. The original language here speaks of the most severely purifying process known to the ancients through which silver was passed when the greatest possible purity was desired; the dross was all consumed, and only the bright and precious metal remained.

The Bible has passed through the furnace of persecution, literary criticism, philosophic doubt, and scientific discovery, and it has lost nothing but those human interpretations which clung to it as alloy to precious ore. If we would be Godlike in conversation, we must maintain the strictest purity of integrity and holiness in all we say.

Psalm 12:2–8

How Long, Lord?

> *Today's Faith Builder:*
> Consider and hear me, O LORD my God;
> Enlighten my eyes,
> Lest I sleep the sleep of death. (Psalm 13:3)

David doubtless prayed this prayer more than once while in danger and it is intended to express the feelings of the people of God in their ever-returning trials.

"How long?" is repeated four times and reveals an intense desire for deliverance, a great anguish of heart. And what if there is some impatience mingled with it? Is this not a true picture of our own experience? Oh, for grace that, while we wait on God, we may be kept from indulging a complaining spirit!

How long our days seem when our soul is cast down within us! Time flies like a bird in our summer days but in our winters like one that flutters painfully. A week within prison walls is longer than a month at liberty.

Ah, David, how like a fool you talk, accusing God of forgetting you! Can God forget? Can the memory of Omniscience fail? Above all, can Jehovah's heart forget His own beloved child? Oh, dark thought! It was surely bad enough to suspect a temporary forgetfulness, but shall we imagine that the Lord will forever cast away His people? No, His anger may endure for a night, but His love will abide forever.

But now faith lifts up her voice. Now the tide will turn, and the weeper shall dry his eyes. Note the cry of faith, "O LORD my God"! It is glorious that our position in God is not destroyed by all our trials and sorrows. The title deed of heaven is not written in the sand but in eternal brass.

Psalm 13:1–3

The Song Returns

⟩ *Today's Faith Builder:*
I will sing to the Lord,
Because He has dealt bountifully with me. (Psalm 13:6)

What a change is here! The rain is over and gone, and the time of the singing of birds has come. Prayer has so refreshed the poor weeper that he clears his throat for a song. If we have mourned with him, let us now dance with him.

David's heart was more out of tune than his harp. He begins many of his psalms sighing and ends them singing; and others he begins in joy and ends in sorrow. Here the joy is all the greater because of the previous sorrow, as a calm is more delightful after a storm.

For many years, it had been his habit to make the Lord his castle and tower of defense, and he smiles from behind the same protection still. He is sure of his faith and his faith makes him sure; had he doubted the reality of his trust in God he would have blocked up one of the windows through which the sun of heaven delights to shine.

All the powers of his enemies had not driven the psalmist from his stronghold. As the shipwrecked sailor clings to the mast, so did David cling to his faith; he neither could nor would give up his confidence in the Lord his God. Oh, that we may profit from his example, and hold to our faith as we hold to our very life!

Now listen to the music faith makes in the psalmist's soul. The bells of his mind are all ringing. Sweet music sounds from the strings of his heart. His voice joins in the song and his tongue keeps tune with his soul while he declares, "I will sing to the Lord." The Lord returns our song after sorrow.

Psalm 13:3–6

Expecting Better Times

> *Today's Faith Builder:*
>   Oh, that the salvation of Israel would come out of Zion!
>   When the LORD brings back the captivity of His people,
>   Let Jacob rejoice and Israel be glad. (Psalm 14:7)

Sin is always folly, and it is the height of sin to attack the very existence of God. Though fools themselves, the wicked mock the truly wise as if the wise were foolish. The reason for their mockery seems to be the confidence of the godly in their Lord, so they ask, "What can your God do for you now? Where is the reward of all your praying and begging?"

Taunting questions like these are thrust into the faces of weak but gracious souls, tempting them to feel ashamed of their faith. But let us not be laughed out of our confidence in God. Instead, let us scorn their scorning and defy their jeers. In a short time the Lord, our refuge, will avenge His own elect (Luke 18:7) and free Himself of His adversaries, who once made light of Him and His people.

This psalm closes with a fitting prayer, for what could so effectively convince atheists, overthrow persecutors, halt sin, and secure the godly as Israel's salvation? The coming of Messiah was the desire of the godly in all ages, and though He has already come with a sin offering to purge away iniquity, we look for Him to come a second time.

What happy, holy, heavenly days await us! Blessed are all those who daily look for His appearing.

Psalm 14

Who Walks with God?

❯ *Today's Faith Builder:*

    LORD, who may abide in Your tabernacle?

    Who may dwell in Your holy hill? (Psalm 15:1)

A sense of the glory of the Lord and of the holiness of His house, His service, and His attendants moves the humble mind to ask the solemn question before us.

Considering the law, no one can dwell with God, for there is not one person on the earth who lives up to the requirements mentioned in this psalm. We must learn from the Lord of the tabernacle the qualifications for His service and when we have been taught of Him, we will clearly see that only our spotless Lord Jesus, and those who are conformed to His image, can ever be accepted before our holy and majestic Lord.

In answer to the question, the Lord informs us of the character of the one who alone can dwell in His holy hill. This perfect holiness is found only in the Man of Sorrows, but in a measure it is developed in all His people by the Holy Spirit. Faith and the graces of the Spirit are not mentioned because this is a description of outward character, and where fruits are found the root may not be seen, even though it is surely there.

He only is right who is upright in walk and downright in honesty. His faith shows itself by good works and therefore is not dead faith. Saints not only desire to love and speak truth with their lips, but they seek to be true within; they will not lie even in the closet of their hearts, for God is there to listen.

Jesus was the mirror of sincerity and holiness. Let us be more like Him!

Psalm 15

A Psalm of the Savior

❭ *Today's Faith Builder:*
Preserve me, O God, for in You I put my trust. (Psalm 16:1)

We are not left to human interpreters for the key to this psalm, for, speaking by the Holy Spirit, Peter tells us David was writing about Jesus (Acts 2:25–36). Nor is this our only guide, for the apostle Paul, also directed by the Holy Spirit, quotes from this psalm and testifies that David wrote of the Man through whom is preached to us the forgiveness of sins (Acts 13:35–38).

Tempted in all points as we are, the manhood of Jesus needed to be preserved from the power of evil. Though pure Himself, the Lord Jesus, as an example to His followers, looked to the Lord His God for preservation. Having been preserved, He is able to preserve those who trust in Him.

When He says, "preserve Me," He means His members, the mystical body, Himself, and all in Him. But while we rejoice in the fact that the Lord Jesus used this prayer for His members, we must not forget that He employed it most surely for Himself; He had so emptied Himself and so truly taken on Him the form of a servant (Phil. 2:7) that as a man He needed divine keeping even as we do and often cried out for strength. If Jesus looked out of Himself for protection, how much more must we, His imperfect followers do so!

As chickens run beneath the hen in danger, so do we flee quickly to our Lord. He is our great, overshadowing protector. As the Savior prayed, so let us pray, and as He became more than a conqueror, so shall we also through Him. Let us when buffeted by storms bravely cry to the Lord as He did, "In You do I put my trust."

Psalm 16:1–6

Pleasure Forever

❯ *Today's Faith Builder:*
> You will show me the path of life;
> In Your presence is fullness of joy;
> At Your right hand are pleasures forevermore. (Psalm 16:11)

Praise as well as prayer was presented to the Father by our Lord Jesus, and we are not truly His followers unless our resolve is, "I will bless the Lord." Jesus is called Wonderful and Counselor, but as man He spoke not of Himself, but as His Father had taught Him. It would be good for us to follow His example of lowliness, cease from trusting in our own understanding, and seek to be guided by the Spirit of God.

The communion of the soul with God brings inner spiritual wisdom. He who learns from God will soon find wisdom within himself growing in the garden of his soul.

The work of faith is not merely to create a peace which passes all understanding (Phil. 4:6–7), but to fill the heart full of gladness until the tongue breaks forth in notes of harmonious praise. Faith gives us living joy and bestows dying rest. Christ's resurrection is the cause, the promise, the guarantee, and the proof of the coming resurrection of all His people.

Christ, being raised from the dead, ascended into glory to dwell in constant nearness to God, where joy is at its full forever; the vision of this urged Him onward in His glorious but grievous work. To bring His chosen to eternal happiness was the high ambition which inspired Him and made Him wade through a sea of blood. We have a preview of heaven by tasting God's love here below.

Psalm 16:7–11

Safe in Slippery Places

> *Today's Faith Builder:*
> Uphold my steps in Your paths,
> That my footsteps may not slip. (Psalm 17:5)

D avid would not have been a man after God's own heart if he had not been a man of prayer. He was a master in the art of praying, flying to his Lord in all times of need, as a pilot speeds to the harbor in the stress of a storm. The smell of the furnace is upon this psalm, but there is evidence in the last verse that he who wrote it came unharmed out of the flame.

If our God could not or would not hear us, we would be in deep trouble. Some believers give so little time to prayer that God does not hear them for the simple reason that they neglect to pray. It is more likely that we will not hear the Lord than that He will not hear us.

The psalmist has grown bold by the strengthening influence of prayer, and he now calls upon the Judge of all the earth to give a verdict on his case. He has been libeled, basely and maliciously; and having brought his action to the highest court, he, like an innocent man, has no desire to escape the inquiry but even invites and asks for justice. With Jesus as our complete and all-sufficient righteousness we need not fear, though today should be the Day of Judgment.

It is most assuring to be able to appeal immediately to the Lord and call upon our Judge to be a witness for our defense. "Beloved, if our heart does not condemn us, we have confidence toward God" (1 John 3:21).

In difficult times it is especially important to pray.

Psalm 17:1–5

Under His Wings

❭ *Today's Faith Builder:*
    Keep me as the apple of Your eye;
    Hide me under the shadow of Your wings. (Psalm 17:8)

Experience is the best teacher. He who has been taught the faithfulness of God in hours of need has great boldness in prayer. The psalmist here comes back to his first prayer and teaches us by example, to pray again and again, until we are sure that our prayers are answered. That marvelous grace which has redeemed us with the precious blood of God's Son is here asked to come to the rescue.

What a prayer this is! Consider its moving requests: "O Lord, show Your marvelous lovingkindness; show it to my intellect, and remove my ignorance; show it to my heart, and revive my gratitude; show it to my faith, and renew my confidence; show it to my experience, and deliver me from all my fears."

The title here given to our gracious God is extremely comforting. He is the God of Salvation; it is His present and perpetual habit to save believers. He puts forth His best and most glorious strength, using His right hand of wisdom and might, to rescue all those of whatever rank or class who trust in Him.

Even as the parent bird completely shields her brood from evil and meanwhile cherishes them with the warmth of her own heart by covering them with her wings, so do with me, most gracious God, for I am Your child and You have a parent's perfect love.

This last clause is in the future tense in Hebrew as if to show that what the writer asked, he was now sure would be granted to him. Confident expectation should keep pace with earnest prayer.

Psalm 17:6–12

Satisfied

❯ *Today's Faith Builder:*
As for me, I will see Your face in righteousness;
I shall be satisfied when I awake in Your likeness. (Psalm 17:15)

The more furious the attack, the more fervently the psalmist prays. His eye rests only upon the Almighty, and he feels that God has but to rise and the answer will come at once.

Let the lion spring upon us; if Jehovah steps between we need no better defense. When God meets our foe face to face in battle the conflict will soon be over. We are weak and foolish like sheep, but we have a Shepherd wise and strong who knows the old lion's wiles and is more than a match for him; therefore we will not fear, but rest safely in the fold. What a moving sight it will be to see Satan prostrate beneath the feet of our glorious Lord!

Gold and silver are often given to the wicked liberally and they therefore enjoy all manner of carnal delights. But in contrast with the glories of the world to come, what are these paltry, molehill joys? Self, self, self—all these joys begin and end in selfishness; but, our God, how rich are those who begin and end in You!

As for me, I neither envy or covet these men's happiness, but partly have and partly hope for "far better" things. To see God's face and to be changed by that vision into His image so as to partake of His righteousness—this is my noble ambition, and in the prospect of this I cheerfully give up all my present enjoyments. My satisfaction is to come. I shall awake at the sound of the trumpet, wake to everlasting joy, because I will arise in Your likeness.

Psalm 17:13–15

God Is Enough

> *Today's Faith Builder:*
I will love You, O Lord, my strength. (Psalm 18:1)

Here the psalmist resolves to abide in the closest and most intimate union with his Lord. Our triune God deserves the warmest love of all of our hearts. Love is still the crowning grace.

Dwelling among the crags and mountain fortresses of Judea, David had escaped the malice of Saul, and here he compares his God to a safe place of concealment and security. Believers are often hidden in their God from slander and the fury of the storm of trouble. The clefts of the Rock of Ages are safe hiding places.

The happy poet resolves to call upon the Lord in joyful song, believing that in all future conflicts his God would deal as well with him as in the past. Many are saved mourning and doubting, but David has such faith that he could fight singing and win the battle with a song still on his lips. How good it is to receive fresh mercy with a heart already grateful for mercy enjoyed, and to anticipate new trials with a confidence based upon past experience of divine love!

The courageous man, however, who usually hopes for the best may sometimes fear the worst. Satan knows how to blockade our coasts with the iron warships of sorrow, but the port of prayer is still open, and grace can run the blockade bearing messages from earth to heaven and blessings in return from heaven to earth.

Faith increases by exercise, and He whom we first viewed as Lord is soon seen to be our promise-keeping God. Even fools can believe that God is revealed in the sunshine and calm, but faith is wise and discerns Him in the terrible darkness and threatening storm.

Psalm 18:1–19

February 5

Comfort in Affliction

> *Today's Faith Builder:*
> For You will save the humble people,
> But will bring down haughty looks. (Psalm 18:27)

David's early troubles arose from the wicked hatred of envious Saul, who no doubt persecuted him under the cover of charges brought against the character of the "man after [God's] own heart" (Acts 13:22). These charges David declares to have been utterly false and asserts that he possessed a grace-given righteousness which the Lord had rewarded in defiance of all his slanderers.

A godly man can see that in God's plan uprightness and truth are in the long run sure to bring their own reward. Should he not, when he receives that reward, then praise the Lord for it?

We should keep the image of God so constantly before us that we become conformed to it. This inner love for righteousness must be the motive for Christian integrity in our public walk. The fountain must be filled with love to holiness, and then the streams which flow from it will be pure and gracious.

God first gives us holiness, and then rewards us for it. We are His workmanship, vessels made for honor, and when made, the honor is given to the vessel—though, in fact, it belongs to the Potter. The prize is awarded to the flower at the show, but the gardener deserves it.

This comforts the poor in spirit whose spiritual griefs find solace only from the Lord. They cannot save themselves but God will save them.

A considerable amount of this psalm is in the future tense. We are reminded then that our present joy or sorrow is not nearly as important as our great and eternal future!

Psalm 18:20–28

Strength for the Battle

> *Today's Faith Builder:*
> It is God who arms me with strength,
> And makes my way perfect. (Psalm 18:32)

God's warriors may expect to have a taste of every form of fighting and must by the power of faith determine to conduct themselves like good soldiers; but they must be careful to lay all their laurels at Jehovah's feet. The trophies of our conflicts we dedicate to the God of Battles and ascribe all glory and strength to Him.

Where can lasting hopes be fixed? Where can the soul find rest? Where can stability be found? Where is strength to be discovered? In the Lord Jehovah alone. In Him we find rest and refuge.

Have we been made more than conquerors over sin? Then let us give all the glory to Him who has equipped us with His own inexhaustible strength that we might be unconquered in battle and unwearied in our daily walk.

Climbing into secure fortresses, David had been preserved from slipping and made to stand where a wild goat can scarcely find a footing; this was a perfect example of preserving mercy. Bring out the harp, and let us imitate the psalmist's joyful thanksgiving. If we had fallen, our wailings would have been terrible; since we have survived and stood firm, let our gratitude be equally fervent.

It is a great blessing to be brought into full Christian liberty but it is a greater favor to be able to walk as we ought in such liberty, not being permitted to slip. To stand on the rocks of affliction is the result of sufficient grace, but this aid is needed just as much in the luxurious plains of prosperity.

Sin, death, and hell have been disarmed by our conquering Lord.

Psalm 18:29–42

Our Living Lord

> *Today's Faith Builder:*
> The LORD lives!
> Blessed be my Rock!
> Let the God of my salvation be exalted. (Psalm 18:46)

Internal strife is very hard to deal with. A civil war is war in its most miserable form; we should be grateful when harmony reigns.

If we have peace in the three kingdoms of our spirit, soul, and body, we ought to praise the Lord in song. Unity in a church should especially produce an attitude of gratitude.

Out of their mountain strongholds those in hiding crept in fear to own their allegiance to Israel's king. And from the castles of self-confidence, the dens of carnal security, poor sinners come kneeling before the Savior, Christ the Lord. Our sins, which have entrenched themselves in us as in impregnable forts, shall yet be driven out by the sanctifying energy of the Holy Spirit, and we shall serve the Lord in singleness of heart.

We serve no inanimate, imaginary, or dying God. He only has immortality. Like loyal subjects let us cry, "Live on, O God. Long live the King of kings."

As the Lord our God lives so we would live for Him. He is the ground of our hope, so let Him be the subject of our praise. Our hearts bless the Lord, with holy love exalting Him.

As our Savior, the Lord should more than ever be glorified. He who rescues us from deserved danger should be very dear to us. In heaven they sing, "To Him who loved us and washed us from our sins in His own blood" (Rev. 1:5); this kind of music should also be common in gatherings of the saints here below.

Psalm 18:43–50

Glory All Around

> *Today's Faith Builder:*
> The heavens declare the glory of God;
> And the firmament shows His handiwork. (Psalm 19:1)

I n his youth the psalmist, while keeping his father's flock, had devoted himself to the study of God's two great books; nature and Scripture, and he had so thoroughly entered into the spirit of these two volumes that he was able to compare and contrast them, magnifying the excellency of the Author in both.

The book of nature has three leaves—heaven, earth, and sea—of which heaven is the first and most glorious, and by its aid we are able to see the beauties of the other two. Any book without its first page would be sadly imperfect, and especially the great Natural Bible, since its first pages, the sun, moon, and stars, supply light to the rest of the volume. These are the keys without which the writing that follows would be dark and hard to understand.

Any part of creation has more instruction in it than human minds will ever exhaust, but the celestial realm is peculiarly rich in spiritual truth. Every moment God's existence, power, wisdom, and goodness are being sounded abroad by the heavenly heralds which shine upon us from above.

It is not merely glory that the heavens declare, but the "glory of God," for they deliver to us such unanswerable arguments for a conscious, intelligent, planning, controlling, and presiding Creator that no unprejudiced person can remain unconvinced by them. In the expanse above us God flies, as it were, His starry flag to show that the King is at home. While we bless the God of our days of joy, let us also praise Him who gives songs in the night.

Psalm 19:1–6

The Book of Joy

⟩ *Today's Faith Builder:*
The statutes of the LORD are right, rejoicing the heart;
The commandment of the LORD is pure, enlightening the eyes.

(Psalm 19:8)

The practical effect of the Word of God is to turn man to himself, to his God, and to holiness, and the turn or conversion is not outward alone; the soul is moved and renewed. The great means of the conversion of sinners is the Word of God. Try to reach a man's depraved nature with philosophy and reasoning and it laughs your efforts to scorn, but the Word of God soon transforms him.

God's witness in His Word is so sure that we may draw solid comfort from it both for time and eternity, and no attacks made upon it, however fierce or subtle, can ever weaken its force. What a blessing that in a world of uncertainties we have something sure to rest upon! We hurry from the quicksands of human speculations to the terra firma of Divine Revelation.

As a law or plan the Word of God converts, then as a testimony it instructs. It is not enough for us to be converts, we must continue to be disciples; and if we have felt the power of truth, we must go on to prove its certainty by experience.

As a physician gives the right medicine and a counselor the right advice, so does the Book of God. Notice the progress in this psalm. The writer was converted and was next made wise and now is happy; that truth which makes the heart right then gives joy to the right heart. Free grace brings heart joy. There is no remedy for comfort like that which is poured from the bottle of Scripture.

Psalm 19:7–11

A Prayer for Acceptance

> *Today's Faith Builder:*
> Let the words of my mouth, and the meditation of my heart
> Be acceptable in Your sight,
> O LORD, my strength and my Redeemer. (Psalm 19:14)

M oved by the Scriptures, the psalmist marvels at the number and seriousness of his sins. Augustine wrote, in his older days, a series of retractions; ours might make a library if we had enough grace to be convinced of our errors and confess them. Secret sins, like private conspirators, must be hunted out, or they may do deadly mischief; it is well to be much in prayer concerning them.

Saints may fall into the worst of sins unless restrained by grace and therefore they must watch and pray lest they enter into temptation. There is a natural proneness to sin in the best of us, and we must be held back as a horse is held back by the bit or we will run into it. Every sin has in it the very venom of rebellion against God.

The final verse of this psalm is such a sweet and spiritual prayer that it is almost as commonly used in Christian worship as the apostolic benediction.

Words are mockery if the heart does not meditate on them; the shell is nothing without the kernel; but both together are useless unless accepted. We must in prayer view Jehovah as our strength and our Redeemer, or we shall not pray right.

The psalm began with the heavens, but it ends with Him whose glory fills heaven and earth.

Blessed Redeemer, enable us now to meditate acceptably upon Your sweet love and tenderness.

Psalm 19:12–14

God Hears

❭ *Today's Faith Builder:*
May the LORD answer you in the day of trouble;
May the name of the God of Jacob defend you. (Psalm 20:1)

What a mercy that we may pray in the day of trouble, and what a still more blessed privilege that no trouble can prevent the Lord from hearing us! Troubles roar like thunder, but the believer's voice will be heard above the storm.

We are not to worship "the unknown God," but we should seek to know the covenant God of Jacob who has been pleased to reveal His name and attributes to His people. There may be much to learn about royal or respected names, but it will be a mark of heavenly scholarship to discover all that is contained in the divine name.

The day of trouble is not over, the pleading Savior is not silent, and the name of the God of Israel is still the defense of the faithful. The name "God of Jacob" is suggestive; Jacob had his day of trouble, he wrestled, was heard, was defended, and in due time, was honored, and his God is our God still; He hears and rewards all His wrestling Jacobs.

There is no help like that which God sends, and no deliverance like that which comes out of His sanctuary. The sanctuary to us is our blessed Lord, who was typified by the temple and is the true sanctuary which God has built, and not man. Let us fly to the Cross for shelter in all times of need, and help will be sent to us.

Those who rest on the Lord are often cast down at first, but an Almighty arm lifts them, and they joyfully stand upright. The victory of Jesus is the inheritance of His people.

Psalm 20

Strength from Above

> *Today's Faith Builder:*
>> The king shall have joy in Your strength, O LORD;
>> And in Your salvation how greatly shall he rejoice! (Psalm 21:1)

Let every subject of King Jesus imitate the King; let us lean upon Jehovah's strength, let us rejoice in it with unstaggering faith, let us exalt it in our thankful songs. We shall rejoice more and more as we learn by experience more fully the strength of the arm of our covenant God.

Our weakness unstrings our harps, but His strength tunes them anew. If we cannot sing a note in honor of our own strength, we can at any rate rejoice in our omnipotent God. Everything here is ascribed to God; the source is *Your strength* and the stream is *Your salvation*. Our Lord planned and ordained it, and therefore it is His salvation.

Let us with our Lord rejoice in salvation, as coming from God, as coming to us, as extending to others, and to all the world.

We need not be afraid of too much rejoicing. The shoutings of the early Methodists in the excitement of their joy were far more pardonable than our own lukewarmness.

He who is a blessing to others cannot but be glad himself; the unbounded goodness of Jesus and the loving favor of His Father give Jesus unlimited joy.

His joy is full. Its source divine. Its duration eternal. Its degree going beyond all bounds.

Let us shout and sing, for Jesus is our King, and in His triumphs we share a part.

Psalm 21:1–6

Exalting God

❯ *Today's Faith Builder:*
Be exalted, O LORD, in Your own strength!
We will sing and praise Your power. (Psalm 21:13)

Our Lord, like a true King and Leader, was a master in the use of weapons and could handle well the shield of faith, for He has set us a brilliant example of unwavering confidence in God. He felt Himself safe in His Father's care until His hour arrived. He knew that He was always heard in heaven; He committed His cause to Him that judges right, and in His last moments He committed His spirit into the same hands. This psalm of triumph was composed long before our Lord's conflict began, but faith leaps over the boundaries of time and chants her triumph while she sings her battle song.

He who is most high in every sense engages all His infinite perfections to maintain the throne of grace. He was not moved from His purpose in His sufferings, nor by His enemies, nor shall He be moved from the completion of His eternal plan. He is the same yesterday, today, and forever.

It is always right to praise the Lord when we remember His goodness to His Son and the overthrow of His foes. The exaltation of the name of God should be the business of every Christian; but since we fail to honor Him as He deserves, we may invoke His own power to aid us. Be high, O God; maintain Your position by Your own almighty power, for none other can do it.

Joy should always flow in the channel of praise. All the attributes of God are fitting subjects to be celebrated by the music of our hearts and voices. He alone delivered us, and He alone shall have the praise.

Psalm 21:7–13

Trusting God

> *Today's Faith Builder:*
> Our fathers trusted in You;
> They trusted, and You delivered them. (Psalm 22:4)

This is most clearly The Psalm of the Cross. It may have been actually repeated word-for-word by our Lord when hanging on the tree. It is a photograph of our Lord's saddest hours, the record of His dying words, the memorial of His expiring joys. David and his afflictions may be here in a very limited sense, but, as the star is concealed by the light of the sun, he who sees Jesus will probably neither see nor care to see David.

Before us we have a description both of the darkness and the glory of the cross, the sufferings of Christ and the glory which shall follow. Oh, for grace to draw near and see this great sight! We should read reverently, taking off our shoes as Moses did at the burning bush, for this is holy ground.

"My God, my God, why have You forsaken me?" was the startling cry of Golgotha. To what extreme grief was our Master driven! What must have been His anguish to find His own beloved and trusted Father standing afar off, neither granting help nor apparently hearing prayer? Yet there was a reason for all this which those who rest in Jesus as their substitute know well. Jesus was forsaken because our sins had separated us from our God.

We may think and speak harshly of God when we are under His afflicting hand, but not so His obedient Son. He knows too well the Father's goodness to let outward circumstances libel His character.

Trust is the rule of life with all in the family of God. Ancient saints cried and trusted, and in trouble we must do the same.

Psalm 22:1–10

Help from God Alone

❭ *Today's Faith Builder:*
Be not far from Me,
For trouble is near;
For there is none to help. (Psalm 22:11)

The nearness of trouble is a powerful motive for God's help; this moves our Heavenly Father's heart and brings down His helping hand. It is His glory to be our very present help in trouble (Ps. 46:1).

In our Lord's case, none either could or would help Him. It was necessary that He should tread the winepress alone; yet it grieved Him that all His disciples had forsaken Him. Being friendless is crushing to the human mind, for man was not made to be alone.

Turning from His enemies, our Lord describes His own personal condition in words which should bring tears into every loving eye. He was utterly spent, like water poured upon the earth; His heart failed Him and had no more firmness in it than running water. His whole being was made a sacrifice, like a drink offering poured out before the Lord. Pause, dear reader, and view the wounds of your Redeemer.

Unholy eyes gazed insultingly upon the Savior's nakedness and shocked the sacred delicacy of His holy soul. The sight of His agonizing body ought to have insured sympathy from the throng, but it only increased their savage laughter as they gloatingly looked upon His miseries. The first Adam made us all naked, and therefore the second Adam became naked that He might clothe our naked souls.

Now invincible faith repeats the prayer so pitifully offered before. He wants nothing but His God, even in His deepest humiliation. Imitating Him, the believer can sing, "When I am weak, then I am strong."

Psalm 22:11–21

Good News for God's People

> *Today's Faith Builder:*
> I will declare Your name to My brethren;
> In the midst of the assembly I will praise You. (Psalm 22:22)

Jesus delights in His church, so His thoughts, after much distraction, return at the first moment of relief to His beloved ones. He is not ashamed to call them brothers. Jesus anticipates happiness in having communication with His people; He is pleased to be their teacher and minister.

We may learn from our Lord that one of the best methods of showing our thankfulness for deliverance is to tell others what the Lord has done for us. We mention our sorrows readily enough; why are we so slow in declaring our deliverances?

The spiritually poor find a feast in Jesus; they feed upon Him to the satisfaction of their hearts. They were famished until He gave Himself for them, but now they are filled at the King's table. The thought of the joy of His people gave comfort to our dying Lord. Note who partakes of the benefit of His passion: the poor, the humble, and the lowly. Lord, make us so.

Grace now finds most of its jewels among the poor, but in the latter days the mighty of the earth shall taste of redeeming grace and shall worship with all their hearts the God who deals so bountifully with us in Christ Jesus.

Jesus has provided joy for good times and consolation when we are troubled. Amid the tumults and disasters of the present the Lord reigns. In His coming peaceful kingdom, the rich fruit of His dominion will be seen by all.

Psalm 22:22–31

My Shepherd

❭ *Today's Faith Builder:*
The LORD is my shepherd;
I shall not want. (Psalm 23:1)

The position of this psalm is worthy of notice. It follows The Psalm of the Cross. There are no green pastures, no still waters on the other side of the Twenty-second Psalm. It is only after we have read "My God, My God, why have You forsaken me?" that we come to "The LORD is my shepherd." We must by experience know the value of the good Shepherd's blood shed on the cross before we shall be able truly to know the sweetness of the good Shepherd's care.

What condescension is this, that the infinite Lord assumes toward His people the office and character of a shepherd! David himself had been a keeper of the sheep and understood both the needs of the sheep and the many cares of a shepherd. He compares himself to a creature weak, defenseless, and foolish, and he takes God to be his Provider, Preserver, Director and indeed, his everything.

We must cultivate the spirit of complete dependence upon our heavenly Father. The sweetest word of all here is that monosyllable, *my.* He does not say, "The Lord is the shepherd of the world at large and leads forth the multitude as His flock," but "The Lord is my shepherd"; if He be a shepherd to no one else, He is a shepherd to me; He cares for me, watches over me, and preserves me.

I might want otherwise, but when the Lord is my shepherd He is able to supply my needs, and He is certainly willing to do so, for His heart is full of love, and therefore I shall not want. I know that His grace will be sufficient for me. He will say to me, "As your day so shall your strength be." I may not have all that I wish for, but I shall not want.

Psalm 23:1–3

Unafraid

> *Today's Faith Builder:*
> Yea, though I walk through the valley of the shadow of death,
> I will fear no evil;
> For You are with me;
> Your rod and Your staff, they comfort me. (Psalm 23:4)

This unspeakably delightful verse has been sung on many a death bed and has helped to make the dark valley bright. Each word in it has a wealth of meaning.

"Yes, though I walk," as if the believer did not quicken his pace when he came to die but still calmly walked with God. To walk indicates the steady advance of a soul which knows its road, knows its end, resolves to follow the path, feels quite safe, and is therefore perfectly calm and composed.

Observe that it is not walking "in" the valley but "through" the valley. We go through the dark tunnel of death and emerge into the light of immortality. Death is not the house but the porch, not the goal but the passage into it.

And then, it is not "the valley of death" but "the valley of the shadow of death." When there is a shadow there must be a light somewhere, and so there is. Death stands by the side of the road on which we travel and the light of heaven shining on him throws a shadow across our path; let us then rejoice that there is a light beyond.

Nobody is afraid of a shadow; a shadow cannot stop us for a moment. The shadow of a dog cannot bite; the shadow of a sword cannot kill; the shadow of death cannot destroy us. Let us therefore not be afraid.

Psalm 23:4

Full and Running Over

> *Today's Faith Builder:*
> You prepare a table before me in the presence of my enemies;
> You anoint my head with oil;
> My cup runs over. (Psalm 23:5)

The Twenty-third Psalm is not worn out; it is as sweet to believers now as it was in David's time. May we live in the daily enjoyment of this blessing. David had not only enough, a cup full, but more than enough, a cup which overflowed.

"What, all this, and Jesus Christ too?" said a poor woman as she broke a piece of bread and filled a glass with cold water. One may be ever so wealthy, but if he is discontented his cup cannot run over; it is cracked and leaks. Contentment is more than a kingdom, it is another word for happiness.

"Surely goodness and mercy shall follow me all the days of my life" is a fact as indisputable as it is encouraging, and therefore a heavenly "surely" is set as a seal upon it. These twin guardian angels will always be at my back and beck.

When princes travel they must not go unattended, and so it is with the believer. Goodness and mercy follow him always—the black days as well as the bright days, the days of fasting as well as the days of feasting, the dreary days of winter as well as the bright days of summer. Goodness supplies our needs and mercy blots out our sins.

While I am here I will be a child alone with my God; the whole world shall be His house to me; and when I ascend into the upper chamber I shall not change my company, nor even change the house. I shall only go to dwell in the upper story of the house of the Lord forever.

Psalm 23:5–6

Who Owns All This?

> *Today's Faith Builder:*
> The earth is the LORD's, and all its fullness,
> The world and those who dwell therein. (Psalm 24:1)

Man lives on the earth and parcels out its soil among his kings and autocrats but the earth is not man's. He is but a tenant, a leaseholder for an uncertain time, open to immediate eviction. The great Landowner and true Proprietor holds His court above the clouds and laughs at the title deeds of men.

The "fullness" of the earth may mean its harvests, its wealth, its life, or its worship; in these senses the Most High God is Possessor of all.

The sea is full, despite all the clouds which rise from it; the soil is full, though millions of plants derive their nourishment from it. Under man's tutored hand the world is coming to a greater fullness than ever, but it is all the Lord's. We look also for a future fullness when the true ideal of a world for God shall have been reached in millennial glories, and then the earth and all its fullness will clearly be the Lord's.

He who rules the fish of the sea and the fowl of the air should not be disobeyed by man, His noblest creature. We do not belong to the world nor to Satan, but by creation and redemption we belong to the Lord.

The Christian looks forward to a more stable world and rests his hopes on a more stable foundation than this world affords. Those who trust in worldly things build upon the sea; but we have laid our hopes, by God's grace, on the Rock of Ages; we are resting on the promise of an immutable God, we are depending on our faithful Redeemer.

Psalm 24:1–2

A Question of Holiness

❯ *Today's Faith Builder:*
Who may ascend into the hill of the LORD?
Or who may stand in His holy place? (Psalm 24:3)

Outward practical holiness is a very precious evidence of grace. It is vain to speak of inward experience unless the daily life is free from impurity, dishonesty, violence, and oppression. Those who draw near to the Lord must have clean hands.

If our hands are now unclean, let us wash them in the precious blood of Jesus and let us pray to God, lifting up pure hands.

But clean hands would not be enough unless they were connected to a pure heart. True religion is heart-work. We may wash the outside of the cup and the platter as long as we please but if the inner parts are filthy, we are filthy altogether in the sight of God, for our hearts are more truly ourselves than are our hands.

There must be a work of grace in the core of the heart as well as in the palm of the hand, or our professed faith is a delusion. May God grant that our inward powers may be cleansed by the sanctifying Spirit, so that we may love holiness and abhor all sin. The pure in heart shall see God (Matt. 5:8), all others are but blind bats. Stone-blindness in the eyes arises from stone in the heart. Dirt in the heart throws dust in the eyes.

The soul must be delivered from delighting in the temporary toys of earth. All men have their joys by which their souls are lifted up; the worldling lifts up his soul in carnal delights but the saint is lifted up in the ways of the Lord.

To desire communion with God purifies us. Awakened souls seek the Lord above all; they are despised by men but loved by God.

Psalm 24:3–6

The King of Glory

> *Today's Faith Builder:*
  Who is this King of glory?
  The LORD strong and mighty,
  The LORD mighty in battle. (Psalm 24:8)

Our Lord Jesus Christ could ascend into the hill of the Lord because His hands were clean and His heart was pure. We have here a picture of our Lord's glorious ascent. We see Him rising from amidst the little group on Olivet, and as the cloud receives Him, angels reverently escort Him to the gates of heaven.

He who, fresh from the cross and the tomb, now rides through the gates of the New Jerusalem is higher than the heavens. The watchers at the gate look over the battlements and ask, "Who is this King of glory?"—a question full of meaning and worthy of the meditations of eternity. Who is He in person, nature, character, office, and work? What is His pedigree? The answer given in a mighty wave of music is, "The LORD strong and mighty, the LORD mighty in battle."

We know the might of Jesus by the battles which He has fought, the victories which He has won over sin, death, and hell, and we clap our hands as we see Him leading captivity captive in the majesty of His strength. Oh, for a heart to sing His praises!

It is possible that you are saying, "I shall never enter into heaven, for I have neither clean hands nor a pure heart." Look then to Christ. He has entered as the forerunner of those who trust Him. Follow in His footsteps, and rest upon His merit. He rides triumphantly into heaven and you shall ride there too if you trust Him.

Faith stands by the fountain filled with blood, and as she washes in it, clean hands and a pure heart are given to her.

Psalm 24:7–10

Uplifting Thoughts

> *Today's Faith Builder:*
To You, O LORD, I lift up my soul. (Psalm 25:1)

It is but mockery to lift up our hands and eyes unless we also bring our souls into our devotions. True prayer may be described as the soul rising from earth to heaven; it is taking a journey up Jacob's ladder, leaving our cares and fears at the foot, and meeting with our Lord at the top.

When the storm winds are blowing, the Lord's vessels turn and make for their well-remembered harbor of refuge. What a blessing that our Lord will hear our cries in times of trouble although we may have almost forgotten Him in days of prosperity.

Faith is the cable which binds our boat to the shore, and by pulling at it we draw ourselves to the land. Faith unites us to God and then draws us near to Him. As long as the anchor of faith holds there is no need to fear in any storm.

Patience is the daughter of faith; we cheerfully wait when we are certain that we shall not wait in vain. It is our duty and our privilege to wait on the Lord in service, in worship, in expectancy, in trust all the days of our life.

Our faith will be tried, and if it is true, it will bear continued trial without being overcome by doubts and fears. We will not grow weary of waiting on God if we remember how long and how graciously He once waited for us.

What gems are these two expressions: tender mercies and lovingkindnesses! They are the virgin honey of language; no words are sweeter. Often the workings of God in our lives are mysterious, but in time He will make all things plain.

Psalm 25:1–7

God Is Good

> *Today's Faith Builder:*
>   Good and upright is the LORD;
>   Therefore He teaches sinners in the way. (Psalm 25:8)

Here the goodness and righteousness of God appear in friendly union. To see them united one must stand at the foot of the cross and view them blended in the sacrifice of the Lord Jesus. It is truly wonderful that through the atonement the justice of God pleads as strongly as His grace for the salvation of the sinners whom Jesus died to save.

We must not conclude that God's goodness will cause Him to save sinners who continue to wander in their own ways, but we may be sure that He will renew transgressors' hearts and guide them into the way of holiness. Let those who desire to be delivered from sin take comfort from this: God Himself will be the teacher of sinners. What a ragged school this is for God to teach in! God's teaching is practical; He teaches sinners not only the doctrine, but the way.

Meek spirits are highly favored with the Father of the meek and lowly Jesus for He sees in them the image of His only begotten Son. They know their need of guidance and are willing to submit their own understanding to God's will, so He has promised to be their guide. Humble spirits are endowed with a rich inheritance; let them be of good cheer.

This is a rule without exception: God is good to those who are good. Mercy and faithfulness will abound to those who through mercy are made faithful. Whatever approaching storms may threaten we can rest assured that while grace enables us to obey the Lord's will, we need not fear that Providence will cause us any real loss.

Psalm 25:8–11

Learning God's Secrets

❯ *Today's Faith Builder:*
The secret of the LORD is with those who fear Him,
And He will show them His covenant. (Psalm 25:14)

When God sanctifies the heart He enlightens the head. We all wish to choose our way, but how good it is when the Lord directs our choice! God does not violate our will but He instructs it, so we choose that which pleases Him.

Having learned by grace both to abound and to be empty, the believer dwells at ease, and his soul will be at ease forever! In heaven, ease and glory will unite. Like a warrior whose battles are over, or a farmer whose barns are full, his soul will take its ease and be merry forever.

The secret of the Lord is with those who fear Him. This signifies confidential intimacy and select fellowship. Carnal minds cannot guess what is intended by it and even believers cannot explain it in words, for it must be felt to be known. Neither wisdom nor strength can force a door into this inner chamber. Saints can understand heavenly mysteries. They have been initiated into the fellowship of the skies.

Our Lord has been pleased to show believers the designs of His love in the Book of Inspiration, the Bible, and by His Spirit He leads us into the hidden mystery of redemption. He who does not know the meaning of this will never learn it from a commentary; let him look to the cross, where the secret lies.

We may add to this look of faith and hope the obedient look of service, the humble look of reverence, and the tender look of affection. Happy are those whose eyes are never turned away from their God.

Psalm 25:12–15

Distress Signals

> *Today's Faith Builder:*
>   The troubles of my heart have enlarged;
>   Bring me out of my distresses! (Psalm 25:17)

Sometimes unbelief suggests that God has turned His back on us. If we turn to God we need not fear that He will ever turn from us. The reason for a lack of fellowship with God is always in us, and when that is removed nothing can keep us from fully enjoying communion with Him.

When trouble penetrates the heart it is trouble indeed. Here the psalmist's heart was filled with grief like a lake overflowing with water because of enormous floods; this is used as an argument for deliverance and it is a powerful one. When the darkest hour of the night arrives, we may expect the dawn; when the sea is at its lowest ebb, the tide must surely turn; and when our troubles are enlarged to beyond anything we could have imagined, we may hopefully pray, "Bring me out of my distresses."

Note the many trials of the saints: desolate and afflicted, troubles enlarged, distresses and pain. But note also the submissive and believing spirit of the true saint; all he asks for is a look from God upon his troubled condition. A look from God will make him content, and that being granted, he asks no more.

Even more noteworthy is the way in which the afflicted believer discovers the true source of all difficulties and removes it. "Forgive all my sins" is the cry of a soul that is more sick of sin than of pain, and that would rather be forgiven than healed. Blessed is the man to whom sin is more unbearable than disease. Few see the connection between sin and sorrow; only a grace-taught heart feels it.

Psalm 25:16–22

God's Lovingkindness

> *Today's Faith Builder:*
> For Your lovingkindness is before my eyes,
> And I have walked in Your truth. (Psalm 26:3)

The sweet singer of Israel appears before us in this psalm as one enduring reproach; in this he was a type of the great Son of David and is an encouraging example to us to find comfort at the throne of grace when we are slandered.

Worried and worn out by the injustice of his critics, the innocent spirit flies from its false accusers to the throne of Eternal Right. He was a man of integrity; he had not used any traitorous or unrighteous means to gain the crown or to keep it.

What a comfort it is to have the approval of one's own conscience! If there is peace within the soul, the blustering storms of slander which howl about us will be harmless as summer breezes. When the little bird in my bosom sings a merry song, it is of no matter to me if a thousand owls hoot at me from without.

Faith trusts in God to accomplish His own decrees. Slippery though the way may be, so that I walk like a man on ice, faith keeps me from falling. Straight paths and simple faith bring the pilgrim happily to his journey's end.

Dwell on that heavenly word *lovingkindness*. Is it not an unmatchable word, unexcelled, unrivaled? The goodness of the Lord to us should be the motive for our conduct; we are not under the bondage of the law, but under the sweet constraints of grace, which are far more mighty, although far more gentle.

If we were not so forgetful of the way of God's mercy to us, we would be more careful to walk in the ways of obedience to Him.

Psalm 26:1–5

Integrity and Mercy

> *Today's Faith Builder:*
> But as for me, I will walk in my integrity;
> Redeem me and be merciful to me. (Psalm 26:11)

To tell the worthy praises of the God of all grace should be the perpetual purpose of a pardoned sinner. Let people slander us as they please, we should not cease to praise the Lord. Let dogs bark, but let us like the moon shine on.

God's people should not be silent. The wonders of divine grace are enough to make the tongue of the mute sing. God's works of love are wonderful if we consider the unworthiness of their objects, the high cost of their provision, and the glory of their result. And as people find great pleasure in discussing things that amaze them, believers rejoice to tell of the great things which the Lord has done for them.

Here the lover of godliness states his personal protest against unrighteous gain. He is a nonconformist and is ready to stand alone in his nonconformity. Like a live fish, he swims against the stream. Trusting in God, the psalmist resolves that the plain way of righteousness shall be his choice, even if others may prefer the sinful paths of violence and deceit. Still he does not speak proudly nor proclaim his own strength, for he cries for redemption and pleads for mercy.

Our integrity is neither absolute nor inherent. It is a work of grace in us and is marred by human infirmity. We must, therefore, trust in the redeeming blood and God's mercy, confessing that though we are saints by faith we must still bow as sinners before God. Established in Christ Jesus by being vitally united to Him, we have nothing left to occupy our thoughts but the praises of our God.

Psalm 26:6–12

Our Lord to the Rescue

❭ *Today's Faith Builder:*

The Lord is my light and my salvation;
Whom shall I fear?
The Lord is the strength of my life;
Of whom shall I be afraid? (Psalm 27:1)

Salvation finds us in the dark, but it does not leave us there; it gives light to those who sit in the valley of the shadow of death.

After conversion our God is our joy, comfort, guide, teacher, and in every sense our light. He is light within, light around, light reflected from us, and light to be revealed to us. Notice that it is not said merely that the Lord gives light, but that He *is* light; nor that He gives salvation, but that He *is* salvation. He, then, who by faith has laid hold on God, has all covenant blessings in his possession.

The powers of darkness are not to be feared, for the Lord our light destroys them; and the damnation of hell is not to be dreaded by us, for the Lord is our salvation. Our life derives all its strength from Him who is the author of it; if He is pleased to make us strong we cannot be weakened by all the efforts of the adversary. "If God is for us, who can be against us" (Rom. 8:31), either now or in time to come?

It is a good sign if the wicked hate us. If our foes were godly people, we would have cause for concern, but the hatred of the wicked is better than their love.

Before the actual conflict, the warrior's heart may be filled with fear. The shadow of anticipated trouble is, to timid minds, a more powerful source of anxiety than the trouble itself. But when the battle begins, faith's shield will ward off the blows and faith's banners will wave in spite of our foes.

Psalm 27:1–3

Heart's Desire

> *Today's Faith Builder:*

  One thing I have desired of the Lord,
  That will I seek:
  That I may dwell in the house of the Lord
  All the days of my life,
  To behold the beauty of the Lord,
  And to inquire in His temple. (Psalm 27:4)

Divided goals bring distraction, weakness, disappointment. The man of one Book and one pursuit is successful. Let all our affection become one affection, and that be set on heavenly things.

God judges us by the desire of our hearts. Our desire of the Lord should be sanctified, humble, constant, submissive, fervent, and focused on one goal. This is the right target for desires, the right well into which to dip our buckets, the door to knock at, the bank to draw on.

Under David's painful circumstances we might have expected him to desire rest, safety, and a thousand other good things, but he has set his heart on the pearl and leaves the rest. David desired above all things to be one of the household of God, a home-born child, living at home with his Father.

We must not attend the meetings of believers to see and be seen or merely to hear the minister. Instead, we must gather with the saints intent upon learning more of our loving Father, more of the glorified Jesus, more of the mysterious Spirit, in order to more lovingly admire and more reverently adore our glorious God.

We should make our visits to the Lord's house inquirers' meetings where we sit at Jesus' feet and give our full attention to learning of Him.

Psalm 27:4–6

Strength for Fainting Hearts

❯ *Today's Faith Builder:*
> Wait on the LORD;
> Be of good courage,
> And He shall strengthen your heart;
> Wait, I say, on the LORD! (Psalm 27:14)

We may expect answers to prayer, but if we would have the Lord hear our voice, we must be responsive to His voice. The true heart should echo the will of God as the rocks among the Alps repeat the sweetest music, the notes of the peasant's horn. Would to God that we were more sensitive to His Spirit.

Faintness of heart is a common weakness; even he who slew Goliath was subject to its attacks. Faith prevents fainting. Hope is heaven's comfort for present sorrow.

We must believe to see, not see to believe; we must await the appointed time and satisfy our soul's hunger with foretastes of the Lord's eternal goodness, which will soon be our feast and song.

Wait at the Lord's door with prayer; wait at His feet with humility; wait at His table with service; wait at His window with expectancy. Those seeking help often receive nothing but a cold shoulder from earthly benefactors after long and patient waiting; he has a better hope whose Benefactor is in the skies.

Let the heart be strengthened and the whole body is filled with power; a strong heart makes a strong arm.

What strength is this which God Himself gives to the heart? Consider the martyrs and see their glorious deeds. Go to God and get such power yourself. "Wait, I say, on the LORD!"

Psalm 27:7–14

A Troubled Believer's Cry

> *Today's Faith Builder:*
> Hear the voice of my supplications
> When I cry to You,
> When I lift up my hands toward Your holy sanctuary. (Psalm 28:2)

A cry is a natural expression of sorrow, but to bring help the cry must be directed to the Lord. When we consider the readiness of the Lord to hear and His ability to aid, we will see good reasons for directing all our appeals at once to the God of our salvation.

The unchanging Lord is our rock, the immovable foundation of all our hopes and our refuge in trouble. We will flee to Him in every hour of danger. It will be useless to cry to the rocks when the day of His wrath has come (Rev. 6:14–17), but today our Rock responds to our cries.

When God seems to close His ear, we must not close our mouths, but rather cry more earnestly. Those to whom prayer is but a religious exercise may be content without answers to prayer but not those who pray in faith. They are not satisfied with prayer being only a way to calm the mind and subdue the will—they must go further and obtain actual replies from heaven.

How sad if the Lord should become forever silent to our prayers! This thought suggested itself to David, and he turned it into a plea, teaching us to argue and reason with God in our prayers.

Uplifted hands have ever been a form of devout posture and are intended to signify a reaching upward toward God, an eagerness to receive the blessing being sought. We stretch out empty hands, we lift them toward the mercy seat of Jesus, from there expecting answers to our prayers.

Psalm 28:1–5

A Time for Prayer and Praise

> *Today's Faith Builder:*
> Blessed be the LORD,
> Because He has heard the voice of my supplications! (Psalm 28:6)

Believers are full of benedictions; they are blessed and a blessing; but they give their best blessings to their glorious Lord.

Our psalm was a prayer up to this point, and now it turns to praise. They who pray well will soon praise well. Prayer and praise are the two lips of the soul: two bells to ring out sweet and acceptable music in the ears of God; two angels to climb Jacob's ladder; two altars smoking with incense; two of Solomon's lilies dropping sweet-smelling myrrh. They are two young deer that are twins, feeding on the mountain of myrrh and the hill of frankincense.

Real praise is based on reason; it is not irrational emotion but rises like a pure spring from the depths of experience. Answered prayers should be acknowledged. Do we not often fail to give thanks?

Would it not greatly encourage others and strengthen us if we faithfully recorded God's goodness, and made a point of voicing our praise for it? We should shun ingratitude and live daily in the heavenly atmosphere of thankful love.

The Lord uses His power on our behalf and infuses His strength into us in our hours of weakness. Every day the believer may say, "I am helped."

We serve a great God. Let us greatly rejoice in Him. A song is the soul's finest method of expressing its happiness.

When the heart is glowing, the lips should not be silent. When God blesses us, we should bless Him with all our heart.

Psalm 28:6–9

Glory to God!

> *Today's Faith Builder:*
> Give unto the LORD the glory due to His name;
> Worship the LORD in the beauty of holiness. (Psalm 29:2)

This psalm is meant to express the glory of God as heard in the pealing thunder. Just as the Eighth Psalm is to be read by moonlight, when the stars are bright, as the Nineteenth needs the rays of the rising sun to bring out its beauty, so this one can be best understood beneath the dark clouds of a storm, by the glare of lightning, or in that descending dusk which announces the war of elements.

God is seen everywhere, and all the earth is hushed by the majesty of His presence. The Word of God in the law and the gospel is here also depicted in its majesty of power. The voice of God in Jesus Christ is full of majesty, so we have God's works and God's Word joined together.

Neither men nor angels can confer anything upon Jehovah, but they should recognize His glory and might and give Him glory in their songs and in their hearts.

Many are backward in glorifying God; especially successful people, who are often too taken with their own glory to spare time to give God His rightful praise. We should not need to be pressured to give what is due, especially when the payment is so pleasant.

In the past, worship was cumbered with ceremony, and men gathered around one dedicated building, which was symbolic of the beauty of holiness. But now our worship is spiritual, and the architecture of the house and the garments of the worshipers are of no importance; the spiritual beauty of inward purity and outward holiness is far more precious to our holy God.

Psalm 29:1–4

Strength and Peace

> *Today's Faith Builder:*
> The LORD will give strength to His people;
> The LORD will bless His people with peace. (Psalm 29:11)

The voice of our dying Lord split the rocks and opened the graves; His living voice still works wonders. The hills of our sins leap into His grave and are buried in the red sea of His blood when the voice of His intercession is heard.

Flames of fire attend the voice of God in the gospel, illuminating and melting the hearts of men; by these He consumes our lusts and kindles in us a holy flame of ever-inspiring love and holiness.

Power was displayed in the hurricane whose course this psalm so clearly pictures; and now, in the cool calm after the storm, that power is promised to be the strength of the chosen. He who wings the unerring lightning bolt will give His redeemed the wings of eagles. He who shakes the earth with His voice will terrify the enemies of His saints and give His children peace.

Why are we weak when we have divine strength available? Why are we troubled when the Lord's own peace is ours? Jesus the mighty God is our peace. What a blessing this is today! What a blessing it will be to us in that day of the Lord which will bring darkness to the ungodly!

Is this not a great psalm to be sung in stormy weather?

Can you sing during the thunder?

Will you be able to sing when the last thunders are let loose, and Jesus judges the living and the dead?

If you are a believer, your heritage of strength and peace will surely start you singing.

Psalm 29:5–11

He Lifts Us Up

⟩ *Today's Faith Builder:*
I will extol You, O Lord, for You have lifted me up,
And have not let my foes rejoice over me. (Psalm 30:1)

The psalmist had a reason for the praise that was in his heart. He had been drawn up like a prisoner from a dungeon, like Joseph out of the pit, and therefore he loved His Deliverer.

Grace has lifted us out of the pit of hell, from the ditch of sin, from the "Slough of Despond," from the bed of sickness, from the bondage of doubts and fears. Have we no song to offer for all this?

How has our Lord lifted us? He has lifted us up from our sins and placed us in the family of God; lifted us up into union with Christ to sit together with Him in heavenly places (Eph. 1:3). Lift high the name of our God, for He has lifted us above the stars.

The devil and all our spiritual enemies have not been permitted to rejoice over us. Let us give all the glory to Him who has sustained us in our integrity.

David is sure, beyond a doubt, that God has done great things for him, so he is glad. He had descended to the brink of the grave and yet was restored to tell of the patience of God with him. Nor was this all; he admitted that nothing but grace had kept him from the lowest hell, and this made him doubly thankful.

To be spared from the grave is much; to be delivered from the pit is more. We have cause for praise, since both deliverances are traceable to the glorious right hand of the Lord, who is the only Preserver of life, and the only Redeemer of our souls from hell.

Psalm 30:1–3

God Gives a Song

> *Today's Faith Builder:*
> Sing praise to the Lᴏʀᴅ, you saints of His,
> And give thanks at the remembrance of His holy name.
>
> (Psalm 30:4)

"Join my song; assist me in expressing my gratitude," urges the psalmist. David felt that he could not praise God enough himself, and therefore he would enlist the hearts and voices of others. He would not fill his choir with hypocrites but with sanctified people who could sing from their hearts. He calls to you, people of God, because you are saints; and if sinners are wickedly silent, let your holiness move you to sing.

You are His saints: chosen, blood-bought, called, and set apart for God; sanctified on purpose that you should offer the daily sacrifice of praise. Abound in this heavenly duty.

Singing to the Lord is a pleasing exercise, a profitable engagement. Do not require others to stir you up to so pleasant a service.

Let your songs express thankfulness in which the Lord's mercies live again in joyful remembrance. Remembering the past should tune our harps, even if present joys are lacking.

Holiness is an attribute which inspires the deepest awe. "Holy, holy, holy!" is the song of the seraphim and cherubim; let us join in it not reluctantly, as though we trembled at the holiness of God, but cheerfully, as humbly rejoicing in it.

Even in the dreary winter the daystar lights his lamp. When the Sun of Righteousness comes, we wipe our eyes and joy chases out intruding sorrow. Mourning only lasts till morning.

Psalm 30:4–6

He Makes Us Glad

❯ *Today's Faith Builder:*
You have turned for me my mourning into dancing;
You have put off my sackcloth and clothed me with gladness.
(Psalm 30:11)

Prayer is the unfailing resource of God's people. If they are driven to their wits' end, they may still go to the mercy seat.

When an earthquake makes our mountain tremble, the throne of grace still stands firm, and we may come to it. Let us never forget to pray nor doubt the success of prayer. Prayer will succeed when all else fails.

"Hear, O LORD, and have mercy upon me" is a short and comprehensive petition, available at all seasons. Let us use it often.

"LORD, be my helper" is another compact, expressive, ever fitting prayer. It is suitable to hundreds of experiences of the Lord's people; it is fitting for the minister when he is going to preach, to the sufferer upon a bed of pain, to the toiler in the field of service, to the believer under temptation, to the man of God under adversity. When God helps, difficulties vanish. He is the help of His people, a very present help in trouble (Ps. 46:1).

God takes away the mourning of His people, and what does He give them instead? Quiet and peace? Yes, and a great deal more. He makes their hearts dance at the sound of His name.

He takes off their sackcloth. That is good. What a delight to be rid of the garments of woe! But what then? He clothes them with that royal vestment which is the garment of glorified spirits in heaven.

Glory be to You, O God, by a sense of full forgiveness and present justification, You have filled me with all Your fullness.

Psalm 30:7–12

The One to Trust

❯ *Today's Faith Builder:*
    In You, O LORD, I put my trust;
    Let me never be ashamed;
    Deliver me in Your righteousness. (Psalm 31:1)

The psalmist has but one refuge, the best one. Though other things be doubtful, he relies on Jehovah. David states this positively; he begins with it, lest by the stress of his trials he should forget it.

This statement of faith is the support by which he intends to be delivered from his trouble. He dwells on it as a comfort for himself and as a plea with God. No mention is made of merit; his faith relies on divine favor and faithfulness, and on these alone.

How can the Lord permit anyone to be ultimately put to shame who depends on Him alone? This would not be dealing like a God of truth and grace. It would bring dishonor to God Himself if faith were not in the end rewarded. Faith dares to look even to the sword of justice for protection; while God is righteous, faith will not be proven futile and fanatical.

Faith is the foundation of prayer. Our appeal is not to any supposed virtue in ourselves, but to the glorious goodness and grace in the character of God.

The enemies of David were cunning as well as strong; if they could not conquer him by power, they would capture him by craft. Our spiritual foes are the same; like their leader, the Serpent, they seek to trap us by deceit.

Past deliverances are strong pleas for present assistance. What the Lord has done He will do again, for He does not change.

Psalm 31:1–6

Hope in Adversity

⟩ *Today's Faith Builder:*

> I will be glad and rejoice in Your mercy,
> For You have considered my trouble;
> You have known my soul in adversities. (Psalm 31:7)

The psalmist is grateful for mercy in the past and joyfully anticipates mercy in the future, so he praises God in spite of his problems. He finds hope and rejoices in adversity. In our most earnest prayers, we must bless the Lord. Praise is never a hindrance to prayer, but rather a refreshment to it.

God acknowledges His own when others are ashamed to admit they know them. He never refuses to know His friends. He does not think less of them for their poverty and does not misjudge them and cast them off when their faces are lean with sickness or their hearts heavy with depression.

Moreover, the Lord Jesus knows us in our sorrows, having a deep sympathy for us in them. When others cannot enter into our griefs for lack of understanding, Jesus dives into the lowest depths with us, comprehending our deepest woes, because He has experienced them all.

Jesus is a Physician who knows every case; nothing is new to Him. When we are so bewildered that we do not know our own condition, He knows us completely. Oh, for grace to know more of Him!

The enemy may get a temporary advantage over us, but we are like men in prison with the door open. God will not let us be kept in bondage; He always provides a way of escape.

Many saints have had their greatest spiritual growth while going through their most serious difficulties. They have discovered that God is equal to every emergency.

Psalm 31:7–14

His Marvelous Kindness

❭ *Today's Faith Builder:*
Blessed be the LORD,
For He has shown me His marvelous kindness in a strong city!
(Psalm 31:21)

The sovereign Determiner of destiny holds all the issues of life in His own power. We are not strays on the ocean of fate but are steered by infinite wisdom toward our desired haven. Providence is a soft pillow for anxious heads, a grave for despair.

Give me the sunshine of heaven in my soul, and I will defy the storms of earth. Permit me to know a sense of Your favor, O Lord, and a consciousness that You are pleased with my manner of life, and all may frown and slander as they will. It is always enough for a servant if he pleases his master; others may be dissatisfied, but he is not their servant, they do not pay his wages, and their opinions carry no weight with him.

Truly the life of faith is a miracle. We serve a good Master. Faith receives a large reward even now but looks for her full inheritance in the future.

Dwellers at the foot of the cross of Christ are not bothered by the sneers of the proud. The wounds of Jesus heal all the scars which the jagged weapons of contempt can inflict upon us. When armed with the mind which was in Christ Jesus, the heart is invulnerable to all the darts of pride.

Keep up your spirit. Fear weakens, courage strengthens.

Our Lord will draw very near to us in our adversity and put His own power into us. God is faithful and does not fail His children; why then should we be afraid?

Psalm 31:15–24

Forgiveness

> *Today's Faith Builder:*
> Blessed is he whose transgression is forgiven,
> Whose sin is covered. (Psalm 32:1)

Like the Sermon on the Mount, this psalm begins with beatitudes. This is the second Psalm of Benediction.

Pardoning mercy is of all things in the world most to be prized, for it is the only sure way to happiness. Blessedness is not promised to one who has been a diligent law-keeper, for then it would never come to us, but rather to a lawbreaker, who by grace most rich and free has been forgiven.

Self-righteous Pharisees have no part in these blessings. Over the returning prodigal the word of welcome is here pronounced, and the music and dancing begin. A full, instantaneous, irreversible pardon of transgressions turns the poor sinner's hell into heaven and makes the heir of wrath a partaker in blessings.

What a miracle of deliverance! It cost our Savior a sweat of blood to bear our load. It cost Him His life to take it away. Samson carried the gates of Gaza, but what was that to the weight which Jesus bore on our behalf?

Christ's atonement is the propitiation, the covering, the making of an end of sin. When a sinner sees this, believes it, and trusts in Christ as Savior he is accepted into the family of God and therefore enjoys a foretaste of heaven.

The three words to denote our disobedience, transgression, sin, and iniquity are the three-headed dog at the gates of hell, but our glorious Lord has silenced its barkings forever against His own believing ones. The trinity of sin is overcome by the Trinity of heaven.

Psalm 32:1–2

Confession and Cleansing

> *Today's Faith Builder:*
> I acknowledged my sin to You,
> And my iniquity I have not hidden.
> I said, "I will confess my transgressions to the LORD,"
> And You forgave the iniquity of my sin. (Psalm 32:5)

What a killing thing is sin! It is a pestilent disease, a fire in the bones! While we cover our sin it rages within, and like a wound it swells horribly and torments terribly.

David's horror at his great guilt drove him to continual remorse. His voice was now unlike the speech of man but was so full of sighing and groaning that it resembled the hoarse roaring of a wounded animal.

None know the pangs of conviction but those who have endured them. Under terrors of conscience, men have little rest by night, for the grim thoughts of the day pursue them to their bedrooms and haunt their dreams, or else they lie awake in a cold sweat of anxiety.

Unconfessed transgression, like poison, dried up the fountain of the psalmist's strength and made him like a tree blasted by lightning or a plant withered by the scorching heat of a tropical sun.

The first thing we can do, if we would be pardoned, is to acknowledge our sin; if we are too proud for this we deserve punishment. We must, as far as possible, unveil the secrets of the soul. A full confession softens and humbles the heart.

When the soul determines to plead guilty, forgiveness is near; so David wrote, "And You forgave the iniquity of my sin." Not only was the sin pardoned, but the virus of guilt was put away as soon as the acknowledgment was made.

Psalm 32:3–5

God Makes Us Glad

> *Today's Faith Builder:*
> Be glad in the LORD and rejoice, you righteous;
> And shout for joy, all you upright in heart! (Psalm 32:11)

Here and hereafter the way of the wicked is unprofitable. He who sows sin will reap sorrow. Sorrows of conscience, of disappointment, of terror, are the sinner's sure heritage in time, and in eternity sorrows of remorse and despair. Let those who boast of present sinful joys remember what shall be in the future and take warning.

Faith in God is the great reliever of life's cares, and he who possesses it lives in an atmosphere of grace surrounded by a bodyguard of mercies. May the Lord enable us at all times to believe in His mercy even when we cannot see evidences of it, for to the believer, mercy is as all-surrounding as omniscience, and every thought and act of God is perfumed with it. The wicked have a hive of wasps around them, but we have a swarm of bees storing honey for us.

Happiness is not only our privilege but our duty. We serve a generous God who makes being joyful a part of our obedience. How sinful is our rebellious complaining! How natural it seems that we who have been forgiven should be glad!

We are not to be glad in sin, or to find comfort in prosperity, but in our God, the garden of our soul's delight. That there is a God and such a God, and that He is ours and ours forever, our Father and our reconciled Lord, is matter enough for a never-ending psalm of joy.

Redouble your rejoicing. Since God has clothed His choristers in the white garments of holiness, let them not restrain their joyful voices but sing aloud and shout as those who find a priceless treasure.

Psalm 32:6–11

Sing a New Song

> *Today's Faith Builder:*
> Sing to Him a new song;
> Play skillfully with a shout of joy. (Psalm 33:3)

Joy is the soul of praise. To rejoice in earthly comforts is dangerous, to rejoice in self is foolish, to rejoice in sin is fatal, but to rejoice in God is heavenly. He who would have a double heaven must begin to rejoice below like those above. Praise is the clothing of the saints in heaven; it is fitting that they should try it on below.

The Lord must have a full octave, for all notes are His, and all music belongs to Him. All songs of praise should be to Him. We ought to make every hymn of praise a new song. To keep up the freshness of worship is a great thing, and in private it is indispensable.

Let us not present old, worn-out praise, but put life and soul and heart into every song, since we have new mercies every day and see new beauties in the work and word of our Lord. The sweetest tunes and the sweetest voices with the sweetest words are all too little for the Lord our God.

It is natural for great praise to express itself loudly. Men shout at the sight of their kings; shall we not offer loud hosannas to the Son of David?

The character of God is a sea, every drop of which should become a well of praise for His people. Come astronomers, geologists, naturalists, botanists, chemists, miners—all you who study the works of God—for your true reports confirm this declaration.

Earth might have been as full of terror as of grace, but instead it teems and overflows with kindness. If earth is full of mercy, what must heaven be?

Psalm 33:1–5

Our Wise Creator

> *Today's Faith Builder:*
> The counsel of the LORD stands forever,
> The plans of His heart to all generations. (Psalm 33:11)

The angelic heavens, the starry heavens, and the atmospheric heavens were brought into existence by a word. What if we say by "The Word"? "Without Him nothing was made that was made" (John 1:3).

How easy it was for the Lord to make paths for the planets and the glorious angels! A word, a breath could do it. It is as easy for God to create a universe as for a man to breathe; no, far easier, for man does not breathe independently, but borrows the breath in his nostrils from his Maker.

Creation came into existence out of nothing. The same power which first created the universe now sustains it. Happy is the one who has learned to lean his all on the sure Word of Him who built the skies.

Men's purposes are blown to and fro like the thread of a spider's web or the down of a thistle, but the eternal purposes are firmer than the earth. Men come and go; children follow their parents to the grave; the undisturbed mind of God moves on in unbroken serenity, producing ordained results with unerring certainty.

No man can expect his will or plan to be carried out from age to age; the wisdom of one period is the folly of another, but the Lord's wisdom is always wise and His designs run on from century to century. His power to fulfill His purposes is by no means diminished by the passing of years. He who was sovereign over Pharaoh in Egypt is still the King of kings and Lord of lords. Let us rejoice and show the world that we serve a glorious Master.

Psalm 33:6–12

Who's Watching?

❭ *Today's Faith Builder:*
Behold, the eye of the LORD is on those who fear Him,
On those who hope in His mercy. (Psalm 33:18)

It is one of our choicest privileges to be always under our Father's eye, to be never out of the sight of our best Friend.

The all-seeing God preserves the poorest of His people when they are alone and friendless, but ten thousand armed men cannot guarantee safety to him whom God leaves to destruction. The weakest believer dwells safely under the shadow of Jehovah's throne while the strongest sinner is in peril every hour. Why do we talk so much of our armies and heroes? The Lord alone has strength, and let Him alone have praise.

"The eye of the LORD is on those who fear Him." That eye of special care is their glory and defense. None can take them by surprise, for the celestial Watcher sees the designs of their enemies and thwarts them. They who fear God need not fear anything else; let them fix their eye of faith on Him, and His eye of love will always rest upon them.

The Lord's hand goes with His eye; He lovingly preserves those whom He graciously observes. Rescues and restorations await the saints. Death cannot touch them until the King allows it.

To wait is a great lesson.

To be quiet in expectation, patient in hope, confident in waiting reveals the maturity of a Christian.

We who trust cannot but be glad of heart—our inner nature triumphs in our faithful God. The root of faith in due time bears the flower of rejoicing. Doubts breed sorrow; confidence creates joy.

Psalm 33:13–22

Unending Praise

> *Today's Faith Builder:*
> I will bless the LORD at all times;
> His praise shall continually be in my mouth. (Psalm 34:1)

The Lord has the right to a monopoly on His creatures' praise in every situation, under every circumstance, before, in, and after trials, on bright days of happiness and dark nights of fear. Happy is he whose fingers are wedded to his harp. He who praises God for mercies will never be without a mercy for which to praise.

To bless the Lord is never unseasonable. Our thankfulness is not to be kept secret. What a blessed mouthful is God's praise! If people's mouths were always filled with praise there would be no complaining against God or slander of neighbors.

God deserves thankfulness from the heart and praise with the mouth: good thoughts in the closet and good words in the world.

When we feel our own inability to adequately glorify the Lord and therefore stir up others to take part, this is good both for us and for our friends. Congregational worship is the outgrowth of one of the instincts of the new life. In heaven it is enjoyed to the full, and earth is most like heaven where it abounds.

He who trusts God has no need to be ashamed of his confidence; time and eternity will both justify his reliance.

Finally, David was rid of all his woes. The Lord sweeps our griefs away as men destroy a hive of hornets, or as the winds clear away the mists. Prayer can clear us of troubles as easily as the Lord rid Egypt of the frogs and flies when Moses prayed for them. We ought to talk of the Lord's goodness that others may trust our faithful God.

Psalm 34:1–7

Blessings Guaranteed

❭ *Today's Faith Builder:*
Oh, taste and see that the LORD is good;
Blessed is the man who trusts in Him! (Psalm 34:8)

Try an inward, experimental test of the goodness of God. You cannot see how good God is except by tasting for yourself. Faith is the soul's taste; they who test the Lord by their confidence always find Him good, and they are blessed.

Fear not the wrath of men. Fear God and nothing else.

To trust God is better policy than the smartest politicians can teach or practice. No really good thing will be denied those whose first and main goal in life is to seek the Lord. People may call them fools, but the Lord will prove them wise. They will win where the worldly-wise lose their all, and God will have the glory.

Guard your tongue from speaking evil, for evil words will return to you and take the joy out of living. We cannot spit forth poison without feeling some of the venom burning our own flesh. Clean and honest conversation, by keeping the conscience at ease, promotes happiness, but lying and wicked talk stuffs our pillow with thorns and makes life a constant whirl of fear and shame.

Depart from evil. Avoid the lion's den, leave the viper's nest. Distance yourself from temptation. Be practical, active, energetic, persevering in good.

Seek peace with God, with your own heart, with others; search after it as a businessman seeks a precious pearl. Nothing can more effectively promote our own happiness than peace. Hunt for it; chase it with eager desire. The peace which you promote will return to your own heart and be a perennial spring of comfort to you.

Psalm 34:8–14

Never Alone, Never Forsaken

> *Today's Faith Builder:*
>
> Many are the afflictions of the righteous,
> But the LORD delivers him out of them all. (Psalm 34:19)

The Lord observes the righteous with approval and tenderness; they are so dear to Him that He cannot take His eyes off them. He watches each one of them as carefully and intently as if there were only one creature in the universe.

The eyes and ears of the Lord are turned to His people, His whole mind is occupied about them; if slighted by all others they are not neglected by Him. He hears their cry at once, as a mother is sure to hear her sick child; the cry may be broken-hearted, sad, feeble, unbelieving, yet the Father's alert ear catches each note of any groan or prayer and He is not slow to answer.

Like Israel in Egypt, they cry out under the heavy yoke of oppression, temptation, care, and grief. And the Lord hears them. He is like a night watchman who no sooner hears the alarm bell than He flies to rescue those who need Him. Our afflictions may be many and difficult but prayer can set us free from them all.

Broken hearts think God is far away when He is really very near to them. They run here and there, seeking peace in their own works, in experiences, or in proposals and resolutions while the Lord is near them and simple faith will reveal Him.

Our afflictions come from all points of the compass and are as many and as tormenting as mosquitoes in the tropics. *But,* blessed *but,* how it takes the sting out of the previous sentence: "But the LORD delivers him out of them all."

Psalm 34:15–22

Protection

> *Today's Faith Builder:*
>> Plead my cause, O LORD, with those who strive with me;
>> Fight against those who fight against me. (Psalm 35:1)

Every child of God has this protection: The accuser of believers is always met by their Advocate. Jesus does this for His beloved. He is their intercessor and champion; whatever aid they need they will receive from Him, and in whatever way they are attacked they will be defended.

Let us leave our safety in the Lord's hand. The help of man is vain, but the intervention of heaven is always effective.

Besides holding off the enemy the Lord can also calm the mind of His servant by assurance from His Word that he is, and shall be, safe under the Almighty wing. An inner persuasion of security in God is of all things the most precious in the furnace of persecution. One word from the Lord quiets all our fears.

God's judgments are often sudden and powerful. Death enters the persecutor's house without pausing to knock at the door. The thunderbolt of judgment leaps from its hiding place, and in one crash the wicked are broken forever.

Men set traps and catch their own fingers. They throw up stones that fall upon their own heads. How often Satan outwits himself and burns his fingers with his own coals!

Upon being rescued, David gives all honor to the Lord. We do not triumph in the destruction of others but in the salvation given to us by God. Prayer heard should always produce praise. We rob God by suppressing our gratefulness.

Psalm 35:1–10

Praise During Persecution

❭ *Today's Faith Builder:*
> I will give You thanks in the great assembly;
> I will praise You among many people. (Psalm 35:18)

Rewarding evil for good is devilish but men have learned this lesson well from the old Destroyer and practice it perfectly. The wicked would strip the righteous naked to their very soul: They know no pity. The only limits to human malice are those God Himself may choose to place on it.

David had been a man of sympathy; he had mourned when Saul was in ill health, sorrowing for him as though he were a near and dear friend. His heart went into mourning for his sick master. He prayed for his enemy and made the sick man's condition his own, pleading and confessing as if his own personal sin had brought the evil.

Prayer is never lost: If it does not bless those for whom intercession is made, it will bless the intercessors. Clouds do not always descend in showers upon the same spot from which the vapors ascended, but they do come down somewhere. In some place or other prayers yield their showers of mercy. If our dove finds no rest among our enemies, it will return to us, bringing an olive branch of peace in its mouth.

It is such delicate and addictive work to tear a good person's character in pieces that when slanderers start they do not wish to stop. A pack of dogs tearing at their prey is nothing compared with a group of malicious gossips mauling the reputation of a worthy man.

Even so, the slandered psalmist chooses to praise God.

Praise—personal praise, public praise, perpetual praise—should be the daily revenue of the King of heaven.

Psalm 35:11–18

Our Lord Is Near

❭ *Today's Faith Builder:*
This You have seen, O LORD;
Do not keep silence.
O Lord, do not be far from me. (Psalm 35:22)

Out of the mouth comes what is in the heart. When mischief is meant, mischief is soon made. Jesus was charged with trying to overturn Caesar—much more will some accuse His people.

David's enemies set no bounds to their infamous charges but poured out wholesale abuse, trusting that if all did not stick, some of it would. They were glad to find a fault or misfortune or to swear they had seen evil where there was none.

Malice has but one eye and it is blind to all virtue in its enemy. Eyes can generally see what hearts wish. A man with a speck in his eye sees a spot on the sun. Malice is folly.

Here is comfort: Our heavenly Father knows all our sorrow.

The psalmist claims a nearness to his God; he leaves his case with the righteous Judge. He begs that the suit may be brought, heard, tried, and the verdict given. It is well with a man when his conscience is so clear that he dares to make such an appeal.

God will not give His sheep over to the wolfish jaws of persecutors. Just when they are tuning their instruments to celebrate their victory, they will be made to laugh on the other side of their mouths. They are too sure and boastful; they reckon without God. Little do they dream of the end which will be put to their scheming.

The day is coming when shouts of victory shall be raised by all who are on Christ's side, for the battle will turn and the foes of truth shall be routed. Jesus will arrange all things for our good.

Psalm 35:19–28

Mercy Higher Than Our Clouds

> *Today's Faith Builder:*
> Your mercy, O LORD, is in the heavens;
> Your faithfulness reaches to the clouds. (Psalm 36:5)

This is a song of happy service that all may sing who bear the easy yoke of Jesus. The wicked are contrasted with the righteous and the Lord of the devout is heartily praised; obedience to so good a Master is insisted on, and rebellion against Him is plainly condemned.

People who dare to sin constantly and presumptuously cannot respect the great Judge of all. Unholiness is proof of ungodliness. Wickedness is the fruit of an atheistic root. Those eyes which have no fear of God before them now shall have the terrors of hell before them forever.

Those who fear God proceed from strength to strength in the right path, but the godless soon forsake what little good they once knew. God-fearing people meditate upon God and His service, but those who turn all their thoughts and inventive faculties toward evil demonstrate their godlessness. He has the devil for his bedfellow who lies in bed and schemes how to sin. God is far from him.

The sky above is ever clear, and mercy calmly smiles above the noise and smoke of this poor world. Darkness and clouds are but of the earth's lower atmosphere; the heavens are always serene and bright with innumerable stars. Divine mercy abides in its vast expanse unaltered by the rebellions of man.

When we can measure the heavens, we will understand the mercy of the Lord. In salvation, the Lord Jesus has displayed grace higher than the heaven of heavens and wider than the universe. As the sea mirrors the sky, so the mercy of the Lord is seen in His works.

Psalm 36:1–5

God Is Always Right

> *Today's Faith Builder:*
> Your righteousness is like the great mountains;
> Your judgments are a great deep;
> O Lord, You preserve man and beast. (Psalm 36:6)

As winds and hurricanes shake not a mountain, so the righteousness of God is never in any degree affected by circumstances: He is always just. Who can bribe the Judge of all the earth or who can, by threatening, compel Him to pervert judgment? Not even to save His elect would the Lord allow His righteousness to be compromised.

The Lord is not to be questioned as to why this and why that. He has reasons, but He does not choose to submit them to our consideration. Far and wide, awesome and irresistible like the ocean are the providential workings of God; at one time they appear as peaceful as the unrippled sea of glass, at another tossed with tempest and whirlwind, but evermore most glorious and full of mystery. Yet as the sea mirrors the sky, so the mercy of the Lord is to be seen reflected in all the working out of His will on the earth. The Lord is faithful in all that He does.

Those who put their trust in God shall be received into His house and shall share in the provision laid up there. The dwelling place of the Lord is not confined to any location, so we may regard our dwelling, if we be believers, as one room in the Lord's great house; and we will, both in providence and grace, find a satisfying amount supplied to us as the result of living near to the Lord by faith. God's everlasting love brings ample comfort to us, and the richest pleasure. Happy is the person who can drink in the gospel. Nothing else can so completely fill the soul.

Psalm 36:6–12

Don't Fret

> *Today's Faith Builder:*
> Do not fret because of evildoers,
> Nor be envious of the workers of iniquity. (Psalm 37:1)

This psalm was written by David in his old age. The great riddle of the prosperity of the wicked and the affliction of the righteous, which has perplexed so many, is here answered in the light of the future, and fretfulness and complaining are forbidden. It is a psalm in which the Lord sweetly quiets the common complaints of His people, calming their minds as to His present work regarding His chosen flock and the wolves by which they are surrounded.

We urgently need the command, "Do not fret because of evildoers." To fret is to worry, to have an unsettled heart, to fume, to become angry. Nature is likely to kindle a fire of jealousy when it sees criminals riding on horses and law-abiding people walking in the mire. When one is poor, despised, and in deep trouble, our old nature becomes envious of the rich and famous. To be free from envy at such a time is a lesson learned only in the school of grace.

Faith cures fretting. Sight views things only as they seem, causing envy; faith has clearer vision and sees things as they really are, bringing peace. True faith is actively obedient. There is a joy in holy activity which drives away discontent. Where there is heaven in the heart there will be heaven in the house.

There is no room for fretting if we remember that we belong to the Lord, but there is every incentive to be peaceful, constantly rejoicing and praising Him. People who delight in God desire or ask nothing but what will please Him. Their desires are submitted to God's will.

Psalm 37:1–4

Rest in the Lord

❯ *Today's Faith Builder:*
Commit your way to the LORD,
Trust also in Him,
And He shall bring it to pass. (Psalm 37:5)

Roll the whole burden of life upon the Lord. Cast away anxiety, resign, leave all with the God of all. Our destiny will be a joyful experience if we confidently entrust all to our Lord.

The farmer sows and cultivates and then leaves the harvest to God. What else can he do? He cannot cover the heavens with clouds or command the rain or bring forth the sun or create the dew. He does well to leave the whole matter with God, to leave everything in His hands, expecting a blessed result.

Regarding personal reputation, we can be quietly content and leave our vindication with the Judge of all the earth. The more we fret, the worse for us. Our strength is to sit still. The Lord will clear the slandered. If we look to His honor, He will see to ours.

To hush the spirit is to be silent before the Lord. To wait in holy patience for the Lord to clear up our difficulties should be the aim of every gracious heart. A silent tongue in many cases not only shows a wise head, but a holy heart.

Time is nothing to God; let it be nothing to you. God never is before His time, He never is too late. Patience awards good things last, and they last forever.

There is no good, but much evil, in worrying your heart about the present success of wicked unbelievers. Never allow a question to be raised as to the righteousness and goodness of the Lord.

Psalm 37:5–11

Walking Safely

> *Today's Faith Builder:*
> The steps of a good man are ordered by the LORD,
> And He delights in his way. (Psalm 37:23)

How comforting it is to know that all events are known to our God, and that nothing in our future can take Him by surprise! No arrow can pierce us by accident, no dagger smite us by stealth; neither in time nor eternity can any unforeseen ill happen to us. The future will be but a continual development of the good things which the Lord has in store for us.

Calamities will come, but deliverance will come also. The righteous never expect immunity from trouble, so they will not be discouraged when it comes their way. Rather they will cast themselves anew upon their God, and prove again His faithfulness and love. God is not a friend in the sunshine only, He is a friend at every turn.

No reckless fate, no fickle chance rules us; our every step has been planned by the Lord. All that concerns a saint is of interest to his heavenly Father. God loves to view the holy strivings of a soul pressing forward to the skies. Jesus has fellowship with the faithful in all their trials and joys, and delights to be their sympathizing companion.

Even when we fall the Lord sustains us. Where grace does not keep from going down, it will save from staying down. Job had double wealth at last. Joseph reigned over Egypt. Jonah landed safely. It is not that the saints are strong or wise or meritorious that they rise up after every fall, but because God is their helper and therefore none can prevail against them.

Psalm 37:12–24

Strength for Tough Times

❯ *Today's Faith Builder:*
But the salvation of the righteous is from the LORD;
He is their strength in the time of trouble. (Psalm 37:39)

The gains and pleasures of evil are temporary, but the rewards of grace are eternal. The awarding of honor to whom honor is due is God's delight, especially when the upright person has been slandered by others. It must be a divine pleasure to right wrongs and to defeat the schemes of the unjust. God is as faithful to the objects of His love as He is just to all mankind. Come what may, the saints are preserved in Christ Jesus, and because He lives, they shall live also.

Jesus was watched by His enemies, who were thirsting for His blood; His followers now must not look for favor where their Master found hatred and death. Temporary injustices are tolerated in the order of Providence for wise purposes, but the bitter will not always be called sweet, nor light falsely called darkness. The right will ultimately appear, evil will be unmasked, and the real and true will be revealed.

The little word *wait* is easy to say but hard to carry out, still faith must do it. Continue in the narrow path; let no haste for riches or ease cause unholy action. Let your motto be "On, on, on." Never dream of turning aside.

While trouble overthrows the wicked, it only drives the righteous to their strong Helper, who rejoices to uphold them. In the future Jehovah will stand up for His forces in the heat of the battle. As He rescued Daniel from the lions so will He preserve His beloved from their enemies; they need not therefore fret nor be discouraged.

Psalm 37:25–40

Grace for Groaning Times

> *Today's Faith Builder:*
> Lord, all my desire is before You;
> And my sighing is not hidden from You. (Psalm 38:9)

This psalm begins with a prayer that reveals the writer's distress over his own sinfulness. He expects chastening but in his mental misery pleads for mercy.

Depression is harmful to the body; it is enough to create and foster every disease and is in itself the most painful of all diseases. Soul sickness weakens the body, and then bodily weakness reacts on the mind.

Deeper still the sickness penetrates until the bones, the more solid parts of the system, are affected. Poor health and no rest are two serious problems, and these are both the experience of every awakened conscience until Jesus gives relief.

A man who has pain in his bones tosses to and fro in search of rest, but finds none. He becomes worn out with agony and, in many cases, a sense of sin creates in the conscience a terrible sense of unrest which can only be exceeded in anguish by the torture of hell itself. The heart groans and sighs silently and the voice fails to speak.

When our prayers appear to be more habitual than spiritual, they still prevail with our loving Father. He hears the murmur of the heart and the roaring of the soul because of sin and comes to relieve His afflicted right on time.

Praise God! He reads the longings of our hearts. Nothing can be hidden from Him; what we cannot tell Him, He understands.

Psalm 38:1–9

Hope for the Weak and Wounded

❯ *Today's Faith Builder:*
For in You, O LORD, I hope;
You will hear, O Lord my God. (Psalm 38:15)

A s we remember the lovingkindness of the Lord we see how good it was for our own strength to fail us, since this drove us to the Strong for strength; how right it was that our light should be quenched, that the Lord's light should be all in all to us.

Hope in God's intervention and belief in the power of prayer are two of the greatest comforts to the soul in times of adversity. Turning away from the hope of help from people to the sovereign Lord of all, and to Him as our own promise-keeping God, we shall find perfect peace in waiting upon Him.

Reputation like a fair pearl may be cast into the mire, but when the Lord makes up His jewels, godly character will shine with unclouded splendor. Rest then, slandered one, and let not your soul be tossed to and fro with anxiety.

The least flaw in a believer is sure to be noticed; a slight slip of the foot sets all the dogs of hell barking. When we are weak and feel like we are dying, the evils which oppose us are sure to be lively enough. If the devil were sick or our lusts feeble, we might stop praying so fervently, but with such lively and vigorous enemies we must not cease to cry mightily unto our God.

When sickness, slander, and sin all beset a saint, he requires the special aid of heaven, and he shall have it. He is afraid of nothing since God is always with him.

We will not be forsaken by our Lord. In heaven we will see that we had not one trial too many, or one pain too severe.

Psalm 38:10–22

When to Be Silent

❯ *Today's Faith Builder:*
> I said, "I will guard my ways,
> Lest I sin with my tongue;
> I will restrain my mouth with a muzzle,
> While the wicked are before me." (Psalm 39:1)

The psalmist's greatest fear was that he would sin, therefore, he looked for the best way to avoid it and he determined to be silent. It is good when we can strengthen ourselves in doing right by remembering a wise resolution.

To avoid sin we have to be very circumspect, keeping all actions under control. Unguarded ways are generally unholy ones. *Careless* is another word for *graceless*.

In times of sickness or other trouble we must watch for the sins consistent with such trials, especially murmuring and complaining. Tongue sins are great sins: like sparks of fire careless words spread and do great damage. If believers speak bitter words against God in times of depression, the ungodly will take them up and use them as a justification for their sinful ways. If a man's own children rail at him, it is no wonder if his enemies' mouths are full of abuse.

One's tongue always needs watching, for it is as unruly as an unbroken horse. But especially must the tongue be kept under control when the wounds of the Lord's chastening rod excite it to rebel.

When David went so far as to discipline himself to entire silence "even from good," there must have been at least a little sullenness in his soul. In trying to avoid one fault, he fell into another. To use the tongue against God is a sin of commission, but not to use it at all is a serious sin of omission.

Psalm 39:1–6

Better Things Ahead

> *Today's Faith Builder:*
> And now, Lord, what do I wait for?
> My hope is in You. (Psalm 39:7)

What is there in this world to enchant me? Why should I linger where the prospect is so uninviting and the present so trying?

Pondering these questions, the psalmist turns to his God. He has thought about the world and all things in it and is relieved to know that such vain things are temporary; he has therefore cut all cords that bound him to earth and is ready to leave for heaven.

The Lord is self-existent and true, and therefore worthy of the confidence of men. He will live when all the creatures die, and His fullness will abide when all second causes are exhausted. To Him, therefore, let us direct our expectation, and on Him let us rest for our confidence.

Let all wise builders turn themselves from sand to rock, for if not today, yet surely before long a storm will rise before which nothing will be able to stand but that which has the lasting element of faith in God to hold it firm. David had but one hope, and that hope was in God. This enabled him to anchor his soul safely and after a little drifting, all was peace.

Tears speak more eloquently than ten thousand tongues. When our sorrows fill our eyes with tears, God will soon turn our mourning into joy. Though He may be quiet for a long time, as though He were unaware of our troubles, the hour of deliverance will come like the morning when dewdrops cover the grass.

David uses the fleeting nature of our life as an argument for the Lord's mercy. We show mercy to the poor and so will our Lord to us.

Psalm 39:7–13

Waiting

> *Today's Faith Builder:*
> I waited patiently for the LORD;
> And He inclined to me,
> And heard my cry. (Psalm 40:1)

Patient waiting on God was a special characteristic of our Lord Jesus. Impatience never lingered in His heart and never escaped His lips. All through His agony in the garden, His trial of cruel mockings before Herod and Pilate, and His passion on the tree, He waited in omnipotence of patience.

No glance of anger, no word of complaining, no act of vengeance came from God's patient Lamb. He waited and continued to wait; was patient to perfection, excelling all others who have glorified God in the fires.

Job in the ash pit does not equal Jesus on the cross. Christ wears the royal crown among the patient. Did Jesus wait, and shall we be impatient and rebellious? Neither Jesus the Head, nor any one of the members of His body, will ever wait on the Lord in vain. What a wonder it is that our Lord should have to cry and wait as we do and should receive the Father's help through the same process of faith and pleading as we must go through! The Son of David was brought very low, but He rose to victory; and here He teaches us how to conduct our conflicts so that we will succeed in the same wonderful way that He succeeded in His triumph over suffering, death, and the grave.

Jesus is the true Joseph taken from the pit to be Lord of all. If we, like our Lord, are cast into the lowest pit of shame and sorrow, we will, by faith, rise to stand on the same elevated, sure, and everlasting Rock of divine favor and faithfulness.

Psalm 40:1–5

Delighting in God's Will

> *Today's Faith Builder:*
> I delight to do Your will, O my God,
> And Your law is within my heart. (Psalm 40:8)

Faith obtains promises. A simple, single-eyed confidence in God is the sure badge of blessing. A man may be as poor as Lazarus, as hated as Mordecai, as sick as Hezekiah, as lonely as Elijah, but while his hand of faith can keep its hold on God, none of his outward afflictions can prevent his being numbered among the blessed. But the wealthiest and most prosperous man who has no faith is accursed.

Believing men are too noble to honor mere moneymaking or cringe before boasted dignity. The righteous pay their respect to humble goodness rather than to inflated pride. Our Lord Jesus was our best example of this. No flattery of kings and great ones ever fell from His lips.

Our blessed Lord alone could completely do the will of God. The law is too perfect for such poor creatures as you and me to hope to fulfill. Jesus not only did the Father's will, but found delight in it.

From eternity past He had desired the work set before Him; in His human life He moved ever forward until He reached the baptism of agony in which He magnified the law, and even in Gethsemane He chose the Father's will and set aside His own.

Here then is the essence of obedience, namely in the soul's cheerful devotion to God. Our Lord's obedience, which is our righteousness, is in no way lacking in this eminent quality. In spite of His measureless griefs, our Lord found delight in His work. We must each be like Him in this or there will be no evidence that we are His disciples.

Psalm 40:6–10

Our Gladness His Glory

❯ *Today's Faith Builder:*
    Let all those who seek You rejoice and be glad in You;
    Let such as love Your salvation say continually,
    "The Lord be magnified!" (Psalm 40:16)

What riches of grace that in His bitterest hour Jesus should remember the lambs of His flock! And what does He ask for them? That they may be doubly glad, intensely happy, emphatically joyful.

Jesus would have all who seek Him made happy by finding what they seek and by experiencing peace through His grief. As deep as were His sorrows, so high would He have their joys. He groaned that we might sing and was covered with a bloody sweat that we might be anointed with the oil of gladness.

Our sins were innumerable and so were His griefs. He had no sin, but our sins were laid on Him, and He took them as if they were His own: He was made sin for us (2 Cor. 5:21). O my soul, what would my sins have done for me eternally if the Friend of sinners had not condescended to take them all upon Himself?

Another result of the Redeemer's passion is the promotion of the glory of God by those who gratefully delight in His salvation. Our Lord's desire should be our joy; we love His great salvation with all our hearts; let us then proclaim His glory.

The suffering Redeemer regarded the consecration of His people to the service of heaven as a grand result of His atoning death; it is "the joy that we set before Him" (Heb. 12:2). God being glorified is the reward of the Savior's suffering and sacrifice.

Psalm 40:11–17

Blessings for Those Who Help the Poor

> *Today's Faith Builder:*
> Blessed is he who considers the poor;
> The LORD will deliver him in time of trouble. (Psalm 41:1)

This is the third psalm beginning with a benediction and it progresses beyond the first two. To search the Word of God comes first, pardon for sin is second, and now the forgiven sinner honors God by living for the good of others.

Those who partake of divine grace receive a more tender nature and are not hardened against those in need; they take up the cause of all the downtrodden and make a serious effort to help them. They do not toss them a small gift and go on their way but ask about their sorrows, discover their needs, study the best ways to bring them relief, and find practical ways to come to their rescue.

The compassionate lover of the poor thinks of others and therefore God will think of him. God gives to us as we give to others. Days of trouble come to the most generous and they have made the wisest provision for rainy days who have provided shelter to others when times were better for them. The promise is not that the generous saint will have no trouble but that he will be preserved in it, and in due time, brought out of it.

Selfishness bears a curse in itself; it is a cancer in the heart. Liberality brings happiness and deep inner peace. Here are the rewards of those who are like Jesus in caring for others; they bless and shall be blessed; they preserve and shall be preserved; they watch over the lives of others and they shall be precious in the sight of their Lord.

Psalm 41:1–3

Gossip and Grace

> *Today's Faith Builder:*
>> By this I know that You are well pleased with me,
>> Because my enemy does not triumph over me. (Psalm 41:11)

D avid's enemies spoke evil of him; the viper fastened on Paul's hand; the better the man the more likely he is to be attacked and the more venomous the slander.

Evil tongues are busy tongues and they are never truthful. Jesus was completely misrepresented, although no offense was in Him. If persecutors could have their way the church would have but one neck and that would be on the chopping block, but the Lord lives and preserves both believers and their names.

Out of the sweetest flowers chemists can distill poison and from the purest words and deeds malice can gather evidence for defamatory reports. It is amazing how spite spins webs out of no materials whatever. It is a severe trial to have wicked people around you waiting for every word which they may pervert into evil. The Master whom we serve was constantly subject to this affliction.

How far people will go to publish their slanders! They would gladly write their falsehoods in the sky. A little fault is magnified, a slip of the tongue is a libel, a mistake a crime, and if a word can have two meanings the worse is always given to it.

David rejoiced that he lived under divine surveillance, tended, cared for, and smiled upon by his Lord, and that it would always be so. None can bless the Lord so sweetly as those who have experienced His faithfulness in times of trouble.

Psalm 41:4–13

Thirsting for God

❯ *Today's Faith Builder:*

As the deer pants for the water brooks,
So pants my soul for You, O God. (Psalm 42:1)

Although David is not mentioned as the author, this psalm bears the marks of his style and experience in every letter. It is the voice of a spiritual believer who is depressed, longing for the renewal of God's presence, struggling with doubts and fears, yet holding his ground by faith in the living God. Most of the Lord's family have sailed on the sea that is here so graphically described.

David was heartsick. He did not seek ease nor covet honor but the joy of communion with God was an urgent need of his soul, viewing this not merely as the sweetest of all luxuries but as an absolute necessity for life.

Like the parched traveler in the wilderness whose bottle is empty and who finds the wells dry, he must drink or die; he must have God or faint. His soul, his very self, his deepest life was thirsty for a sense of God's presence.

Give David his God and he is as content as a thirsty deer which finally, after a long search, quenches its thirst and is perfectly happy. But deny him his Lord and his heart sinks, his bosom palpitates, his whole frame is convulsed, like one who gasps for breath or pants after long running.

Oh, to have the highest craving after the highest good! This is a sure evidence of grace. The psalmist longs not merely for the temple and the ordinances but for fellowship with God Himself. He lives and gives living water to all believers; therefore eagerly desire Him.

Psalm 42:1–5

When You're Feeling Down

❯ *Today's Faith Builder:*
Why are you cast down, O my soul?
And why are you disquieted within me:
Hope in God;
For I shall yet praise Him,
The help of my countenance and my God. (Psalm 42:11)

A s though he were two men, the psalmist talks to himself. His faith reasons with his fears, his hope argues with his sorrows. Are these present troubles to last forever? Why this deep depression, this faithless fainting, this chicken-hearted melancholy?

Here David scolds David out of the dumps. And he is an example for all depressed ones. To search out the cause of our sorrow is often the best remedy for grief. In this case, ignorance is not bliss; it is misery. The mist of ignorance magnifies the causes of our alarm; a clearer view will make our monsters disappear.

If every evil is let loose from Pandora's box, there will still be hope at the bottom. Grace swims to our aid though the waves roar and be troubled (Ps. 46:3). God is unchangeable, and therefore His grace is the ground for unshaken hope. Even if everything is now dark, the day will come. Meanwhile, hope carries stars in her eyes; her lamps are not dependent on oil from without, her light is fed by secret communion with God, which sustains the spirit.

The main hope and chief desire of David rests in the smile of God. His face is what he seeks and hopes to see; this will revive him. He who can use such heroic language in his gloomy hours will surely overcome his despair.

Psalm 42:6–11

Longing for Light

> *Today's Faith Builder:*
> Oh, send out Your light and Your truth!
> Let them lead me;
> Let them bring me to Your holy hill
> And to Your tabernacle. (Psalm 43:3)

As the sun sends forth its beams, so the Lord sends forth His favor and His faithfulness to all His people. And as all nature rejoices in the sunshine, the saints triumph in the love and faithfulness of their God, which, like a golden sunbeam, lights up even the darkest surroundings with delightful splendor.

We seek not light by which to sin, nor truth that we may be exalted, but that they may become our practical guides to the closest communion with God; only the light and truth He sends will do this. Common light is not strong enough to show the road to heaven, but the light of the Holy Spirit and the truth as it is in Jesus are elevating, sanctifying, perfecting; and they lead us to the glorious presence of God.

If David should be delivered from his enemies and allowed to return home, he would not go first to his own house, but his willing feet would carry him to the altar of God. His whole heart would go as a sacrifice to the altar, counting it his greatest happiness to be permitted to lie there as a burnt offering wholly dedicated to the Lord.

With what joy should believers draw near to Christ, who is the antitype of the altar! It is beautiful to observe how David's longing to escape from the oppression of man always leads him to sigh more intensely for communion with God.

Psalm 43

God of Our Fathers

> *Today's Faith Builder:*
> We have heard with our ears, O God,
> Our fathers have told us,
> The deeds You did in their days,
> In days of old. (Psalm 44:1)

Godly fathers are, by the order of both nature and grace, the best instructors of their sons; they cannot delegate this sacred duty. When fathers are tongue-tied religiously, need they wonder if the hearts of their children remain sin-tied?

Note that the main point of the history transmitted from father to son was the work of God; this is the core of history, and therefore no one can write history correctly who is a stranger to the Lord's work. It is delightful to see the footprints of the Lord on the sea of changing events, to behold Him riding on the whirlwind of war, pestilence, and famine, and above all to see His unchanging care for His chosen people. Those who are taught to see God in history have learned a good lesson from their fathers.

The Lord alone was exalted in bringing His people into the land which flowed with milk and honey. The tribes fought for their allotments, but their success was due to the Lord who worked through them. The warriors of Israel were not inactive, but their valor was secondary to that miraculous working by which Jericho's walls fell down. Canaan was not conquered without the armies of Israel, but it is equally true that it was not conquered by them; the Lord was the conqueror, and the people were but instruments in His hands. They could not ascribe their memorable victories to themselves; He who made the sun and moon stand still for them was worthy of all their praise.

Psalm 44:1–3

Boasting in the Lord

❯ *Today's Faith Builder:*
  In God we boast all day long,
  And praise Your name forever. (Psalm 44:8)

I n union and communion with God saints work wonders; "If God is for us, who can be against us?" (Rom. 8:31).

Note that all the conquests of these believers are said to be "through You," "through Your name." Never let us forget this, lest going to battle in our own strength we fail most miserably. Let us not, however, fall into the equally dangerous sin of distrust, for the Lord can make the weakest of us equal to any emergency.

Though today we may be timid and defenseless sheep, He can by His power make us strong and cause us to push as with the horns of unicorns until those who rise up against us shall be crushed and battered, never to rise again.

Those who are so weak that they can scarcely stay on their feet, but, like little babes, totter and fall, are by divine assistance able to overthrow their foes and proclaim complete victory. This double action of God in blessing His people and confounding His enemies should always be kept in mind; Pharaoh is drowned, while Israel passes through the sea.

We have abundant reason for boasting in the Lord when we recall His mighty acts. What blessed boasting! It is the only sort of boasting that is bearable. Just as manna bred worms and stank except that which was laid up before the Lord, all boasting is loathsome except glorying in the Lord, which is commendable and pleasing to God.

Praise should be perpetual. If there are no new acts of love, the Lord ought to be praised for what He has done for His people.

Psalm 44:4–8

When Trouble Gets Us Down

> ❭ *Today's Faith Builder:*
> Arise for our help,
> And redeem us for Your mercies' sake. (Psalm 44:26)

It always encourages a troubled believer when he can see that God's great name will be honored through his trials, but our misery is increased when we appear to be suffering in vain. For our comfort, let us rest in the confidence that the Lord is glorified in our difficulties and know that even when no evidence of His glory is seen, He is accomplishing His own secret purposes, which will be revealed in due time. We do not suffer for nothing, nor are our griefs without eternal rewards.

The world does not recognize its real nobility, having no eye for true excellence; it found a cross for the Master, and it cannot be expected to award crowns to His disciples.

When enduring many griefs, if we can still cling to God in loving obedience, it will be well with us. True faithfulness can put up with rough treatment. Those who follow God for what they get will leave Him when persecution comes, but not sincere believers: They will not forget their God, even in the most trying times.

Those who are true to God will never find Him false to them.

When the heart sinks, the troubled one is down indeed. Heart sorrow is the very heart of sorrow. It is miserable when the heart cannot escape from itself, being shut up in its own dejection and bound with the cords of despondency. God's people may be down, not only in the dust but in the ash pits with Job and Lazarus, but their day is coming; their tide will turn, and they shall have a bright summer after their bitter winter.

Psalm 44:9–26

The King

> *Today's Faith Builder:*
> My heart is overflowing with a good theme;
> I recite my composition concerning the King;
> My tongue is the pen of a ready writer. (Psalm 45:1)

There is no writing like that dictated by the heart. A good heart will only be content with good thoughts. Good streams flow from a good fountain.

It is sad when the heart is cold with a good subject, and worse when it is warm with a bad subject, but especially good when a warm heart and a good subject come together. This song has "the King" for its only subject and it was composed for the King's honor alone; well might the writer call it a good theme.

The psalmist did not write carelessly; he calls his poem his work. We are not to offer the Lord that which cost us nothing. Good material deserves good workmanship. We should carefully consider our heart's affections and our mind's meditations on any discourse or poem in which we speak of One so great and glorious as our royal Lord.

As though the King Himself had suddenly appeared before him, the psalmist turns to address his Lord. A loving heart has the power to envision its object. The eyes of a true heart see more than the eyes of the head. Jesus reveals Himself when we are pouring forth our affections to Him. Usually when we are ready Christ appears.

Through grace, many have been made lovely in character, yet they have each had a flaw; but in Jesus we behold every feature of a perfect character. Grace of person and grace of speech reach their highest point in Him.

Psalm 45:1–2

Who's on the Throne?

❭ *Today's Faith Builder:*
   Your throne, O God, is forever and ever;
   A scepter of righteousness is the scepter of Your kingdom.
                                        (Psalm 45:6)

Christ is the true champion of the church. Others are but underlings who must borrow strength from Him.

Jesus is the truest of heroes. Hero worship in His case alone is commendable. He is mighty to save, mighty in love. Love delights to see the Beloved arrayed as fits His excellency; she weeps when she sees Him in the garments of humiliation; she rejoices to behold Him in the garments of His exaltation.

Our precious Christ can never be exalted too much. Heaven itself is but just good enough for Him. All the pomp that angels and archangels and thrones and dominions and principalities and powers can pour at His feet is too little for Him. Only His own essential glory fully answers to the desire of His people. We can never praise Him enough.

The psalmist cannot restrain His adoration. His enlightened eye sees God in the royal Husband of the church: God to be adored, God reigning everlastingly.

Blessed sight!

Blind are the eyes that cannot see God in Christ Jesus!

What a mercy for us that our Savior is God! What a glad thing it is that He reigns on a throne which will never pass away, for we need both sovereign grace and eternal love to secure our happiness. Could Jesus cease to reign we would cease to be blessed. All the just rejoice in the government of the King who reigns in righteousness.

Psalm 45:3–6

April 17

Our Righteous Redeemer

> *Today's Faith Builder:*
> You love righteousness and hate wickedness;
> Therefore God, Your God, has anointed You
> With the oil of gladness more than Your companions. (Psalm 45:7)

Christ Jesus is not neutral in the great contest between right and wrong; as warmly as He loves the one He abhors the other. What qualifications for a King! What grounds of confidence for a people!

The whole of our Lord's life on earth proved the truth of these words; His death to put away sin and bring in the age of righteousness sealed the fact beyond all question. His providence, by which He rules from His mediatorial throne, when rightly understood reveals the same. We should imitate Him both in His love and hate; they are both needed to complete a righteous character.

Names well-known in one generation have been unknown to the next, but the praise of Jesus will ever be fresh, His renown ever new. God will see to this; His providence and His grace will make it so.

The fame of Messiah is not left to human guardianship; the Eternal guarantees it, and His promise never fails. All through the ages the memories of Gethsemane and Calvary will glow with eternal light; nor will the lapse of time, the smoke of error, or the malice of hell be able to dim the glory of the Redeemer's name.

Praise is due from every heart to Him who loved us and redeemed us by His blood; this praise will never be fully paid, but will always be a debt. Age to age reveals more of His love. Let every year increase the volume of music of earth and heaven, and let thunders of song roll up to the throne.

Psalm 45:7–17

God's Timely Protection

> *Today's Faith Builder:*
>   God is our refuge and strength,
>   A very present help in trouble. (Psalm 46:1)

Others boast of their safe castles on inaccessible rocks, secured with gates of iron, but God is a far better refuge from distress than all of these. Remember this and consider yourselves safe; make yourselves strong in God.

Neither forget that God is our refuge right now, in the immediate present, as surely as when David wrote these words. God alone is our protection. All other refuges are unsafe, all other strength is weakness, for power belongs to God. He is all-sufficient and equal to all emergencies.

God has been tried and proven by His people. He never forsakes His afflicted ones. He is their help, truly, effectively, constantly; He is always present and near them, close at their side and ready for their rescue. He is more present than any friend or relative can be, more present than even the trouble itself. To all this comforting truth is added the consolation that His assistance comes at the time of need. He is not as the swallows that leave us in winter. He is a friend in need and a friend in deed.

With God on our side, how irrational fear would be! Where He is all power and love are; why then should we be afraid? Since God remains faithful, there can be no danger to His cause or people. When all things seem to be crashing down around us, faith smiles serenely. We need not be afraid of the storms of life with all their noise and force to destroy. Our Lord stills the raging of the sea and holds the waves in the hollow of His hand.

Psalm 46:1–7

Be Still

❯ *Today's Faith Builder:*
Be still, and know that I am God;
I will be exalted among the nations,
I will be exalted in the earth! (Psalm 46:10)

The Lord rules the angels, the stars, the elements, and all the hosts of heaven; the heaven of heavens is under His control. The General of all the forces of the land and the Lord High Admiral of the seas is on our side: our powerful ally. Woe to those who fight against Him, for they shall blow away like smoke before the wind when He gives the word to scatter them. He destroys the destroyer. In every place where His cause and crown have been disregarded, ruin has followed; sin has been a blight on nations throughout history and has left their palaces to lie in ruins.

God's voice quiets the noise of war and calls for the silence of peace. He crushes great powers until they cannot cause trouble again; He gives His people rest. How glorious will be the ultimate victory of Jesus in the day of His appearing, when every enemy will be destroyed.

Relax and wait in patience, you believers! Acknowledge that Jehovah is God, you who feel the terrors of His wrath! Adore Him and Him only, you who share in the protections of His grace.

The boasts of the ungodly and the timid forebodings of the saints should be hushed by remembering what the Lord has done in past ages. The whole earth shall yet reflect the light of His majesty.

Even man's history of sin, obstinacy, and pride will bring glory to God when grace reigns, bringing eternal life throughout the whole earth.

Psalm 46:7–11

Sing Praises

> *Today's Faith Builder:*

  Sing praises to God, sing praises!
  Sing praises to our King, sing praises! (Psalm 47:6)

G od's service is such a delight that it cannot make us weary, and that choicest part, the singing of praises, brings so much pleasure that we cannot have too much of it.

Clapping our hands, the most natural and enthusiastic expression of praise, is fitting in view of the Lord's victories and His universal reign. Our joy in God may be too emotional for some but He will not criticize us for it.

Our God is no local deity, no petty ruler; in infinite majesty He rules the mightiest realms. He is the sole monarch of all lands, King of kings and Lord of lords. Not a village or island is excluded from His reign. How glorious will that time be when this is seen and known by all, when in the person of Jesus everyone will behold the glory of the Lord!

The battle is not ours but the Lord's. He will take His own time, but He will achieve certain victory for His church. Truth and righteousness will climb to the top through grace.

There is no doubt about the outcome of this war. The most rebellious hearts and the most stubborn wills shall submit to all-conquering grace. All the Lord's people, both Jews and Gentiles, may clap their hands at this, for God's victory will be theirs, but those who suffer and labor most will have the largest share of joy.

We feel His reign to be so gracious that even now we long to be fully obedient to it. We submit our will, our choice, our desire wholly to Him.

Psalm 47

Praise Him!

> *Today's Faith Builder:*
>> Great is the LORD, and greatly to be praised
>> In the city of our God,
>> In His holy mountain. (Psalm 48:1)

None can conceive how great Jehovah is, but we can see that He is great in delivering His people, great in the love of those delivered, and great in the hearts of the enemies whom He scatters, as measured by their fears. Instead of the mad cry of Ephesus, "Great is Diana," we say, "Great is the Lord!"

Jesus is the "great Shepherd" (Heb. 13:20), our great God and Savior, our great High Priest. His Father has divided Him a portion with the great, and His name shall be great over all the earth. There is none like the Lord, and there should be no praises like His praises. The Lord can only be fittingly praised by holy people and they should continually be occupied with His worship.

Jerusalem was beautiful for location; she was called the Queen of the East. The Church is beautiful spiritually, being near God's heart, within the mountains of His power, upon the hills of His faithfulness, in the center of His providential operations. The elevation of the Church is her beauty. The more she is above the world the fairer she is.

We worship no unknown god. We know Him as our refuge in distress, in whom we delight, and run to Him in every time of need. We have no other refuge. Even if we were made kings and our houses were to become palaces, we would have no confidence in ourselves but trust in the Lord as our protector; His well-known power is our sure defense.

Psalm 48:1–8

Our Faithful Guide

> *Today's Faith Builder:*
>   For this is God,
>   Our God forever and ever;
>   He will be our guide
>   Even to death. (Psalm 48:14)

Holy people do not forget God's wonders; they meditate deeply on them. Devout minds never tire of so great a subject. It is good to think of past mercies in times of trial and equally profitable to remember them in seasons of prosperity. Grateful memories sweeten sorrows and sober joys.

Where God is most seen He is best loved. When saints assemble they constitute a living temple and our deepest thoughts when gathered together should center on the lovingkindness of the Lord revealed in the experiences of us all. Memories of mercy should be associated with continuing praise.

All the Church, and each individual member, should rejoice in the Lord and magnify His name. The righteous acts of the Lord are proper subjects for joyful praise.

The security of the people of God is not a doctrine to be kept in the background. It may be safely taught and should be frequently pondered. We give thanks for the hope of eternal joy.

Throughout life to our dying day, God will graciously guide us, and after death He will lead us to the fountains of living water awaiting in heaven. We look to Him for resurrection and eternal life. This comforting hope is clearly consistent with what He has done for us in the past.

Farewell, fear. Come gratitude and faith, and sing joyously.

Psalm 48:9–14

Wise Words

⟩ *Today's Faith Builder:*
My mouth shall speak wisdom,
And the meditation of my heart shall give understanding.
(Psalm 49:3)

All people are concerned with wisdom. It is wise to feel, "Everything which concerns people is of personal interest to me." We must all appear before the judgment seat (2 Cor. 5:10), so we all should pay attention to any advice which may help us prepare for it.

Sons of great men, wicked men, men of great wealth, and you who experience the pains of poverty are all invited to hear the inspired minstrel as he plays a mournful but instructive song on his harp. The low will be encouraged, the high will be warned, the rich will be sobered, the poor consoled; there will be a useful lesson for each one willing to learn it.

Inspired and therefore lifted beyond himself, the prophet is not praising his own accomplishments but giving glory to the Holy Spirit who taught him. He knew that the Spirit of truth and wisdom spoke through him.

He who would have others hear begins by hearing himself. The truth came to the psalmist as a parable, and he attempted to interpret it so that all could understand. He would not leave the truth in obscurity but listened to its voice until he understood it so well that he could translate it into the common language of the people.

The psalmist was no mystic, delighting in deep and cloudy things, yet he was not afraid of the most profound topics; he tried to open the treasures of darkness to discover pearls from the deep. Let us gather around this minstrel of the King of kings and hear his psalm.

Psalm 49:1–4

Why Should We Be Afraid?

> *Today's Faith Builder:*
> Why should I fear in the days of evil,
> When the iniquity at my heels surrounds me? (Psalm 49:5)

The man of God looks calmly forward to dark times when those evils which have dogged his heels shall temporarily overtake him—that evil which tries to trip him up or slow him down.

In some dreary part of our road ahead evil people may grow stronger and bolder and, gaining on us, openly attack us. Those who followed us like a pack of wolves may overtake us and surround us. What then? Shall we become cowards? Shall we be victims of their violence? God forbid. What are these foes but mortal men who will die and pass from this earthly scene?

There can be no reason for the faithful to be alarmed. Their enemies are too insignificant to be worthy of fear. Does not our Lord say to us, "I, even I, am He who comforts you" (Isa. 51:12)?

What if our enemies are among the important people of the earth? When we contrast our Rock with theirs, it would be foolish to be afraid of them. Even though they brag loudly, we can smile. What if they glory "and boast [themselves] in the multitude of their riches"? While we glory in our God we will not be frightened by their proud threats.

Great strength, position, and wealth make wicked men very high in their own opinion, but the heir of heaven is not awed by their false dignity or frightened by their pride. Never, therefore, will we fear those evil nibblers at our heels, whose boasted treasure proves to be so powerless to save.

Psalm 49:5–14

True Riches

› *Today's Faith Builder:*
But God will redeem my soul from the power of the grave,
For He shall receive me. (Psalm 49:15)

We shall come forth from our temporary resting place in due time, made alive by God's power. Like our risen Head we cannot be held by the grip of the grave; redemption has freed us from the slavery of death. No earthly redemption could make us rich, but God has made it possible through the blood of His dear Son.

We are the redeemed of the Lord. He will take me out of the grave, take me up to heaven. God will receive my spirit and my body will sleep in Jesus until, being raised in His image, it will also be received into Glory.

Do not be concerned when you see the godless prosper. Raise no questions as to divine justice; allow no envy to cloud your mind. Temporary prosperity is too small a matter to be worth fretting about. Though the sinner and his family are held in great esteem and stand tall in the community, all things will finally be made right. Only those of poor judgment will give people greater respect because they have greater wealth than others.

All must pass through the river of death naked. Not a rag of clothing, not a coin of treasure, not a bit of honor can the dying person carry with him. Why then fret ourselves over such fleeting prosperity?

Comforting as the theme of his psalm is to the righteous, it is full of warning to the worldly. Hear it, all you rich and poor. Give ear to it, all nations of the earth.

Psalm 49:15–20

Who Owns All This?

For every beast of the forest is Mine,
And the cattle on a thousand hills. (Psalm 50:10)

Jehovah's dominion extends over the whole earth, and therefore this decree is directed to all people. The east and the west are called to hear the God who makes His sun rise on every quarter of the globe.

The psalmist speaks of himself and all believers as anticipating the immediate appearing of their Lord upon the scene. "He comes," they say, "our covenant God is coming." They can hear His voice from afar and envision the splendor of all who are coming with Him. Like them, we should await the long-promised appearing of the Lord from heaven. He comes to speak, to plead with His people, to accuse and judge the ungodly. The Lord Jesus will be "revealed from heaven with His mighty angels, in flaming fire taking vengeance on those who do not know God" (2 Thess. 1:7–8).

How could Israel imagine that the Most High God, possessor of heaven and earth, had need of beasts for offerings when all the countless herds and flocks that find shelter in a thousand forests and wildernesses belong to Him? Not only the wild animals but also the tamer creatures are all His own. Their cattle were not, after all, their own, but were still the great Creator's property. What a mistake is made about divinely commanded sacrifices when they are wrongly viewed as in themselves being pleasing to God!

A spiritual God demands other life than that which is seen in animals; He looks for the spiritual sacrifices of love, trust, and praise, the life of your hearts.

Psalm 50:1–11

Sacrifices of Praise

> *Today's Faith Builder:*
> Whoever offers praise glorifies Me;
> And to him who orders his conduct aright
> I will show the salvation of God. (Psalm 50:23)

Israel was not blamed for lack of animal sacrifices on the altar, but for want of thankful adoration of the Lord. She excelled in the visible, but in inward grace, which is the one thing needed, she sadly failed. Too many today are like her.

Let your sacrifice be presented to God, who sees the heart; pay to Him the love you promised, the service you agreed to give, the loyalty of heart you vowed to maintain.

Oh, for grace to do this!

Oh, that we may be graciously enabled to love God and live up to our profession! Our main concern is to be the servants of the Lord Jesus and to love Him.

To some it seems a small and expected thing to pray when we are distressed, yet this is more acceptable worship than the formalistic presentation of bulls and goats on the altar of sacrifice. This is our Lord's command concerning worship; see how full of mercy it is.

Praise is the best sacrifice: true, hearty, gracious thanksgiving from a renewed mind. Sacrifice your loving gratitude, and God will be honored by it.

Holy living is a good evidence of salvation. He who submits his whole way to God's guidance and is careful to honor Him in his life brings an offering which the Lord accepts through His dear Son. God's blessing is not promised to ceremonies nor to impure lips, but to grateful hearts and holy lives.

Psalm 50:12–23

Cleanse Me

❭ *Today's Faith Builder:*
Wash me thoroughly from my iniquity,
And cleanse me from my sin. (Psalm 51:2)

Pardon of sin must always be an act of pure mercy and therefore the awakened sinner flees to his pardoning Lord.

The hypocrite is content if his garments are washed, but the truly repentant one cries, "wash me." The careless soul is content with others thinking he is clean, but the truly awakened conscience desires a real and practical washing.

His one sin against Bathsheba served to show the psalmist the whole mountain of his iniquity, of which that foul deed was but one falling stone. He desires to be rid of the whole mass of his filthiness, which, though once so little observed, had become a hideous, haunting terror to his mind.

"Cleanse me from my sin" is a broad expression that goes beyond the original cry for washing. It is as if the psalmist, longing to be totally clean, said, "Lord, if washing will not do, try some other process; if water will not avail, let fire, let anything be tried, so that I may be purified. Rid me of my sin by some means, by any means, by every means, only do purify me completely, and leave no guilt upon my soul."

It is not the punishment he cries out against, but the sin. David is sick of sin as sin; his loudest outcries are against the evil of his transgression and not against the painful consequences of it.

When we deal seriously with our sin, God will deal gently with us. When we hate what the Lord hates, He will soon make an end of it, giving us joy and peace.

Psalm 51:1–3

What God Wants to Do in Us

> *Today's Faith Builder:*
>   Behold, You desire truth in the inward parts,
>   And in the hidden part You will make me to know wisdom.
>   (Psalm 51:6)

The virus of sin lies in its opposition to God; the psalmist's sense of sin against others increased his awareness of his sin against God. All his wrongdoing centered, culminated, and came to a climax at the foot of God's throne. To injure others is sin, mainly because in doing so we violate the law of God. The psalmist's heart was so filled with a sense of the wrong he had done to the Lord Himself that all other confession was swallowed up in a brokenhearted acknowledgment of his offense against Him.

God desires not only outward virtue but inward purity, and the penitent's sense of sin is greatly deepened as, astonished, he discovers this truth and how far he falls short in pleasing his Lord. Reality, sincerity, true holiness, and faithfulness are the demands of God. He cares not for the pretense of purity; He looks to the mind, heart, and soul.

The penitent feels that God is teaching him truth concerning his nature, which he had not known before: the love of his heart, the mystery of its fall, and the way to inward purity.

No one but the Lord can teach our innermost nature. The Holy Spirit can write the law of God on our heart, which provides practical wisdom. He can put the fear of the Lord within, and that is the beginning of wisdom. He can reveal Christ in us and He is essential wisdom. Our poor foolish souls shall yet be right with God, and truth and wisdom will reign within us.

Psalm 51:4–6

Our Source of Joy

> *Today's Faith Builder:*
>   Restore to me the joy of Your salvation,
>   And uphold me by Your generous Spirit. (Psalm 51:12)

David prays about his sorrow late in this psalm. He begins with his sin; he asks for pardon and then for joy. He seeks comfort at the right time and from the right source. No voice could revive his dead joys but the one which awakens the dead. Pardon from God would give him double joy: "joy and gladness."

No partial blessing awaits the forgiven one; he will not only have a double-blooming joy but will hear it singing songs of praise. Some joy is felt but not heard, for it is silenced by the noise of fears, but the joy of pardon has a voice louder than the voice of sin. God's voice speaking peace is the sweetest music an ear can hear.

The psalmist is making a great request: He seeks joy for a sinful heart, music for crushed bones—an absurd prayer anywhere but at the throne of God! Absurd there most of all but for Jehovah Jesus bearing our sins in His own body on the tree (1 Peter 2:24).

One who returns to the heavenly Father need not ask to be one of His hired servants or live in perpetual mourning over past sins. He may ask for gladness and he will have it, for if when prodigals return the father is glad and the neighbors rejoice with music and dancing, what need can there be for the restored one to be miserable?

Praying for joy and strength is fitting. Joy will not last if we are not kept from wandering. On the other hand, joy is a very strengthening thing and greatly aids holiness. Joy and strength to overcome are both provided by the Holy Spirit.

Psalm 51:7–13

Praise and Prayer Bring Spiritual Growth

> *Today's Faith Builder:*
> O Lord, open my lips,
> And my mouth shall show forth Your praise. (Psalm 51:15)

Honest penitents come to the point, call a spade a spade, and are completely open with God. What other course is rational in approaching our omniscient Lord?

A great sinner pardoned makes a great singer. Sin has a loud voice, as should our thankfulness. We who are saved should not sing our own praises, but those of the Lord our righteousness, in whose merits we stand righteously accepted.

How marvelously the Lord can open our lips, and what great things we poor simpletons pour forth under His inspiration! If God opens a mouth the fruit of the Spirit will flow from it. When vanity, anger, falsehood, or lust unbar the door of our lips the foulest words storm out; but if the Holy Spirit opens the gate, then grace, mercy, peace, and all the graces come forth in tuneful dances, like the daughters of Israel when they met David returning with the Philistine's head.

A crushed heart is a fragrant heart. God has never yet spurned a lowly, weeping penitent, and He never will while He is love and Jesus is called "the Man who receives sinners." He has no desire for animal sacrifices but seeks after contrite hearts.

God can make His cause to prosper, and in answer to prayer He will do so. Faith grows by the exercise of prayer. A saved soul expects to see its prayers answered in a revived church and then is confident that God will be glorified.

Psalm 51:14–19

Good Reasons for Praise

> *Today's Faith Builder:*
>> I will praise You forever,
>> Because You have done it;
>> And in the presence of Your saints
>> I will wait on Your name, for it is good. (Psalm 52:9)

There are words that, like boa constrictors, swallow people whole, or like lions, tear them to pieces. Evil people love these words; they are sure to use them.

Some say terrible things and then claim they are only speaking out to set the record straight, to promote justice. Actually, they are determined to put down truth and holiness and deceitfully use this excuse to go about it.

The persecutor would destroy the church so God will destroy him, pull down his house, pluck up his roots, and make an end of him. God will turn the tables on those who are malicious and give them what they have given others.

David knew God's mercy to be eternal and perpetual and trusted in it. What a rock to build on! What a fortress for safety!

God's memorable acts of providence, both to saints and sinners, deserve and must have our gratitude. David viewed his prayers as already answered, the promises of God as already fulfilled, and therefore at once lifts up this sacred psalm.

David intended to wait silently before and among the saints, feeling it would be good for both him and them to look to the Lord alone, believing He would ultimately show His character. Our patience will be rewarded and will finally bring us honor.

Psalm 52

Fools and Final Victory

⟩ *Today's Faith Builder:*
The fool has said in his heart,
"There is no God."
They are corrupt, and have done abominable iniquity;
There is none who does good. (Psalm 53:1)

A fool speaks according to his fallen nature; a great fool considers a great subject and comes to a wild conclusion.

The atheist is, morally as well as mentally, a fool, a fool in heart as well as in head; a fool in morals as well as in philosophy. With the denial of God as a starting point, a fool's progress downward is a rapid, riotous, raving, ruinous one. He who begins with impiety is ready for anything.

Every natural man is, more or less, a denier of God. Practical atheism is the religion of the human race.

Those who talk so abominably as to deny their Maker will act abominably. Abounding denial and forgetfulness of God is the source of the unrighteousness and crime which we see around us.

The fallen race of man, left to its own energy, has not produced a single lover of God or doer of holiness, nor will it ever do so. Apart from grace, not one specimen of humanity will be found to follow after the good and true. This is God's verdict after looking down on us all.

David sees the end of the ungodly and the triumph of the saints. Since the yoke of sin has been heavy and the bondage cruel, the coming liberty will be happy and the triumph joyous. The return of Christ and the restoration of Israel are our hope and expectation.

Psalm 53

Help from Above

❭ *Today's Faith Builder:*
Behold, God is my helper;
The Lord is with those who uphold my life. (Psalm 54:4)

As long as God has an open ear we cannot be imprisoned by trouble. All other weapons may be useless, but prayer is always available. No enemy can jam this gun.

Vocal prayer helps the one praying; we keep our minds more fully awake when we use our tongues as well as our hearts. When in danger, David could not afford to pray out of mere custom; he must succeed in his pleadings or become the victim of his adversaries.

The psalmist saw enemies everywhere, and now to his joy, as he looks on his band of defenders, he sees One whose aid is better than all the help of men: He is overwhelmed at recognizing his divine Champion and cries, "Behold." Is this not a time for praise that the great God protects us, His own people? What does the number of our enemies matter when He uplifts the sword of His power to aid us? We care little about the defiance of our foes while we have the defense of God.

Here was a greater champion than all the valiant men who chose David for their captain. It is a great blessing to see our Lord among them.

None can praise the Lord so well as those who have tried and proven the power of His name in times of adversity. God's name is good, and so is His praise. Our souls are strengthened when we are praising God. We are never so holy or so happy as when our adoration of God abounds.

Psalm 54

When You Long to Fly Away

> *Today's Faith Builder:*
> So I said, "Oh, that I had wings like a dove!
> I would fly away and be at rest." (Psalm 55:6)

Believers run as naturally to the Lord in times of trouble as little chickens to a hen when they are in danger. But it is not just the act of prayer that satisfies the godly; they long for an audience with heaven, an answer from the throne, and nothing less will satisfy them.

How comforting that we can be this close to our God! When we are overcome with grief we can bring our sorrowful, wandering thoughts to Him and He will listen so carefully that He will understand what is taking place in our hearts. He will often fulfill desires which we could not have expressed to Him in words. Groanings which cannot be uttered are often prayers that cannot be refused.

The psalmist was so terrified at what might be ahead that he felt like fainting. His fears oppressed him and caused him to tremble. He did not know what would happen to him next, how soon the worst would come.

If David could not resist as an eagle, he would escape as a dove. His love of peace made him sigh for an escape from all strife. We too may be tempted to express a foolish desire to fly away, but neither the wings of doves nor eagles could bear us away from the sorrows of a trembling heart. Besides, it is cowardly to shun the battle which God would have us fight.

Even Noah's dove found no rest until she returned to the ark, and we will only find rest from our sorrows in Jesus. We need not depart; all will be well if we trust in Him.

Psalm 55:1–8

God Is Faithful When Others Let Us Down

> *Today's Faith Builder:*
>   Evening and morning and at noon
>   I will pray, and cry aloud,
>   And He shall hear my voice. (Psalm 55:17)

Attacks by those who have been close to us and trusted by us wound us deeply. They are usually so well-acquainted with our weaknesses that they know how to touch us where we are most sensitive and to say things that do the most damage.

We can find a hiding place from our enemies, but who can escape treacherous friends? If our enemies attack us, we resist them, but where can we go when those who have pretended to love us treat us with contempt? Our blessed Lord had to endure the painful deceit and faithlessness of a favored disciple; let us not be surprised then when we are asked to walk the road marked by His pierced feet.

The psalmist chose not to meet the plots of his adversaries by counterplots, nor to imitate their unceasing violence, but in contrast to their godless behavior would continually turn to his God. Jesus did this and wise believers have always done the same. This shows the contrast of their character to that of their enemies and predicts the contrast of their ends: The righteous will ascend to their God and the wicked will sink to ruin.

Seasons of great need call for frequent seasons of prayer. The three periods named here are most fitting: to begin, continue, and end the day with God is supreme wisdom. Where time has naturally set up a boundary, there let us set up an altar. When our window is open toward heaven, the windows of heaven are open to us. Have a pleading heart and God will have a plenteous hand.

Psalm 55:9–17

What to Do with Our Burdens

❯ *Today's Faith Builder:*
Cast your burden on the LORD,
And He shall sustain you;
He shall never permit the righteous to be moved. (Psalm 55:22)

The voice of slander, malice, and pride is not only heard by those it grieves; it reaches heaven, it enters God's ear, it demands vengeance, and shall have it. God hears and delivers His people; He hears and destroys the wicked. Their cruel jokes, their base falsehoods, their cowardly insults, their daring blasphemies are heard and will be repaid to them by the eternal Judge. All the prayers of saints and profanities of sinners are before His judgment seat, and He will see that justice is done.

The Lord can soon change our condition and He often does so when our prayers become fervent. The crisis of life is usually the secret place of wrestling. Jabbok makes Jacob a prevailing prince. He who stripped us of all friends to make us see Himself in their absence can give them back again in greater numbers that we may see Him more joyfully in their presence.

What God lays on you, lay "on Him." His wisdom casts it on you and it is wise to cast it on Him. He gives your portion of suffering; accept it with cheerful resignation, and then take it back to Him in assured confidence.

He who stands firm stands in God. Like pillars, the godly stand immovable to the glory of the Great Architect.

The Lord is all and more than all that faith can need as the foundation of peaceful trust.

Psalm 55:18–23

Trading Fear for Faith

❯ *Today's Faith Builder:*
    Whenever I am afraid,
    I will trust in You. (Psalm 56:3)

It is sweet to see how the tender, dove-like spirit of the psalmist flies to the tenderest attribute of God for help in the hour of peril. The open mouths of sinners, when they rage against us, should open our mouths in prayer. We may plead the cruelty of others toward us as a reason for God's protection; a father is soon aroused when his children are shamefully treated.

If we may pray for protection from people, how much more can we pray for protection from that great enemy of our souls, the devil. We ask the Lord to forgive us our trespasses, which is another way of saying, "Be merciful to me, O God," and then we say, "Lead us not into temptation, but deliver us from the evil one." The more violent the attack of Satan, the stronger our plea for deliverance. The greatness of God as the Most High is a rich source of consolation to weak believers oppressed by mighty enemies.

Fear that drives us to trust is a blessing in disguise. If I fear people, I have only to trust God and I have the best antidote for fear. To trust when there is no cause for fear is professing faith, but to rely on God when reasons for alarm are many and imminent is the conquering faith of God's elect.

Faith produces praise. He who can trust will soon sing. God's promise, when fulfilled, is a great subject for praise, and even before fulfillment it should give us a song.

When faith is exercised fear is banished and holy triumph follows. Let us maintain faith and we will soon recover courage.

Psalm 56:1–7

God Is Stronger Than Our Enemies

> *Today's Faith Builder:*
> In God I have put my trust;
> I will not be afraid.
> What can man do to me? (Psalm 56:11)

We may be so confused after a long period of trouble that we hardly know where we have or have not been, but our omniscient and considerate Father remembers all in detail. He has counted our troubles as men count their gold, for even the trial of our faith is precious in His sight.

How gracious is our Lord! How exact His knowledge of us! How generous His esteem of His children! How tender His regard!

We may not always understand how prayer works, but it is powerful and effective. God invites us to pray, we cry in anguish of heart, He hears, He acts, and the enemy is turned back. What irresistible artillery this is that wins the battle as soon as we pray! What a God this is who listens to the cry of His children and in a moment delivers them from their mightiest adversaries! Who will seek any other ally than God, who is present as soon as we call, by which we testify of both our need and our confidence in Him?

Faith has banished fear. The least we can do then is to praise Him from whom we receive such valuable favors.

The psalmist now longs to walk in liberty, in holy service, in sacred communion, in continual progress in holiness, enjoying the smile of heaven. Here is the highest reach of a believer's ambition: to dwell with God, to walk in His righteousness, to rejoice in His presence and in the light and glory which it constantly provides.

Psalm 56:8–13

Mercy Enough for Me

> *Today's Faith Builder:*
> I will cry out to God Most High,
> To God who performs all things for me. (Psalm 57:2)

G od is the God of mercy and the Father of mercies (2 Cor. 1:3); it is fitting, therefore, that in distress we should seek mercy from Him in whom it dwells. How can the Lord be unmerciful to a trusting soul? Our faith does not deserve mercy, but when faith is sincere it always receives mercy from the sovereign grace of God.

Evil will pass away, and until then our Lord's eternal wings will remain over us. Blessed be God, our calamities are but for a time, but our safety is for eternity. When we are under the Lord's shadow, trouble may pass over us but it cannot harm us; the hawk flies across the sky, but no evil can come to the chicks when they are safely nestling beneath the hen.

However high our enemies may be, our heavenly Friend is higher, for He is "Most High" and He can readily send the strength we need from the height of His power.

The believer waits and God works.

We may in times of great difficulties expect remarkable mercies; like the Israelites in the wilderness, we shall have our bread hot from heaven, new every morning. Wherever the battle is more fierce than ordinary, there will come help from headquarters, for the Commander in Chief sees all that happens to us. He will be in time, not only to rescue His servants from being swallowed up, but even from being reproached. Such mercy ought to make us pause to meditate and give thanks.

Psalm 57:1–3

Praise Flows from a Peaceful Heart

> *Today's Faith Builder:*
> My heart is steadfast, O God, my heart is steadfast;
> I will sing and give praise. (Psalm 57:7)

Like the burning bush in Horeb, the believer is often in the flames but never consumed. Faith triumphs when we can lie down among hot coals and find rest because God is our defense.

Malicious men carry weapons in their mouths; their jaws are as dangerous as if every tooth were a javelin or an arrow. As for that busy member, the tongue, it is a two-edged, keen, cutting, killing sword.

No weapon is as terrible as a tongue sharpened on the devil's grindstone; yet we need not fear even this, for "No weapon formed against you shall prosper, and every tongue which rises against you in judgment you shall condemn" (Isa. 54:17).

One might think the psalmist would have said, "My heart flutters," but no, he is calm, firm, happy, resolute, established. He is resolved to trust his Lord and praise Him. Twice he declares this to the glory of God, who comforts His servants.

Imagination fails to guess the height of heaven, just as the riches of mercy exceed our highest thoughts. God's goodness is more vast and sublime than even the vaulted skies. He sets the seal of His truth in the clouds, the rainbow which ratifies His covenant. In the clouds He hides His rain and snow which prove His truth by bringing us seedtime and harvest, cold and heat.

Creation is great but the Creator is far greater. Heaven cannot contain Him; His goodness far exceeds the clouds and stars.

Psalm 57:4–11

A Reward for the Righteous

❭ *Today's Faith Builder:*
So that men will say,
"Surely there is a reward for the righteous;
Surely He is God who judges in the earth." (Psalm 58:11)

He who refrains from defending the right is an accomplice in the wrong. As righteous judges ponder the law, balance the evidence, and weigh the case, so the malicious dispense injustice with intended malice. Like the foes of our Lord, they are a generation of vipers, an evil and adulterous generation. They tried to kill Him because He was righteousness itself, yet they masked their hatred of His goodness by charging Him with sin.

There is no sympathy in Scripture for God's enemies. We shall at last say "Amen" to the condemnation of the wicked and will not question God concerning them. Remember how John put it: "After these things I heard a loud voice of a great multitude in heaven, saying, 'Alleluia! Salvation and glory and honor and power belong to the Lord our God! For true and righteous are His judgments'" (Rev. 19:1–2).

God will triumph over the wicked. They shall be so utterly vanquished that their overthrow will be final and fatal and His deliverance complete and crowning. The godly are not forsaken and given over to their enemies; the wicked are not to have the best of it, truth and goodness are recompensed in the end.

Two things come out clearly after all: There is a God and there is a reward for the righteous. Time will remove doubts, solve difficulties, and reveal secrets; meanwhile faith's foreseeing eye discerns the truth even now and is glad.

Psalm 58

Morning Song

❯ *Today's Faith Builder:*
But I will sing of Your power;
Yes, I will sing aloud of Your mercy in the morning;
For You have been my defense
And refuge in the day of my trouble. (Psalm 59:16)

What a blessed morning will soon break for the righteous, and what a song will be theirs! Sons of the morning, you may sigh tonight, but joy will come on the wings of the rising sun. Tune your harps now for the signal to begin the eternal music will soon be given; morning is coming and your song will go on forever.

The song is for God alone, and it is one which none can sing but those who have experienced His lovingkindness. Looking back on a past full of mercy, the saints will bless the Lord with their whole hearts.

The greater our present trials the louder our future songs and more intense our joyful gratitude will be. Had we no day of trouble, where would our season of retrospective thanksgiving be?

See how the singer equips himself with the almighty power of God and calls it all his own by faith. The music of experience is sweet but it is all for God; there is not even a stray note for man, for self, or human helpers. With full assurance the psalmist claims possession of the Infinite as his protection and security. He sees God in all, even in his trials.

Oh, choice song! My soul will sing it now in defiance of all the dogs of hell. Away, away, you adversaries of my soul, the God of my mercy will keep you all at bay.

Psalm 59

God's Help Our Only Hope

❯ *Today's Faith Builder:*
Give us help from trouble,
For the help of man is useless. (Psalm 60:11)

Before the days of Saul, Israel had been brought very low; during his government it had suffered from internal strife, and his reign was closed by an overwhelming disaster. As a result, David found himself the possessor of a tottering throne, troubled with the double evil of division at home and invasion from abroad. He knew that the displeasure of the Lord had brought calamity upon the nation, and he set out to remove that displeasure by earnest prayer.

God with us is better than strong battalions. The truth of God brought about the triumph of David's armies. He had promised them victory. And in proclaiming the gospel we need not be hesitant, for as surely as God is true He will give success to His own Word. For the truth's sake, and because the true God is on our side, let us imitate the warriors of Israel and unfurl our banners to the breeze with confident joy.

Faith regards God's promise not as fiction but as fact, and therefore drinks in joy from it and grasps victory by it. Faith divides the spoil; she is sure of what God has promised and enters at once into possession.

We may by faith ask for and expect that our extremity will be God's opportunity; special and memorable deliverances will be ours when dire calamities appear to be imminent. Faith is never happier than when it can fall back on the promises of God. She remembers this in all discouraging circumstances. The voice of a faithful God drowns out every sound of fear.

Psalm 60

Sheltered in God

> *Today's Faith Builder:*
> For You have been a shelter for me,
> A strong tower from the enemy. (Psalm 61:3)

Pharisees may rest in their prayers; true believers are eager for an answer to them. Ritualists may be satisfied when they have said or sung their litanies, but living children of God will never rest until their prayers have entered into the ears of the Lord.

Our heavenly Father is not hardened against the cries of His own children. How consoling it is to think that the Lord at all times hears His people's cries and is never forgetful of their prayers! Whatever else fails to move Him, praying breath is never spent in vain. We may call upon God from any place. No spot is too dreary, no condition too deplorable; whether it be the world's end or life's end, prayer is equally available.

It is hard to pray when the heart is overwhelmed, yet people of faith plead best at such times. Tribulation brings us to God and brings God to us. Faith's greatest triumphs are achieved in her heaviest trials. Our prayer by reason of our distress may be like a call to a distant friend, but our faith whispers to the Lord as to one who is very near and ready to help.

How infinitely higher than we are is the salvation of God! We are low but it towers like some tall cliff far above us. This is its glory and is our delight when we have climbed onto the Rock and claimed it as our own.

Experience is the nurse of faith. From the past we gather arguments for present confidence.

Psalm 61

Expecting God to Come Through

> *Today's Faith Builder:*
> My soul, wait silently for God alone,
> For my expectation is from Him. (Psalm 62:5)

True faith rests on God alone; confidence which relies but partly on the Lord is worthless. To wait on God and for God is the holy habit of faith; to wait on Him is sincerity; to wait for Him is spiritual purity.

No eloquence in the world is half as full of meaning as the patient silence of a child of God. A person who trusts God will therefore wait patiently until the answer to his prayer comes. Faith can hear the footsteps of coming deliverance because she has learned to be silent.

If the wicked could but ruin the work of grace in us they would be content; they plan to crush our character, to end our influence. They hate the truth and the truthful and try to bring about their overthrow with lies.

Pure faith is unafraid. Faith with a single focus sees herself secure, but when double-minded she is blind and useless (James 1:8). We expect deliverance from God because we believe in Him.

Expectation is the child of prayer and faith and is acceptable to the Lord. We should desire nothing but what is right for God to give, then our expectation will always be from Him. Concerning truly good things, we should not look anywhere but to the Lord. He gives good gifts to His children (Luke 11:13).

Answers to our prayers of faith are on the way and will arrive in time to satisfy our needs. Happy is the man who feels that all he has, all he wants, and all he expects are to be found in his God.

Psalm 62:1–6

Trusting in God Alone

> *Today's Faith Builder:*
>
> Trust in Him at all times, you people;
> Pour out your heart before Him;
> God is a refuge for us. (Psalm 62:8)

Faith is an abiding duty, a perpetual privilege. We should trust when we can see as well as when we are completely in the dark.

Adversity is a good time for faith, but so is prosperity. God deserves our confidence continually. At all times we need to trust in Him. A day without trust in God is a day of anxiety and anger even if it is a day of laughter.

You to whom His love is revealed, reveal yourselves to Him. His heart is set on you, open your hearts to Him. Turn your soul upside down in His secret presence and let your inner thoughts, desires, sorrows, and sins be poured out like water. Hide nothing from Him, for nothing can be hidden from God.

Unburden your soul to the Lord; let Him be your only Father-confessor, for He is the only one who can forgive you when He has heard your confession. To keep our griefs to ourselves is to hoard up misery. The stream will swell and rage if you dam it up; give it a clear course, and it will leap along harmlessly. We need sympathy; and if we unload our hearts at Jesus' feet, we will obtain a sympathy as practical as it is sincere, as consoling as it is honorable. Prayer is the special duty of those to whom the Lord has revealed Himself as Defender and Friend.

What good reasons for faith are here! It can never be foolish to rest on God's almighty arm. He can release us from all troubles and sustain us under all burdens. From now on may we wait only upon Him!

Psalm 62:7–12

Seeking God First

⟩ *Today's Faith Builder:*
> O God, You are my God;
> Early will I seek You;
> My soul thirsts for You;
> My flesh longs for You
> In a dry and thirsty land
> Where there is no water. (Psalm 63:1)

David did not stop singing because he was in the wilderness, but he made his worship suitable to his circumstances and presented a wilderness hymn to his God. There was no desert in his heart though there was a desert around him. We too may expect to find ourselves in rough places. Even then may the Eternal Comforter abide with us and cause us to bless the Lord at all times.

Full assurance does not hinder diligence but is the reason for it. See how eager David is to seek his Lord; he will not wait for noon or the cool evening. He is up at cockcrow to meet his God. Communion with God is so sweet that the chill of the morning is forgotten and the luxury of oversleeping is despised.

The morning is the time for dew and freshness, and the psalmist consecrates it to prayer for fellowship with God. The word *early* has not only the sense of early in the morning, but that of eagerness, immediateness. He who truly longs for God longs for Him now.

A weary place and a weary heart make the presence of God more desirable. The absence of outward comforts can be endured serenely when we talk with God and the most lavish accommodations do not satisfy when He withdraws. Therefore let all desires become one: seeking first the kingdom of God that all else may be added to us (Matt. 6:33).

Psalm 63:1–6

Rejoicing in God's Faithfulness

⟩ *Today's Faith Builder:*
Because You have been my help,
Therefore in the shadow of Your wings I will rejoice. (Psalm 63:7)

Lying awake, the psalmist gave himself to meditation and then be-gan to sing. He has a feast and a song in the night; he consecrated his pillow. His praise anticipated heaven, for there is "no night there" (Rev. 22:5).

Perhaps the wilderness helped to keep David awake, and if so, all the ages are debtors to it for this delightful hymn. If day's cares tempt us to forget God, it will be good if night's quiet leads us to remember Him. We see best in the dark if there we see God best. Some delight in the night, but they are not nearly as happy as those who meditate on God.

Meditation had refreshed David's memory and reminded him of past deliverances. We ought to read our own diaries often, especially noting the hand of the Lord in helping us in suffering, want, labor, or dilemma. This is the best use of memory, to furnish us with proofs of the Lord's faithfulness and lead us on to a growing confidence in Him.

The shade of God is sweet to a believer. Under the eagle wings of Je-hovah we hide from all fear, and we do this naturally and at once because we have proved both His love and His power in the past. We are not only safe but happy in God; we "rejoice" as well as repose.

O Lord, we seek You and Your truth; deliver us from all malice and slander and reveal Yourself to us, for Jesus' sake. Amen.

Psalm 63:7–11

Glad Day Coming

❯ *Today's Faith Builder:*
The righteous shall be glad in the LORD, and trust in Him.
And all the upright in heart shall glory. (Psalm 64:10)

Praying aloud often helps devotion but even mental prayer has a voice which God hears. Prayers which are unheard on earth may be among the best heard in heaven.

Note how often David turns to prayer as his most powerful weapon. He uses it under the pressures of inward sin or outward wrath, of foreign invasion or domestic rebellion. We act wisely when we make prayer our first and most trusted resource in every hour of need.

The Lord knows how to give His people peace. He is more than a match for all disturbers and can defeat both their best laid plans and their open hostilities.

Slander has always been the master weapon of the enemies of good people and the malicious can be expected to use it effectively. As warriors grind their swords to give them an edge which will cut and wound deeply, so do the unscrupulous invent falsehoods which are calculated to inflict pain, to stab the reputation, to kill the honor of the righteous. What is there that an evil tongue will not say? What misery will it not try to inflict?

The righteous need not learn the arts of self-defense or of attack—their protection is in better hands than their own. While unbelievers fear, the children of God are secure in their Father's power and justice. He will not forget His promises.

Psalm 64

God Hears and Answers Prayer

❯ *Today's Faith Builder:*

By awesome deeds in righteousness You will answer us,
O God of our salvation,
You who are the confidence of all the ends of the earth,
And of the far-off seas. (Psalm 65:5)

Praise pleases our Lord and continues to bless Him. Praise does not grow weary in waiting for answers to prayer but all through the night sings on in sure hope that the morning will come.

God has not only heard but is now hearing prayer and always must hear prayer since He is immutable; He never changes. Every right and sincere prayer is as surely heard as it is offered. Coming to God is the proof that our faith is genuine; we come weeping in conversion, hoping in prayer, rejoicing in praise, and delighting in service.

We do not always know what we are asking for when we pray. Nevertheless, it is good to keep on asking, for nothing our Lord grants in His love can do us any harm.

There is no room for self-confidence on land or sea, since God is the only One worthy of our confidence on earth or ocean. Those who exercise faith in God anywhere will find that He is swift and strong to answer their prayers.

Let us learn that we poor puny ones must go to the Strong for strength. Without Him, the everlasting hills would crumble. The child of God in seasons of trouble should flee at once to Him who stills the seas; nothing is too hard for Him.

Psalm 65:1–8

God Is Good to Us

❯ *Today's Faith Builder:*
You crown the year with Your goodness,
And Your paths drip with abundance. (Psalm 65:11)

God's visits leave a blessing behind; this is more than can be said of other visitors. When the Lord goes on missions of mercy, He carries an abundance of things needed by all His creatures. He is represented here as going around the earth, as a gardener surveying his garden and giving water to every plant that needs it. O Lord, in this manner visit Your church, and my poor, parched, and withering soul. Make Your grace to overflow toward me; water me, for no plant of Your garden needs it more.

The soil is made rich by rain and then yields its riches to the gardener, but God is the first giver of all. How truly rich are those who are enriched with His grace!

Vegetation made alive by the moisture of God's rain leaps into life; the seed germinates, sends forth its green shoot, and becomes the fruit of a field which the Lord has blessed. This furnishes us with a picture of the work of the Holy Spirit in beating down high thoughts, fulfilling our smallest desires, softening the soul, and causing every holy thing to increase and spread.

God's love encircles the year as with a crown; each month has its gems, each day its pearl. Unceasing kindness girdles all time with a belt of love.

The bounty of God makes the earth sing His praise, and in opened ears it lifts up a joyous shout. The world is a hymn to the Eternal. Blessed are all who join in as singers in this mighty chorus.

Psalm 65:9–13

To God Be the Glory

❭ *Today's Faith Builder:*
Make a joyful shout to God, all the earth! (Psalm 66:1)

God is to be praised with our voices, and our hearts should join in holy exaltation. All praise from all nations should be raised to the Lord. The languages of the lands are many, but their praises should be one, addressed only to God.

The honor of God should be our subject and honoring Him our object when we sing. To give glory to God is but to restore to Him His own. It is our glory to be able to give God glory, and all our true glory should be ascribed to God, for it is His glory.

"All worship be to God only" should be the motto of all true believers. The name, nature, and person of God are worthy of the highest honor.

We are to throw so much of heart and holy reverence into all our worship that it becomes the best we can give. Heart worship and spiritual joy make praise more glorious than robes, incense, and music could do.

What a change will have taken place when singing replaces sighing, and music thrusts our misery! The nature and works of God will be the theme of earth's universal song, and He Himself will be the object of the joyful adoration of all who have been set free. May the knowledge of the Lord soon cover the earth so that all may worship Him.

All you who now faintly sing God's praises, awake and give full tongue and volume to your song! Make rocks and hills and earth and sea and heaven itself echo with your joyful shouts!

Psalm 66:1–10

After the Fire and Flood

> *Today's Faith Builder:*
> You have caused men to ride over our heads;
> We went through fire and through water;
> But You brought us out to rich fulfillment. (Psalm 66:12)

God's people and affliction are intimate companions. As in Egypt every Israelite was a burden-bearer, so is every believer while in this foreign land. As Israel cried to God because of their painful bondage, so also do the saints. The time will come when every ounce of our present burdens will bring us greater and more glorious rewards.

Many an heir of heaven has experienced severe trials; the fire through which he has passed has been more terrible than that which burns the bones, for it has been fueled with the marrow of his spirit and burned into the core of his heart. The floods of affliction have been more to be feared than the angry sea, for they have even gone into the soul and carried the inner nature down into horrible depths which cannot be imagined without trembling. Yet each saint has been more than a conqueror in the past and will be in the future.

How wealthy every believer is, and how much he feels it in view of his former slavery! What songs could be sufficient to express our joy and gratitude for such a glorious deliverance and such a bountiful heritage?

More awaits us. The depth of our griefs cannot compare with the height of our happiness.

Over the hills faith sees the daybreak in whose light we will enter into this abundant place.

Psalm 66:11–20

A Prayer for Mercy and Blessings

❯ *Today's Faith Builder:*
God be merciful to us and bless us,
And cause His face to shine upon us. (Psalm 67:1)

This psalm begins with a cry for mercy. Forgiveness of sin is always the first link in the chain of mercies extended to us. Mercy is a foundational attribute of our salvation. The best saints and the worst sinners may unite in this prayer. It is addressed to the God of mercy by those who feel their need of mercy, and it implies the death of all legal hopes or claims of merit.

When we bless God we do but little, for our blessings are only words, but when God blesses He enriches us indeed, for His blessings are gifts and deeds. But His blessing alone is not all His people crave—they desire a personal consciousness of His favor and pray for a smile from His face. These three petitions include all that we need here or hereafter: mercy, blessing, and the smile of God.

Abundant love is shown in this psalm, but it begins at home. The whole church, each church, and each little group in the church may rightly pray, "Bless us." It would, however, be very wrong to let our love end where it begins, as some do; our love must make long marches, and our prayers must have a wide sweep—we must embrace the whole world in our intercessions.

As showers which first fall on the hills and afterward run down in streams into the valleys, so the blessing of the Most High comes to the world through the church. We are blessed for the sake of others as well as ourselves. God deals mercifully with believers, then they are merciful to others, so the Lord's name is honored in the earth.

Psalm 67

Be Glad for His Guidance

> *Today's Faith Builder:*
>   But let the righteous be glad;
>   Let them rejoice before God;
>   Yes, let them rejoice exceedingly. (Psalm 68:3)

We should always desire the Lord's leading. Our glorious Captain clears the way, no matter how many may seek to obstruct it; He has but to arise and they flee. He has easily overthrown His enemies in the past and will do so all through the ages. Sin, death, and hell know the terror of His power; their ranks are broken by His presence.

How fitting a prayer this is for starting a revival! How it shows the right method of conducting one: The Lord leads the way, His people follow, the enemies flee!

The presence of God on the throne of grace is a constant delight to believers; let them not fail to drink of the streams which are meant to make them glad. The servants of the happy God should wear the garments of gladness, for in His presence is fullness of joy. That presence, which is the dread and death of the wicked, is the desire and delight of the saints.

"Again I will say, rejoice!" says the apostle (Phil. 4:4), as if he would have us add joy to joy without ceasing. Move on, army of the living God, with shouts of triumph, for Jesus leads the way.

Celebrate the character and deeds of God in song. Do it again and again; and let heartfelt praise be all directed to Him. Sing not to impress people, not to be heard of men, but to honor the Lord. Sing not to the congregation, but "to God." Rise to the highest pitch of joyful reverence in adoring Him.

Psalm 68:1–17

Daily Benefits

❯ *Today's Faith Builder:*
Blessed be the Lord,
Who daily loads us with benefits,
The God of our Salvation! (Psalm 68:19)

As great conquerors of old led whole nations into captivity, so Jesus leads forth a great company of people from the territory of His enemy as the trophies of His mighty grace. To be led into captivity by Him is for our captivity to cease; for our captivity itself to be led captive is a glorious result indeed. The Lord Jesus destroys His foes with their own weapons; He puts death to death, entombs the grave, and leads captivity captive (Eph. 4:8).

God's benefits are neither few nor light, there are loads of them; neither are they intermittent, but they come "daily." If He burdens us with sorrow, He gives strength sufficient to bear it; and if others attempt to oppress us, there is no cause for fear, for the Lord will rescue His people. No matter how strong the enemy, we will be delivered out of his hands.

The Almighty who has entered into a covenant with us is the source of our safety, and the author of our deliverances. As surely as He is our God He will save us. To belong to Him is to be safe.

No one but Jesus can open the gates of the grave; we will pass into them only at His bidding; while on the heavenward side He has opened the doors for all His people. He will save His people from their sins and from all evil, whether in life or death.

Our Lord is strong and makes us strong; blessed are they who draw from His resources. While the self-sufficient faint, the All-Sufficient One will sustain the weakest believer.

Psalm 68:18–35

Christ and Our Crises

> *Today's Faith Builder:*
> Save me, O God!
> For the waters have come up to my neck. (Psalm 69:1)

I f any inquire of whom the psalmist is speaking, of himself, or some other man, we would reply, "of himself *and* of some other man." Who the other man is, we need not take long to discover; it is the Crucified alone who can say, "And for My thirst they gave Me vinegar to drink." In the New Testament, the Holy Spirit has pointed out His footprints all through this sorrowful song and therefore we believe and are sure that the Son of Man is here.

This is the second psalm which begins "Save me, O God," and the former (Ps. 54) is but a shortened summary of this more lengthened complaint. It is remarkable that such a scene of suffering should be presented to us immediately after the jubilant ascension hymn of the previous psalm, but this only shows how interwoven are the glories and sorrows of our ever blessed Redeemer.

Our Lord was no fainthearted sentimentalist; His sorrows were real, and though He bore them heroically, they were terrible even to Him. His sufferings were unlike all others in degree, the waters were such as soaked into the soul; the floods were deep and overflowing.

To us the promise is, "The rivers . . . shall not overflow you" (Isa. 43:2), but no such word of comfort was granted to Him. My soul, your Well-Beloved endured all this for you.

Many waters could not quench His love, neither could the floods drown it. He stemmed the torrent of almighty wrath that we might forever rest in Jehovah's care.

Psalm 69:1–3

God Knows All About Us

❯ *Today's Faith Builder:*
O God, You know my foolishness;
And my sins are not hidden from You. (Psalm 69:5)

David's adversaries were on the throne when he was hiding in caves, just as our Lord's enemies held high positions on the earth. He of whom the world was not worthy was reproached and despised by people of His time. Though innocent, He was treated as guilty.

David has no part in plots against Saul, yet he was held accountable for them. Regarding our Lord, it may be said that He restores what He took not away, for He gives back the injured honor of God and returns man's lost happiness, though the insult of the one and the fall of the other were not, in any sense, His doing. Usually, when a ruler sins the people suffer, but here the proverb is reversed: The sheep went astray, and their wandering caused the Shepherd to suffer for them.

Confession of sin should be easy when we know that all is already known. A prayer without confession of sin may please a Pharisee's pride but will never bring justification. Those who have never seen their sins in the light of God's omniscience are unable to appeal to that omniscience in prayer. Only the one who can say, "You know my foolishness" can add, "You know that I love You" (John 21:15).

Reproach is always painful to a man of integrity and it must have been especially so to one of such holy character as our Lord, but see how He turns to His God and finds comfort in enduring all for His Father's sake. This same comfort belongs to all misrepresented and persecuted saints.

Psalm 69:4–9

The Tender Mercies of Our Lord

> *Today's Faith Builder:*
>> Hear me, O LORD, for Your lovingkindness is good;
>> Turn to me according to the multitude of Your tender mercies.
>>> (Psalm 69:16)

Our Savior wept much in secret for our sins, and, no doubt, frequently endured suffering and anguish of soul for us. Lonely mountain and desert places saw His repeated agonies which, if they could disclose them, would astonish us indeed.

Prayer is never out of season; it aids us in every trial. Our Lord's prayers were well timed and always accepted. Even the perfect One made His appeal to the rich mercy of God; much more should we.

No attribute of God is more sweetly comforting than mercy, and when sorrows multiply, we prize His multitude of mercies more than ever. Our enemies may sometimes outnumber the hairs of our head, but God's mercies cannot be numbered. Let us never forget that each one of them is an available and powerful argument for deliverance when we pray in faith.

It always strengthens the soul to dwell on the importance and sufficiency of the Lord's mercy. If ever a man needs the comforting presence of God it is when he is in distress; and being in distress is a reason to be pleaded with our merciful God as to why He should rescue us. The nearness of God is all a sufferer needs; one smile from heaven will still the rage of hell.

This is a deeply spiritual prayer and one very appropriate for one who feels alone. In renewed communion we will experience the comfort of redemption every day.

Psalm 69:10–19

A Song for Sufferers

> *Today's Faith Builder:*
> I will praise the name of God with a song,
> And will magnify Him with thanksgiving. (Psalm 69:30)

The psalmist was severely afflicted, but his faith was in God. You poor and sorrowful ones, lift up your heads; your Lord suffered and so will you. You are trodden down today as mud in the streets, but you will ride on mountaintops before long; and even now you are raised up together and made to sit together in the heavenlies in Christ Jesus (Eph. 2:6).

He who sang after the Passover sings even more joyously after the Resurrection and Ascension. He leads eternal melodies, and all His saints join in the chorus. Faith foresees the happy end of all affliction and makes us even now begin the music of gratitude which will go on increasing in volume forever.

We have sunshine after rain in these verses. The darkness is past and a glorious light now shines as the sun. All honor is given to Him to whom the prayer was presented; He alone could deliver and did deliver, and therefore, let all the praise be given to Him.

Grateful hearts are always looking for others to join them, and the rejoicing psalmist is delighted that other poor and oppressed people, observing the Lord's dealings with His servants, are encouraged to look for similar comfort and help in their own trials. The continual consolation of the godly is the experience of their Lord, for as He is so are we also in this world; moreover, His triumph has secured ours, and therefore, we have solid reasons to rejoice in Him.

Psalm 69:20–36

A Cause for Joy

> *Today's Faith Builder:*
> Let all those who seek You rejoice and be glad in You;
> And let those who love Your salvation say continually,
> "Let God be magnified!" (Psalm 70:4)

We are not forbidden, in hours of distress, to ask God to speed His coming to rescue us. When in a hurry, a person uses as few words as possible. It is perfectly all right to cry to God daily for speedy deliverance and help; our weakness and our many dangers make this a perpetual necessity.

The psalmist's enemies desire to put his faith to shame so he earnestly prays that they may be disappointed and confused. This will certainly be so at that dread day when the wicked awake to shame and everlasting contempt, if not sooner. When men try to turn others back from the right road, God retaliates by driving them back from their goal. They thought they would shame the godly, but instead they were ashamed and will be forever.

How fond men are of mocking believers, but their taunts are meaningless and more like animal cries than human words! Rest assured that the enemies of Christ and His people will have wages for their work; they will be paid in their own coin. They loved scoffing and they will be filled with it; they will become a proverb and a byword forever.

All true worshipers will have cause for joy. Those who have tasted divine grace will not only feel joy but will continually tell others of it and call upon them to glorify God.

Psalm 70

Trusting God Every Day

❯ *Today's Faith Builder:*
In You, O LORD, I put my trust;
Let me never be put to shame. (Psalm 71:1)

Jehovah deserves our confidence; let Him have it all. Every day we must guard against every form of reliance on ourselves or others and hourly place our faith in our ever-faithful God.

Not only must we rest on God as a man stands on a rock, but we must trust in Him as a man hides in a cave. The more intimate we are with the Lord, the firmer our trust will be.

Here we see a weak man, but he is in a strong place; his security rests in the tower in which he hides and is not placed in jeopardy through his own weakness. This castle is securely shut against all adversaries, they cannot burst its gates open. The drawbridge is up, the bars are firmly in their places; but there is a secret door by which friends of the great Lord can enter at all hours of the day or night as often as they please.

There is never an hour when it is unlawful to pray. Mercy's gates stand wide open and shall do so until at last the Master of the house has risen up to shut the door. Believers find their God to be their strong and accessible refuge and this is for them a sufficient remedy for all the ills of life.

Happy is the man who can use "my" as many times as the many aspects of the Lord's character make it desirable. Is He a strong *refuge*? I will call Him "*my* strong refuge." He shall be *my* rock, *my* fortress, *my* God, (vv. 3–4), *my* hope, *my* trust (v. 5), *my* praise (v. 6).

If we are strong, it is in God; if we are safe, our Refuge shelters us; if we are calm, our soul has found her security in Him.

Psalm 71:1–8

The Strength of the Lord

> *Today's Faith Builder:*
>   I will go in the strength of the Lord GOD;
>   I will make mention of Your righteousness, of Yours only.
>   (Psalm 71:16)

The Lord our God is our only and all-sufficient refuge from every form of persecution. Nearness to God makes us feel secure. A child in the dark is comforted by grasping his father's hand.

When I cannot rejoice in what I have, I will look forward to what shall be mine and will still rejoice. Hope will live on a bare lot, and sing on a branch laden down with snow. No date and no place are unsuitable for hope. Hope is a dweller in all regions, hell alone excepted. We may always hope, for we always have grounds for it.

In our own strength we will fall, but when we hear the voice which says, "Go in this might of yours" (Judg. 6:14), we may advance without fear. Though hell itself were in the way, believers would pursue the path of duty, crying: "I will go in the strength of the Lord GOD; I will make mention of Your righteousness, of Yours only."

Man's righteousness is not fit to be mentioned; filthy rags are best hidden. Neither is there any righteousness under heaven or in heaven comparable to the divine. As God Himself fills all space and is, therefore, the only God, leaving no room for another, so God's righteousness in Christ Jesus fills the believer's soul and he counts all things but dross and rubbish that he "may gain Christ and be found in Him, not having [his] own righteousness, which is from the law, but that which is through faith in Christ" (Phil. 3:8–9).

Forever dedicated to You, my Lord, be this poor, unworthy tongue, whose glory it shall be to glorify You.

Psalm 71:9–16

God Is Faithful to People of All Ages

> *Today's Faith Builder:*
> O God, You have taught me from my youth;
> And to this day I declare Your wondrous works. (Psalm 71:17)

It was comforting to the psalmist to remember that from his earliest days he had been the Lord's disciple. None are too young to be taught of God; they make the most successful scholars who begin early.

There is something touching in the sight of hair whitened with snows of many winters. When our infirmities multiply, we may with confidence expect greater privileges in the world of grace to make up for our declining physical strength. Nothing will make God forsake those who have not forsaken Him. Our fear is that He should do so, but His promise kisses that fear into silence.

The psalmist had leaned on the almighty arm, so he could speak from experience of its sufficiency, and he longed to do so before his life came to a close. He would leave a record for unborn ages to read. He thought the Lord's power to be so worthy of praise that he would make the ages ring with it until time would be no more. This is the purpose of life for believers, so they should labor zealously for the accomplishing of this, their most important work. Blessed are they who begin in youth to proclaim the name of the Lord and do not stop until their last hour brings their last word for their Master.

When we are laid low in the tomb, it is a blessing that we can go no lower but will then mount to better lands; and all this, because the Lord is ever mighty to save. It is safe to lean on Him, since He bears up the pillars of both heaven and earth.

Psalm 71:17–24

The King and His Peaceful Kingdom

> *Today's Faith Builder:*
> In His days the righteous shall flourish,
> And abundance of peace, until the moon is no more. (Psalm 72:7)

Solomon was both king and king's son; so also is our Lord. He has power and authority in Himself, and also royal dignity given Him by His Father. He is the righteous King; He is the Lord our righteousness. We are waiting until He shall be manifested as the ever-righteous Judge. May the Lord hasten that long-awaited day.

What a consolation that none can suffer wrong in Christ's kingdom! He sits on the Great White Throne, unspotted by a single deed of injustice or even mistake of judgment; reputations are safe with Him. We do not always understand what He is doing, but the King of the last and best of monarchies deals out equal justice to the delight of the poor and oppressed.

Where Jesus is there is peace—lasting, deep, eternal. Even those things which we once dreaded lose all terror when Jesus is owned as King of the heart. When the Lord is with us trials and afflictions increase, rather than decrease, our peace.

In a spiritual sense, peace is given to the heart by the righteousness of Christ; all the powers and passions of the soul are filled with a holy calm when the way of salvation, by divine righteousness, is revealed. Then we go forth with joy and are led forth with peace; the mountains and the hills break forth before us into singing. Sin, Satan, and all our enemies will be crushed by the iron rod of King Jesus. We have, therefore, no cause to fear but great reasons to sing.

Psalm 72:1–7

June 6

Our Compassionate King

> *Today's Faith Builder:*
    For He will deliver the needy when he cries,
    The poor also, and him who has no helper. (Psalm 72:12)

The rule of Messiah will be widespread. From Pacific to Atlantic, and from Atlantic to Pacific, He will be Lord, and the oceans which surround each pole will be under His control. All other power will be subordinate to His.

Start where you will, by any river you choose, and Messiah's kingdom will reach to all the earth. As Solomon's realm embraced all the land of promise and left no unconquered territory, so will the Son of David rule all lands given Him in the better covenant. No nation will suffer beneath the tyranny of the Prince of Darkness.

The extent of our Lord's rule is set forth by two far-reaching "alls," all kings and all nations. We do not yet see all things put under Him, but since we see Jesus crowned with glory and honor in heaven, we have no doubts about His universal kingdom. Every knee shall bow to Him and every tongue shall confess that Jesus Christ is Lord to the glory of God the Father (Phil. 2:10–11).

Who would not trust a Prince so good that He makes the needy His special care and pledges Himself to be their deliverer in times of need? A child's cry touches a father's heart, and our King is the Father of His people. If we can do no more than cry it will bring omnipotence to our aid.

All helpless ones are under the special care of Zion's compassionate King; let them place themselves in fellowship with Him. Let them look to Him, for He is looking for them.

Psalm 72:8–12

Living in Kingdom Come

> *Today's Faith Builder:*
> Blessed be the LORD God, the God of Israel,
> Who only does wondrous things! (Psalm 72:18)

Jesus calls not the righteous but sinners to repentance. He does not attempt the needless work of aiding proud Pharisees to display their self-righteousness, but He cares about poor publicans who dare not look up to heaven because they are convicted of their sins. We ought to be eager to be among these needy ones whom the Great King so highly favors.

The fox and the lion have joined forces against Christ's lambs, but the Shepherd will defeat them and rescue the defenseless from their teeth. A soul hunted by the temptations of satanic deceptions and the accusations of people filled with malice will do well to fly to the throne of Jesus for shelter.

God's church is not to be considered unimportant; its beginnings were small, but its growth has been astonishing. The subjects of Christ will be numbered like blades of grass. We need not fear for the cause of truth in the land; it is in good hands, where the will of the Lord is sure to be fulfilled. "Do not fear, little flock, for it is your Father's good pleasure to give you the kingdom" (Luke 12:32).

The saving power of the name of Jesus makes it the rallying point of believers. His name shall be exalted and glorified and shall remain forever the same. As long as time is measured by days, Jesus will be glorious. He will be earth's greatest blessing; when people wish to bless others they will bless in His name. His name is glorious and that glory will fill the whole earth. Our hearts yearn daily for so great a future, and we cry "Amen, and amen!"

Psalm 72:12–20

God Is Good to Us

> *Today's Faith Builder:*
> Truly God is good to Israel,
> To such as are pure in heart. (Psalm 73:1)

The theme of this psalm is that ancient problem which Job's friends could not understand: the present prosperity of the wicked and the sorrows of the godly. Unbelieving philosophers have been puzzled by this, and even believers have too often been tempted to doubt God's goodness by it. The psalmist declares his confidence in God and plants his foot on a rock while he explains his inner conflict.

God is only good, nothing else but good to His children. He cannot act unjustly or unkindly to them; His goodness to them is beyond dispute and without compromise. The writer does not doubt this but lays it down as his firm conviction.

It is important to be sure of what we know, for this will be a good anchor for us when we are troubled by storms which arise from things we do not understand. Whatever may or may not be the truth about mysterious and seemingly incredible things, there are certainties somewhere. Experience has placed some tangible facts within our grasp; let us then cling to these, and they will prevent our being carried away by those hurricanes of infidelity which still come from the wilderness, and like whirlwinds, smite the four corners of our house and threaten to overthrow it.

O my God, however perplexed I may be, let me never think ill of You. If I cannot understand You, let me never cease to believe in You. It must be so, it cannot be otherwise; You are good to those whom You have made good and where You have renewed the heart You will not leave it to its enemies.

Psalm 73:1

Wrong Conclusions

❭ *Today's Faith Builder:*
>   But as for me, my feet had almost stumbled;
>   My steps had nearly slipped. (Psalm 73:2)

Here is the account of a great battle within the psalmist's soul, a spiritual marathon, a hard and well-fought conflict in which the one who was nearly defeated finally won the victory.

The psalmist contrasts himself with his God who is ever good; he admits his personal shortcomings, compares himself with the clean in heart, and goes on to confess his sins. The Lord is good to His saints, "but as for me," am I one of them? Can I expect to share His grace? Yes, I do share it; but I have acted unworthily, very unlike one who is truly pure in heart.

Errors of heart and head soon affect conduct. There is an intimate connection between the heart and the feet. When people doubt the righteousness of God, their own integrity begins to waver. How we ought to watch the inner man, since it has such a powerful effect on the outward character!

It is pitiful that an heir of heaven should have to confess, "I was envious at the foolish." Yet this acknowledgment is, we fear, due from most of us. The psalmist's eye was fixed too much on one thing: He saw their present and forgot their future, saw their outward display and overlooked the discomfort of their souls.

Here the case is stated in the plainest manner, and many a Christian will now recognize his own experience. Wisdom has been expensive, but we have bought it and no longer fret because of evildoers, for the Lord has shown us what their end will be.

Psalm 73:2–14

A Time to Keep Silent

❯ *Today's Faith Builder:*

   If I had said, "I will speak thus,"
   Behold, I would have been untrue to the generation of
   Your children. (Psalm 73:15)

It is not always wise to speak one's thoughts; if they remain within, they will only injure us; but once spoken, they may cause many problems for others. From such a man as the psalmist, complaining and fault finding would have brought deep disappointment to the whole family of God.

We ought to look at the consequences of what we say to others, especially to believers. Rash, undigested, ill-considered speech is responsible for much of the trouble in the churches. Would to God that men would bridle their tongues.

Where we have any suspicion of being wrong, it is better to be silent; it can do no harm to be quiet, and it may do serious damage to spread our hastily formed opinions. Expressions which convey the impression that the Lord acts unjustly or unkindly, especially if they fall from the lips of people of known character and experience, are as dangerous as torches among dry stubble; the timid and trembling are sure to be discouraged by such talk and this will give them reasons for even deeper distress of soul.

The psalmist could not bear the thought of scandalizing the family of God, and yet his seething inner thoughts caused him great anguish. Then his mind entered eternity where God dwells; his heart gazed within the veil, he stood where the thrice-holy God stands. This changed his point of view and brought him peace. He had seen too little to be able to judge; a wider view changed his outlook.

Psalm 73:15–17

God Guides Us All Through Life

> *Today's Faith Builder:*
> You will guide me with Your counsel,
> And afterward receive me to glory. (Psalm 73:24)

The holy poet reviews his inner struggle and criticizes himself for his folly. His pain had been intense. It was a deep-seated sorrow, one which penetrated his very soul. His spirit had become bitter; he had judged others in a harsh, critical, mean manner. He had poisoned his own life at the source and made all its streams as bitter as gall. A false philosophy tortures the mind but true faith drives away doubts and sets captives free!

The wisest of men are foolish enough to ruin themselves unless grace prevents it. The psalmist had acted as if he knew nothing. He had judged happiness by this mortal life, by outward appearances and fleshly enjoyments. He had, for a time, renounced the dignity of an immortal spirit, and, like a mere animal, judged by outward appearances. It was an evidence of his true wisdom that he was so conscious of his own errors. Oh, for grace to hate the very appearance of evil!

The writer here does not give up his faith, though he confesses his former folly. He puts his hand into that of the great Father, asking to be led and agreeing to follow. Our former mistakes are a blessing when they drive us to Him. The end of our own wisdom is the beginning of our being wise. With Him is counsel, and when we come to Him, we are sure to be led in the right path.

Afterward! Blessed word. We can cheerfully put up with the present when we foresee the future and know it is bright.

Psalm 73:18–24

Drawing Near to God Is Good for Us

⟩ *Today's Faith Builder:*

    My flesh and my heart fail;
    But God is the strength of my heart and my portion forever.
                       (Psalm 73:26)

The psalmist now turns away from the glitter that fascinated him to the true gold that was his real treasure. He felt that his God was better to him than all the wealth, honor, and peace he had envied in prosperous unbelievers. He emptied himself of all earthly desires, that he might be filled with his God. No longer would his wishes wander, no other object would tempt them to stray. Now the Ever-living One would be his all in all.

The flesh and heart of this good man had failed him but his God would not fail him. God would be his protection and joy. His heart would be kept by divine love and filled eternally with God's glory. After having been driven far out to sea, Asaph casts anchor in the old port. We will do well to follow his example. There is nothing desirable except God; let us, then, desire only Him. All other things must pass away; let our hearts abide in Him who alone abides forever.

We must be near God to live; to be far off, caught up in wicked works is death. If we profess to be the Lord's servants, we must remember that He is a jealous God and requires spiritual purity from all His people.

The nearer we are to God, the less we are affected by the attractions and distractions of earth. Access into the most holy place is a great privilege and a cure for a multitude of ills. It is good for all saints and for me in particular. It will always be good for me to approach the source of all good: God Himself.

Psalm 73:25–28

God's People Are Safe

> *Today's Faith Builder:*
> Remember Your congregation, which you have purchased of old,
> The tribe of Your inheritance, which you have redeemed—
> This Mount Zion where You have dwelt. (Psalm 74:2)

There are two questions which allow only negative replies: "Has God cast away His people?" (Rom. 11:1), "Will the Lord cast off forever?" (Ps. 77:7).

God is never weary of His people, and even when He is angry with them it is but for a moment and His goal is their eternal good. Grief asks strange questions and expects unreasonable answers. It is a wonder of grace that the Lord has not long ago put us aside as unwanted garments, but He hates putting away (Mal. 2:16) and will be patient with those He has chosen.

The church is no new purchase of the Lord; from before the world's foundation the chosen were regarded as redeemed by the Lamb slain (Eph. 1:4). Shall ancient love die out and the eternal purpose become frustrated? Can He abandon His blood-bought ones and forsake His redeemed? Impossible! The woes of Calvary, and the covenant of which they are the seal, are the security of the saints.

The Lord's portion is His people; will He lose His inheritance? Will He allow His possessions to be torn from Him?

Will the Spirit of God who dwells in our hearts leave them to become haunts for the devil? Will He vacate the throne?

God forbid.

Psalm 74:1–11

God at Work

❯ *Today's Faith Builder:*
    For God is my King from of old,
    Working salvation in the midst of the earth. (Psalm 74:12)

Having spread his sad case before the Lord, the psalmist now presents a series of arguments for divine help. He reasons from the Lord's former wonders of grace and His deeds of power, asking for a repetition of them.

From the most remote period of Israel's history the Lord had worked out her many salvations, especially at the Red Sea. The world was astonished by His wonders of deliverance. Now, every believer may rest full faith in the ancient deeds of the Lord, the work of Calvary, the overthrow of sin, death, and hell.

He who worked out our salvation in the past will not, cannot, desert us now. Each past miracle of grace assures us that He who has begun to deliver will continue to redeem us from all evil. His deeds of old were public and took place in spite of His foes. They were not delusions and, therefore, in all our trials, we look for His assistance and we will surely receive it.

Land and sea receive their boundaries from the Lord. Continents and islands are mapped by His hand. Our Lord who limits the sea can restrain His enemies; and He who guards the borders of the dry land can also protect His people.

The God of nature is the God of grace and we may argue from the changing seasons that sorrow is not meant to rule the year. The flowers of hope will blossom, and the fruits of joy will ripen. The Lord will not allow those who trust in Him to be put to shame.

Psalm 74:12–23

Giving Thanks for His Wondrous Works

> *Today's Faith Builder:*
>   We give thanks to You, O God, we give thanks!
>   For Your wondrous works declare that Your name is near.
>   (Psalm 75:1)

Let us not neglect thanksgiving or we may fear that in the future our prayers will not be answered. As smiling flowers gratefully reflect in their lovely colors the varied beauties of the sun's rays, so should gratitude spring up in our hearts after the smiles of God's providence.

We should praise God again and again. Faint gratitude is ingratitude. For infinite goodness there should be measureless thanks. Faith promises redoubled praise for greatly needed and remarkable deliverances.

God is at hand to answer and do wonders, and we adore our ever-present Lord. We sing not of an unknown god who sleeps and leaves the church to her fate, but of One who on our darkest days is near, a very present help in trouble (Ps. 46:1).

Baal is on a journey (1 Kings 18:27), but Jehovah dwells in His church. Glory be to the Lord, whose perpetual deeds of grace and majesty are clear evidence that He is with us always, even to the end of the age (Matt. 28:20).

The Lord upholds and sustains the right so there is no real cause for fear. While the pillars stand, and stand they must for God upholds them, our house will stand through the storm.

When the day of the Lord arrives, earth's elements will melt with fervent heat (2 Peter 3:10), but even then we will be confident and secure in the care of our covenant God.

Psalm 75:1–3

Praising God for His Justice and Love

> *Today's Faith Builder:*
>> But I will declare forever,
>> I will sing praises to the God of Jacob. (Psalm 75:9)

There is a God who works in our lives; nothing happens by chance. Though deliverance should seem hopeless from earthly sources, God can come through for His people; though justice comes neither from the rising or the setting of the sun, it will come, for the Lord reigns.

People forget that all things are ordained in heaven; they see only human force and carnal passion, but the unseen Lord is far more real than these. He is at work behind and within the clouds. The foolish dream that He does not exist, but He is near even now and on the way to bring His cup of vengeance in His hand, one drink of which will stagger all His enemies.

Even now He is judging. He has not abdicated His authority; the Lord reigns. Empires rise and fall at His bidding. A dungeon here and a throne there are assigned by His will. Kings are but puppets in His hand, serving His purpose when they rise and fall. All power belongs to God; all else is shadow, unreal, misty, dreamlike.

The punishment of the wicked is prepared; God Himself is ready to send it. But the saints will busy themselves rehearsing Jehovah's praises, while their foes drink the wine of God's wrath (Rev. 14:19).

The promise-keeping God who delivered Jacob from a thousand afflictions will bless our souls. He has kept His covenant, which He made with the patriarch, and has redeemed His seed, therefore we will spread His fame abroad forever.

Psalm 75:4–10

Knowing God

› *Today's Faith Builder:*
> In Judah God is known;
> His name is great in Israel. (Psalm 76:1)

If unknown in all the rest of the world, God has so revealed Himself to His people by His deeds of grace that He is no unknown God to them. To know the Lord is to honor Him: Those who know His name admire its greatness.

The unbelieving world is in darkness, but within the favored circle of those who know Him, Jehovah is revealed and adored. The world knows Him not and therefore blasphemes Him, but His church is full of passion to proclaim His fame to the ends of the earth.

The Lord dwells in His church, and to her He is the Lord and giver of peace. The church glories in the knowledge that the Redeemer inhabits her by His Holy Spirit. Attacks by the enemy are futile, for they not only attack us, but the Lord Himself. Who then will harm us? No weapon that is formed against the church shall prosper, and every tongue that rises against her in judgment she shall condemn (Isa. 54:17).

The fear of man is a snare, but the fear of God is a great virtue and has great power for good over the human mind. Let all worship be only to Him.

The angels fell when their rebellion provoked His justice; Adam lost his place in Paradise in the same manner; Pharaoh and other proud monarchs passed away at His frown; neither are there any on earth or in hell who can survive the terror of His wrath. Blessed are those who are sheltered in the atonement of Jesus and therefore have no reason to fear the righteous anger of the Judge of all the earth!

Psalm 76:1–7

When Wrath Becomes Praise

> *Today's Faith Builder:*
>> Surely the wrath of man shall praise You;
>> With the remainder of wrath You shall gird Yourself.
>> (Psalm 76:10)

People will not hear God's voice if they can help it, but God causes it to be heard. The echoes of judgment executed on the arrogant Assyrians are still heard and will be remembered all through the ages to the praise of divine justice. All nations trembled at the news and sat in humbled awe.

Our Lord has a compassionate eye toward the poor and despised; He makes it His priority to right all their wrongs. "Blessed are the meek, for they shall inherit the earth" (Matt. 5:5). They have little enough of it now, but their Avenger is strong and He will surely care for them.

When man breathes out threats he is but blowing the trumpet of the Lord's eternal fame. Furious winds often drive ships more swiftly into port. The devil blows the fire and melts the iron, and the Lord fashions it for His own purposes. Let men and devils rage as they may; they only fulfill our Lord's plan.

Men of the world are often a sword in the hand of God to punish others. Even the most rampant evil is under the control of the Lord and will in the end be overruled for His praise.

To vow or not is a matter of choice, but to discharge our vows is our duty. He who would defraud God is a thief. Our Lord keeps His promises; let not His people fail in theirs. He is a faithful God and deserves to have faithful people. He who deserves to be praised should be worshiped with more than our words.

Psalm 76:8–12

Where to Turn When Troubled

> *Today's Faith Builder:*
>> I cried out to God with my voice—
>> To God with my voice;
>> And He gave ear to me. (Psalm 77:1)

This psalm has much sadness in it, but we may be sure it will end well, for it begins with prayer and prayer never brings a bad ending. Asaph did not run to man but to the Lord, and he did not go to Him with studied, stately, stilted words, but with a cry, the natural, heartfelt expression of pain. He used his voice also, for though spoken words are not necessary to prayer, they often seem forced upon us by the intensity of our desires. Sometimes the soul feels compelled to speak in order to express its agony.

Since praying once did not seem sufficient, the psalmist prayed again. He needed an answer, he expected one, he was eager to have it soon, therefore he cried out to the Lord again and again, for the sound helped express his earnestness.

All day long his distress drove him to his God, and when night came he continued searching. Day and night his trouble was on his mind and his prayer continued. Some of us know what it is, both physically and spiritually, to be compelled to use these words: No relief has been given by the silence of the night, our bed has been a torture rack to us, our body has been in torment, and our spirit in anguish.

Finally, persistent prayer prevailed.

The gate opened to the steady knock.

The same will be true for us in our hour of trial; the God of grace will hear us and answer right on time.

Psalm 77:1–3

Remembering a Song in the Night

> *Today's Faith Builder:*
> I call to remembrance my song in the night;
> I meditate within my heart,
> And my spirit makes diligent search. (Psalm 77:6)

Sleep is a great comforter, but it departs from the sorrowful and then their sorrow deepens and eats into the soul. How much we owe to Him who gives His beloved sleep (Ps. 127:2)!

Words fail the one whose heart fails him. Sleepless and speechless, Asaph was at the end of himself, yet he rallied, and so will we.

Since nothing good was happening, this troubled one ransacked the past to find comfort. He tried to borrow a light from the altars of yesterday to brighten the gloom of today. It is our duty to search for comfort and not sullenly yield to despair. In quiet meditation thoughts may come to us which will raise our spirits, and there is scarcely any subject more likely to prove comforting than memories of past days when the Lord's faithfulness was tried and proven by His people.

At other times, the psalmist's spirit had a song for the darkest hour, but now he could only recall the tune as a departed memory. Where is the harp which once thrilled sympathetically to the touch of these joyful fingers? My tongue, have you forgotten to praise? Can you sing only sad songs?

Asaph searched his past to find comfort or to discover why it was denied him. No one will die by the hand of the enemy who has enough strength of soul remaining to struggle like this.

Psalm 77:4–9

The God of Wonders

❯ *Today's Faith Builder:*
You are the God who does wonders;
You have declared Your strength among the peoples. (Psalm 77:14)

Fly back, my soul, away from present trials, to the wonderful works of Jehovah, the Lord of Hosts, in history, for He is unchanged and is now ready to defend His servants as in the past. Whatever else may pass into oblivion, the marvelous works of the Lord in ancient days must not be forgotten. Memory is an aid to faith. When faith has its seven years of famine, memory, like Joseph in Egypt, opens her granaries.

Meditation enriches speech; it is sad that so much of the conversation of professing believers is worthless, because they take no time for deep thinking. One who meditates should speak out and share his insights, otherwise he is a mental miser, a mill which grinds corn only for the miller. We should choose our topics for meditation carefully so that our talk will build up others.

In a quiet, holy place we understand our God and rest assured that all His ways are just and right. When we cannot trace His way, we can trust it, for it is holy. We must have fellowship with our holy God if we would understand His ways. He who would be wise must worship.

God's providence and grace are both full of displays of His power. In grace, He is especially revealed as mighty to save. Who will not be strong in faith when there is so strong an arm to lean on? Shall our faith be weak when His power is beyond all question? My soul, allow these thoughts to banish all your doubts.

Psalm 77:10–15

Going Deeper

> *Today's Faith Builder:*
>> Your way was in the sea,
>> Your path in the great waters,
>> And Your footsteps were not known. (Psalm 77:19)

Obedient to the Lord, the lower atmosphere yielded its aid to overthrow the Egyptian army. The cloudy chariots of heaven hurried forward to discharge their floods. From the higher regions the dreaded artillery of the Lord of Hosts thundered over the heads of the routed enemies, confusing their minds and adding to their horror.

Lightnings flew like bolts from the bow of God. Swiftly, here and there, went the red tongues of flame, gleaming on helmet and shield, revealing the innermost caverns of the hungry sea. All heaven resounded with the voice of the Lord.

Far down in secret channels of the deep is Your roadway. You can make the sea a highway for Your glorious march. There where billows surge and swell, You still walk, Lord of each crested wave.

You are alone in Your glory, and Your ways are hidden from mankind. You will accomplish Your purposes, but Your means of doing so are often concealed, even though they need no concealing; they are themselves too vast and mysterious for human understanding.

Quietly, as a flock, Israel was guided on by human agency which veiled the overwhelming glory of the divine presence. The Smiter of Egypt was the Shepherd of Israel. He drove His foes before Him, but went before His people. Therefore, with devout joy and full of comfort we close this psalm, the song of one who forgot how to speak and yet learned to sing far more sweetly than others of his time.

Psalm 77:16–20

Listen! God Is Speaking

⟩ *Today's Faith Builder:*
Give ear, O my people, to my law;
Incline your ears to the words of my mouth. (Psalm 78:1)

The inspired poet calls on his countrymen to pay attention to his patriotic teaching. When God gives His truth a tongue and sends for His messengers trained to declare His word with power, the least we can do is listen with earnest, obedient hearts. Shall God speak, and His children refuse to hear? His teaching has the force of law; let us yield both ear and heart to it.

We readers of the sacred records are obligated to study them deeply, exploring their meaning, and trying to practice their teachings. As the officer of an army begins his drill by calling "Attention!" every trained soldier of Christ is called on to listen to His words. People lend their ears to music; how much more then should they listen to the harmonies of the gospel? They sit enthralled in the presence of an orator; how much rather should they yield to the eloquence of heaven?

The mind of the poet-prophet was so full of ancient lore that he poured it forth in a continual stream of song. Beneath this gushing flood lie pearls and gems of spiritual truth, which will enrich those who dive into the depths and bring them up.

The letter of this song is precious, but the deeper message is priceless. Faith comes by hearing. Those who know the Lord will trust in Him; that they may be led to do so is the goal of all spiritual teaching. The result of this teaching should be holy living, not full heads and empty hearts.

Psalm 78:1–8

Equipped to Fight Both Day and Night

› *Today's Faith Builder:*
In the daytime also He led them with the cloud,
And all the night with a light of fire. (Psalm 78:14)

Well-equipped and furnished with the best weapons of the times, the leading tribe failed in faith and courage and retreated before the enemy. How often have we also, though supplied with every gracious weapon, failed to wage successful war against our sins? We have marched on gallantly enough until the testing hour has come, and then in the day of battle we have failed to carry out good resolutions and holy obligations.

Vows and promises were broken, idols were set up, and the living God was forsaken. The Israelites were brought out of Egypt to be separated to the Lord, but they fell into the sins of other nations and did not maintain a pure testimony for the one true God. Before we condemn them, let us repent of our own wicked forgetfulness and confess the many times we have forgotten past blessings.

Our Lord does not begin a work, then cease from it while it is incomplete. He brought Israel into the wilderness, and He led them through it. The cloud He provided both led and shadowed the tribes. It was a vast sunscreen by day, making the fierce heat of the sun and the glare of the desert sand bearable.

So constant was the care of the Great Shepherd that all night every night the sign of His presence was with His people. That cloud which was a shade by day was as a sun by night, just like the grace which cools and calms our joys, soothes and comforts our sorrows.

Psalm 78:9–14

Grumbling About God's Provision

> *Today's Faith Builder:*
> He also brought streams out of the rock,
> And caused waters to run down like rivers. (Psalm 78:16)

Moses split the rock in the wilderness. He was the instrument, but the Lord did it all. Twice He made the rock a gushing stream. What can He not do?

The streams were so fresh, so abundant, so constant, that they seemed to well up from earth's inner fountains and leap from the deep beneath. This divine supply for Israel's urgent need ought to have kept them forever faithful to their wonder-working God.

The supply of water was as abundant in quantity as it was miraculous in origin. Torrents, not driblets, came from the rock. Streams followed the camp; the supply was not for an hour nor a day. This was a marvel of goodness. If we think about the abundance of divine grace we will be lost in admiration. Mighty rivers of love have flowed for us in the wilderness.

To question the ability of the Almighty is to speak against Him. These people were foolish enough to say that although their God had given them bread and water, He could not properly order or furnish a table. How sad that we have also complained about our blessings and longed for the fulfilling of some dream, counting God's gifts to us to be nothing because they did not happen to be exactly what we had hoped or imagined. Chronic complainers will speak against God even when He daily loads them with benefits (Ps. 68:19).

We are still fools and slow of heart to believe our God (Luke 24:25), and this ought to bring us to repentance.

Psalm 78:15–24

Eating Like Angels

❯ *Today's Faith Builder:*
> Men ate angels' food;
> He sent them food to the full. (Psalm 78:25)

The delicacies of kings were outdone, for the elegancies of angels were supplied to Israel. Bread of the mighty ones fell on feeble man. Those who are lower than the angels dined with them.

It was not for the priests or the princes that the manna fell, but for all the nation, for every man, woman, and child in the camp, and there was enough for them all.

God's banquets are never stinted; He gives the best diet and plenty of it. Gospel provisions deserve every praise that we can heap on them; they are free, full, and abundant; they are of God's preparing, sending, and bestowing.

He is well-fed whom God feeds; heaven's food is nourishing and plentiful. If we have ever fed on Jesus, we have tasted better than angels' food, for:

> *Never did angels taste above*
> *Redeeming grace and dying love.*

Happy are the travelers who, in the desert, have their food sent from the Lord's own palace above; let them eat abundantly of the heavenly banquet and magnify the all-sufficient grace which supplies all their needs, according to His riches in glory, by Christ Jesus (Phil. 4:19).

O Lord Jesus, You blessed manna of heaven; we will now feed on You as our spiritual food and will ask You to put away all wicked unbelief from us. Our fathers ate manna and doubted; we feed upon You and are filled with faith.

Psalm 78:25–31

God's Compassion for Wayward People

> *Today's Faith Builder:*
>> But He, being full of compassion, forgave their iniquity,
>> And did not destroy them.
>> Yes, many a time He turned His anger away,
>> And did not stir up all His wrath. (Psalm 78:38)

Apart from faith, life is empty. To wander up and down in the wilderness was a waste of time, but unbelief had shut the Israelites out of the promised land. Those who wasted their days in sin had little cause to wonder when the Lord shortened their lives and declared that they would never enter into His rest.

Doubtless much of the frustration and failure that many experience results from their being weakened by unbelief and controlled by evil passions. None are as disillusioned and unhappy as those who allow sense and sight to override faith and their reason and appetites to overcome their fear of God.

Hard hearts can sometimes only be moved by death. When thousands died around them, the people of Israel suddenly became religious. Reflection followed affliction. They were led to see that they must place all their trust in their God, for He alone had been their shelter, their foundation, their fountain of supply, and their unchangeable friend.

We see the fullness of God's compassion, but we never see all His wrath. The Israelites were forgetful of God, but He was mindful of them. He knew they were made of earthy, frail, corruptible material, and therefore He dealt tenderly with them. The Lord is always ready to discover some reason to have compassion on us.

Psalm 78:32–39

June 28

Safe in His Care

> *Today's Faith Builder:*
> And He led them on safely, so that they did not fear;
> But the sea overwhelmed their enemies. (Psalm 78:53)

People who forget that being grateful returns blessings may also forget their obligation to be thankful. The plagues were signs of Jehovah's presence and proofs of His hatred of idols; these instructive acts of power were performed in the open view of all as signs to be observed by all people far and near. Miracles took place throughout the land, not in cities alone. The Israelites ought not to have forgotten this, for they were the favored people for whom these memorable miracles were performed.

The wolves were slain in heaps; the sheep were carefully gathered and triumphantly delivered. The tables were turned and the poor slaves were honored, while their oppressors were humbled before them. Israel went out like a flock; they were defenseless in themselves as sheep but they were safe under their Great Shepherd; they left Egypt as easily as a flock leaves one pasture for another.

Knowing nothing of the way before them, they were, nevertheless, rightly directed, for the All-Wise God knew every spot of the wilderness. To the sea, through the sea, and from the sea, the Lord led His chosen, while their former taskmasters were too bowed in spirit and broken in power to dare to attack them.

Well might the master of sacred song select "Israel in Egypt" as a choice theme for his poetic genius; and well may every believing mind linger over each part of this amazing deliverance.

Psalm 78:40–53

From Shepherd to King

> *Today's Faith Builder:*
> He also chose David His servant,
> And took him from the sheepfolds. (Psalm 78:70)

David always considered it a high honor that he was both chosen of God and a servant of God. He had been a shepherd of sheep, and this was a fitting school for a shepherd of people. Lowliness of occupation will not keep us from such honors as the Lord chooses to confer. He delights to bless those who are poor and looked down on (1 Cor. 1:27–31).

Exercising the care and art of those who watch young lambs, David followed the ewes in their wanderings. The tenderness and patience he gained by these experiences would develop in him the characteristics of a great king. This prepared David for the office and dignity which God had appointed for him. It is wonderful how often divine wisdom arranges the early and obscure portion of a choice life to make it a training period for a more active and noble future.

Whatever faults David had, he was totally sincere in his allegiance to Israel's superior King; he shepherded for God with an honest heart. He was a wise ruler and the psalmist magnifies the Lord for having appointed him. After a long voyage over a stormy sea, the ark of the Jewish state rested on its Mount Ararat beneath a wise and gentle reign.

As we conclude this long psalm, may we determine to have less sin and as much grace as are shown in Israel's history, and may we close it under the safe guidance of "that great Shepherd of the sheep" (Heb. 13:20).

Psalm 78:54–72

A Patriot's Prayer

> *Today's Faith Builder:*
>> Help us, O God of our salvation,
>> For the glory of Your name;
>> And deliver us, and provide atonement for our sins,
>> For Your name's sake! (Psalm 79:9)

This is a psalm of sorrow such as Jeremiah might have written among the ruins of Jerusalem. It evidently speaks of times of invasion, oppression, and national overthrow. Asaph was a patriotic poet who was never more at home than when he wrote about the history of his nation.

Generations store up transgressions to be paid for by their successors. This urgent prayer asks God to hasten to the rescue because the nation is hurrying down to destruction.

Here is masterly pleading. No argument has such force as this. God's glory was tarnished in the eyes of other nations by the defeat of His people and the profaning of His temple. Therefore His distressed servants ask for His aid.

Sin, the root of this evil, is seen and confessed; pardon is sought as well as removal of chastisement, and both are asked not as matters of right but as gifts of grace. God's name is again brought into the pleading. Believers will find it wise to frequently use this noble plea: It is the great gun of the battle, the mightiest weapon in the armory of prayer. God's glory springs from difficult circumstances, and the dark days of His people become the prelude to unusual demonstrations of the Lord's love and power.

Psalm 79

The Shepherd of Israel

> *Today's Faith Builder:*
> Give ear, O Shepherd of Israel,
> You who lead Joseph like a flock;
> You who dwell between the cherubim, shine forth! (Psalm 80:1)

The name "Shepherd of Israel" is full of tenderness, so it is selected by the troubled psalmist; broken hearts delight in the Lord's names of grace. We may be sure that He who chose to be a shepherd to His people will not turn a deaf ear to their cries.

The Lord had led, guided, and shepherded all the tribes in the wilderness and therefore the appeal is made to Him. The Lord's miracles and protection in the past are strong grounds for praying with expectation for the present and the future.

The Lord's presence was revealed upon the mercy seat between the cherubim, and in all our prayers we should come to Him this way; only in the mercy shown at the cross will God reveal His grace, and only through the sacrifice there can we hope to commune with Him. Let us always pray in the name of Jesus, who is our true mercy seat, to whom we may come boldly, expecting to see the glory of the Lord in answer to our prayers (Heb. 4:16).

Our greatest dread is the withdrawal of the Lord's presence, and our brightest hope is the prospect of His return. During Israel's darkest times, the light of her Shepherd's face is all she needs.

The psalmist prays that the God of Israel will be mighty on behalf of His people, chasing away their enemies and saving them. Oh, that in these days the Lord may be pleased to remember every part of His church and rescue all of her members from their enemies.

Psalm 80:1–6

The God Who Restores His People

❭ *Today's Faith Builder:*
> Restore us, O God of hosts;
> Cause Your face to shine,
> And we shall be saved! (Psalm 80:7)

A change of character is better than a change of circumstances. When the Lord changes His people He will soon change their condition. Only the Lord can do this, for conversion is as divine a work as creation; and those who have once turned to God, if they backslide, need the Lord to restore them again just as He changed them when they believed. It is a choice mercy that "He restores my soul" (Ps. 23:3).

All that is needed for deliverance is the Lord's favor. No matter how fierce the foe or strong the bondage the shining face of God assures both victory and liberty. Since we too often backslide, let us often with our lips and heart cry, "Restore us again, O God, cause Your face to shine, and we shall be saved."

See how the psalmist addresses God. He is here the God of Hosts. The more we approach the Lord in prayer and meditation the higher we will regard Him.

With God no enemy can harm us, without Him none are so weak as to be unable to do us damage. See what evils follow a path of sin and how terrible it is to be forsaken by God.

Faith's day grows brighter as the hours roll on, and her prayers grow more full and mighty. No emergency is too great for the power of God. He is able to save at the last moment by simply turning His smiling face upon His afflicted ones. We can do little with human strength and resources, but God can do all things with a glance. Oh, to live forever in the light of Jehovah's face!

Psalm 80:7–19

Sing to the Lord!

❯ *Today's Faith Builder:*
  Sing aloud to God our strength;
  Make a joyful shout to the God of Jacob. (Psalm 81:1)

The heartiest praise is due to our good Lord. His acts of love to us speak more loudly than any of our words of gratitude can do for Him. No lack of enthusiasm should ever show in our singing. Sing aloud, you debtors to sovereign grace, your hearts are profoundly grateful; let your voices express your thankfulness.

The Lord was the strength of His people in safely delivering them out of Egypt, sustaining them in the wilderness, placing them in Canaan, preserving them from their foes, and giving them victory. People give honor to those in whom they trust, so let us sing aloud to our God, who is our strength and our song.

The God of the nation, the God of their father Jacob, was praised in joyful music by the Israelites; let no Christian be silent or slack in praise, for this God is our God. It is regretful that the supposed refinements of modern singing frighten our congregations from joining lustily in the hymns. For our part, we delight in full bursts of praise and would rather discover the ruggedness of a lack of musical training than miss the heartiness of congregational song. The gods of Greece and Rome may be worshiped well enough with classical music, but Jehovah can only be adored with the heart, and the best music for His service is that which gives the heart priority and liberty in expression.

God is not to be served with misery but with mirthful music. Let then all of our singing be holiness to the Lord.

Psalm 81:1–7

July 4

What God Wants to Give Us

> *Today's Faith Builder:*
> I am the LORD your God,
> Who brought you out of the land of Egypt;
> Open your mouth wide, and I will fill it. (Psalm 81:10)

We owe all to the God and Father of our Lord Jesus Christ. The world, the flesh, and the devil have been of no service to us; they are aliens, foreigners, enemies, and we should not bow down before them. "Little children, keep yourselves from idols" (1 John 5:21) is our Lord's word to us, and by the power of His Spirit we will cast our every false god from our hearts.

Israel was a thousand times pledged to Jehovah because of His marvelous deeds for them in connection with the Exodus. Because He had brought them out of Egypt, He could do great things for them. He had proven His power and His good will; it remained only for His people to believe in Him and ask in keeping with His ability to respond to their requests. Their expectations, though great, could never exceed the bounty of the Lord.

Little birds in their nests open their mouths wide, and the parent birds may fail to fill them, but this will never be so with our God. His treasures of grace are inexhaustible. The Lord can do great things for an obedient people. When His people walk in the light of His countenance and maintain uncompromised holiness, the joy and consolation He gives them are inconceivable. To them the joys of heaven have already begun. They can sing in the ways of the Lord. The spring of the eternal summer has commenced for them. They are already blessed.

Psalm 81:8–16

A Cry for Justice

> *Today's Faith Builder:*
> Arise, O God, judge the earth;
> For You shall inherit all nations. (Psalm 82:8)

A saph no doubt saw much bribery and corruption around him, and while David punished it with the sword, he resolved to attack it with a prophetic psalm. In doing so, the sweet singer was not forsaking his profession as a musician for the Lord, but rather was simply using his talent for a special purpose. He was praising God when he rebuked the sin which dishonored Him, and if he was not making music, he was hushing discord when he called for rulers to dispense justice impartially.

God is the great overseer, who, from His point of view, sees all that is done by the leaders of governments. When they sit in state He stands over them, ready to correct them if they pervert justice.

Judges will be judged, and justices will receive justice. A higher authority will criticize the decisions of earthly lawmakers, and even the judgments of our most impartial judges will be revised by the High Court of heaven.

Come, Judge of all mankind; bring all bad judges to Your bar and end their corruption and prejudice. Here is the world's true hope of rescue from the fangs of tyranny.

The time will come when all races of men will own their God and accept Him as their King. There is one who is "King by right divine," and He is even now on His way. The last days will see Him enthroned and all unrighteous rulers broken like potter's vessels by His power. The second Advent is still earth's brightest hope. Come quickly, "even so, come, Lord Jesus" (Rev. 22:20).

Psalm 82

Asaph's Prayer for Protection

❭ *Today's Faith Builder:*
Do not keep silent, O God!
Do not hold Your peace,
And do not be still, O God! (Psalm 83:1)

This is the last occasion on which we will meet with this eloquent writer. The patriotic poet sings again of wars and imminent dangers, but it is not a godless song of a thoughtless nation entering into war with a light heart. Asaph is well aware of the serious dangers arising from the powerful confederate nations who are Israel's enemies, but his soul in faith rests on Jehovah while as a poet-preacher he excites his countrymen to prayer with this sacred song.

Here the appeal is to *El*, the Mighty One. He is entreated to act and speak because His nation suffers and is in great jeopardy. Now the psalmist looks entirely to God; he asks not for "a leader bold and brave" or for any human force, but casts his burden upon the Lord, being sure that His eternal power and Godhead could meet every need.

These enemies of Israel were also God's enemies and are here described as such, adding intensity to the argument for intercession. The adversaries of the church are usually a noisy and boastful crowd. Their pride is like brass which is always sounding, a cymbal which is ever clanging (1 Cor. 13:1).

Malice is cold-blooded enough to plot with deliberation, and pride, though it is never wise, is often crafty. Hidden away from all harm are the Lord's chosen. Their enemies don't believe this and hope to destroy them; they might as well attempt to destroy the angels before the throne of God. The Lord can easily defeat the enemies of His people.

Psalm 83

Longing to Be in God's House

⟩ *Today's Faith Builder:*
My soul longs, yes, even faints
For the courts of the LORD;
My heart and my flesh cry out for the living God. (Psalm 84:2)

This psalm has a mild radiance about it, entitling it to be called The Pearl of Psalms. If Psalm 23 is the most popular, Psalm 103 the most joyful, Psalm 119 the most deeply experiential, Psalm 51 the most sorrowful, this is one of the most sweet of the Psalms of Peace.

Lovely to the memory, the mind, the heart, the eyes, to the whole soul, are the gatherings of believers. Earth contains no sight so refreshing to us as the meeting of believers for worship. Only weak Christians see nothing pleasant in the services of the church.

The psalmist says his soul longs, pines, and faints to meet with the saints in the Lord's house. His desire was deep and insatiable; his very soul was yearning for God. To stand once again in those areas which were dedicated to holy adoration was the longing of his heart.

True subjects love the courts of their king. The psalmist declared that he could not remain silent in his desires but began to cry out for God and His house; he wept, he sighed, he pleaded for that privilege.

Some need to be whipped to church, while here David is crying for it. He needed no clatter of bells from the belfry to ring him in, he carried his bell in his heart. A holy appetite is a better call to worship than a church bell.

Psalm 84:1–4

The Believer's Source of Strength

❭ *Today's Faith Builder:*
> Blessed is the man whose strength is in You,
> Whose heart is set on pilgrimage. (Psalm 84:5)

The blessing of worshiping the Lord belongs not to half-hearted, listless worshipers, but to those who throw all their energies into it. Neither prayer, nor praise, nor the hearing of the Word will be pleasant or profitable to persons who have left their hearts behind them. A company of pilgrims who had left their hearts at home would be no better than a caravan of carcasses, quite unfit to unite with living saints in adoring the living God.

Those who love the ways of God are blessed. When we have God's ways in our hearts, and our heart in His ways, we are what and where we should be and will enjoy divine approval.

As men meet around a well and talk cheerfully, being refreshed after their journey, so even when sorrowing or going through any other valley, the pilgrims to the skies find sweet comfort in brotherly communion.

There are joys of pilgrimage which make us forget the discomforts of the road. God gives His people the supplies they need while traveling the roads He points out for them. Christian fellowship and the joys of united worship make duties easy and delightful which have been difficult and painful.

Instead of being wearied, pilgrims gather strength as they proceed. Each individual becomes happier, each company becomes more numerous, each holy song more sweet and full. We grow as we advance if heaven is our goal. If we spend our strength in God's ways we will find it increasing.

Psalm 84:5–8

Our Sun and Shield

❯ *Today's Faith Builder:*
> For the LORD God is a sun and shield;
> The LORD will give grace and glory;
> No good thing will He withhold
> From those who walk uprightly. (Psalm 84:11)

Under the most favorable circumstances, enjoying earth's pleasures cannot be compared to the delights of the service of God. To feel His love, to rejoice in the person of the Savior, to survey the promises and feel the power of the Holy Spirit in applying precious truth to the soul, are joys which unbelievers cannot understand. A brief glimpse of the love of God is better than ages spent in the pleasures of sensual gratification.

The lowest position in the service of the Lord's house is better than the highest position among the lost. Only to wait at His threshold and peep within, so as to see Jesus, is bliss. To bear burdens and open doors for the Lord is more honorable than to reign among the wicked.

Heavenly pilgrims are not left without comfort or protection. The pilgrim nation found both sun and shield in that fiery, cloudy pillar which was the symbol of Jehovah's presence, and the Christian still finds both light and shelter in the Lord his God: a sun for happy days and a shield for dangerous ones. A sun above, a shield around; a light to show the way and a shield to ward off its perils: Blessed are those who journey with such a convoy; the sunny and the shady sides of life are equally happy to them.

The Lord gives both grace and glory in infinite abundance. What more can the Lord give, or we receive or desire?

Psalm 84:9–12

Revive Us Again

⟩ *Today's Faith Builder:*
Will You not revive us again,
That Your people may rejoice in You? (Psalm 85:6)

This psalm is the prayer of a patriot for his afflicted country, in which he pleads the Lord's former mercies and by faith foresees brighter days. The self-existent, all-sufficient *Jehovah* is addressed; by that name He revealed Himself to Moses when his people were in bondage. Sweeter still is the name "Our Father," with which Christians have learned to begin their prayers. It is wise to dwell on that part of the Lord's character which arouses the sweetest memories of His love.

We can wisely plead the Lord's interest in us, lashing our little boat close to His vessel, and experiencing a sacred communion in the tossings of the storm.

Hope here grows almost confident. She feels sure that the Lord will return in all His power to save. When we are dead or dying, faint and feeble, God alone can revive us. He has refreshed His people and He is still the same. He will repeat His acts of love.

Those who were revived would rejoice not only in their new life but in the Lord who was the author of it. Joy in the Lord is the ripest fruit of grace; all revivals and renewals lead up to it. By our possession of it we can measure our spiritual condition; it is a gauge of our inward prosperity.

A genuine revival without joy is as impossible as spring without flowers, as dawn without light. If we are enjoying visitations of the Spirit, let us abound in holy joy.

Psalm 85:1–7

Good Gifts from Above

❯ *Today's Faith Builder:*
  Yes, the LORD will give what is good;
  And our land will yield its increase. (Psalm 85:12)

When we believe that God hears us, it is but natural that we should be eager to hear Him. The word which can speak peace to troubled spirits can come only from Him; our voices are too feeble, a bandage far too narrow for the sore. God's voice is powerful: He speaks and it is done; when we hear Him our distress is ended. Happy is the one who prays and then has grace to lie patiently at the Lord's door and wait until His love will chase all sorrow far away.

Faith knows that a saving God is always near at hand, but only to those who fear the Lord and worship Him with holy awe. If salvation is near to seeking sinners, it is surely very near to those who have once enjoyed it and have lost its present joy because of their backsliding; they have but to turn again to the Lord and they will enjoy it again. Mercy comes hand in hand with Truth to fulfill the faithful promise of their gracious God.

Promises which lie unfulfilled like buried seeds will spring up and yield harvests of joy, and those renewed by grace will learn to be true to one another and their God and abhor the falsehood which they loved before. Being pure goodness, God will readily turn from His wrath and give good things to His repenting people.

Our evil brings evil on us, but when we are brought back to follow that which is good the Lord abundantly enriches us with good things. God's march of right will leave a track in which His people will joyfully follow.

Psalm 85:8–13

God Hears the Poor and Needy

> *Today's Faith Builder:*
> Bow down Your ear, O LORD, hear me;
> For I am poor and needy. (Psalm 86:1)

This psalm consists of praise as well as prayer, but it is all so directly addressed to God that it is properly called a prayer. A prayer is all the more pleasing to God when veins of praise run through it.

When our prayers are timid because of our humility, or feeble because we are sick, or unable to rise in faith because we are depressed, the Lord will still receive them; the infinitely exalted Jehovah will have respect to them. Our distress is a powerful reason for our being heard by our merciful and gracious Lord, for misery is always the master argument for mercy.

He who prays all day every day can have confidence that the Lord will hear him when he is in need. If in times of need we cry out to people, or place our confidence in sources other than the Lord, we may expect to be referred to them when calamity comes, but if it has been our habit in difficult times to look to the Lord alone, we can be sure that He will not desert us now.

See how David pleaded first that he was poor and needy, next that he was the Lord's set-apart one, then that he was God's servant and had learned to trust in the Lord. Finally, he stated that he had been taught by the Lord to pray daily. Any believer who is going through trials may claim these reasons for prayer to be answered when wrestling with our prayer-hearing God. He can also expect answers to his prayers. God's goodness flows in abounding streams to those who pray in adoring worship and make mention of His name.

Psalm 86:1–7

Give Heartfelt Praise to God

> *Today's Faith Builder:*
>   I will praise You, O Lord my God, with all my heart,
>   And I will glorify Your name forevermore. (Psalm 86:12)

It is wonderful when greatness and goodness are united, and only in our Lord do either of them exist absolutely and essentially. Thankfully they both exist in Him to an equal degree. Being good, He is ready to forgive; being great, He works great wonders. And there is no wonder so wonderful as forgiveness of sins.

All that God does or makes has wonder in it. Only fools find anything that God made uninteresting; the world is a world of wonders.

We should never praise God with less than all our heart and soul and strength, or our praise will be unreal and unacceptable. Gratitude will prolong its praise eternally. God never stops blessing us; let us never stop blessing Him. As He ever gives grace, let us ever give Him the glory for it.

Personal experience is always the master singer. The psalmist claims to sing among the loudest, because his debt to divine mercy is among the greatest. From the direst death and the deepest dishonor David had been kept by God, for his enemies would have done more than send him to hell had they been able. His sense of sin also made him feel as if the most overwhelming destruction would have been his portion had not grace prevented it.

Some can join the psalmist in speaking honestly of God's forgiveness, and he who pens these lines humbly confesses that he is one of them.

Psalm 86:8–13

The Foundation of the Church

> *Today's Faith Builder:*
> His foundation is in the holy mountains. (Psalm 87:1)

The foundation of the church, which is the mystical Jerusalem, is laid in the eternal, immutable, and invincible decrees of Jehovah. He wills that the church shall be; He settles all arrangements for her calling, salvation, maintenance, and perfection; and all His attributes, like the mountains around Jerusalem, lend their strength for her support.

The Lord has not founded His church on the sand of carnal policy, nor on the lowlands of human government, but on His own power and Godhead. These are pledged for the establishment of His beloved church, which is to Him the chief of all His works.

God delights in the prayers and praises of Christian families and individuals, but He gives special attention to the assemblies of the faithful; He has a special delight in their devotions when they meet to worship. This should lead each separate believer to identify with the church of God; where the Lord reveals His love the most, there should each believer desire and delight to be found. Our homes are very important to us, but we must not prefer them to the places where Christians gather to worship their Lord.

May it be our happy lot to be numbered with the Lord's chosen both in life and death: on the church roll below, and on the church roll above!

Churches are not so wealthy and powerful that we can look to them for everything, but the Lord, who founded the church, is the eternal source of all our supplies, and looking to Him, we will never faint nor fail.

Psalm 87

A Note of Hope in a Sad Song

> *Today's Faith Builder:*
>> Let my prayer come before You;
>> Incline Your ear to my cry. (Psalm 88:2)

"O LORD, God of my Salvation" is a hopeful title by which to address the Lord and it carries with it the only ray of comforting light that shines through this psalm. The writer has salvation, he is sure of that, and God is the sole author of it. When one can see God as his Savior, he is not entirely in darkness. While the living God can be spoken of as the life of our salvation, our hope will never quite die. One of the characteristics of true faith is that she turns to Jehovah, the saving God, when all other confidences have proved to be liars.

The psalmist's distress had not blown out the sparks of his prayer, but fanned them into a greater flame until they burned perpetually like a furnace at full blast. His prayer was personal; when others had not prayed, he had done so. It was intensely earnest, so that it was correctly described as a cry, the kind of cry that children make to move their parents to come and comfort them. It was also unceasing: Neither the business of the day nor the weariness of the night had silenced it. Surely such praying could not be in vain.

Day and night are both suitable to prayer, therefore let us go with Daniel and pray when men can see us. Yet, since supplication needs no light, let us accompany Jacob and wrestle at Jabbok until daybreak.

There may be obstacles which impede the upward flight of our prayers, so let us ask the Lord to remove them. He who has prayed day and night cannot bear to have his prayers unanswered.

Psalm 88

Perpetual Praise

⟩ *Today's Faith Builder:*

I will sing of the mercies of the Lord forever;
With my mouth will I make known Your faithfulness to
all generations. (Psalm 89:1)

Whatever we may observe or experience, we ought to praise God for His mercies since they always remain the same whether we can understand them or not. Human feelings sing only now and then, but faith is an eternal songster.

When others are silent, believers must keep singing. They should praise God continually since His love for them cannot change, even though Providence may seem to frown.

We are not only to believe in the Lord's goodness, but to always rejoice in it. His goodness is the source of all our joy and since it cannot be dried up, the stream of rejoicing ought never to stop flowing or cease to be fed by sparkling springs of song. We have many mercies in which to rejoice and should therefore multiply our expressions of thankfulness.

Jehovah provides our daily benefits, and He is the all-sufficient and unchanging God; therefore our rejoicing in Him should never cease nor become less enthusiastic. Even time must not place boundaries on our praises; they are to leap into eternity singing. He blesses us with eternal mercies, so let us sing to Him forever.

Because God is and ever will be faithful, we have a theme for song which will not be out of date for future generations. It will never be worn out, never be disproved, never be unnecessary, never be a dull subject without value to mankind.

Psalm 89:1–4

Who Can Still a Raging Sea?

> *Today's Faith Builder:*
>> You rule the raging of the sea;
>> When its waves rise, You still them. (Psalm 89:9)

Earth and heaven unite in admiring and adoring the promise-keeping God. Saints above see clearly into the heights and depths of divine love, therefore they praise its wonders. Saints below, being conscious of their many sins and their frequent grieving of the Lord, admire His faithfulness.

The holiest tremble in the presence of the Holy One; their familiarity with Him is seasoned with the profoundest awe. How reverent our worship should be!

Our Lord controls the ocean at all times, even during violent storms. At the Red Sea the foaming billows saw their God and stood upright in awe. Then the Lord stilled them. No one else can do this; to attempt it would be foolish, but the Lord's "Hush" silences the raging storm. The Lord's Anointed calmed the storms of Galilee, for He is Lord of all. As a mother stills her child to sleep, the Lord calms the fury of the sea, the anger of men, the storm of adversity, the despair of the soul, and the rage of hell.

All things are God's, rebellious earth as well as adoring heaven. Let us not despair because of the power of Satan. The habitable and cultivated earth, with all its produce, knows the Lord as its Creator and Sustainer, Builder, and Upholder.

God as a sovereign is never unjust or unwise. He is too holy to be unrighteous and too wise to be mistaken. Let all the upright in heart be joyful!

Psalm 89:5–14

Who Receives the Blessing of the Lord?

> *Today's Faith Builder:*
> Blessed are the people who know the joyful sound!
> They walk, O LORD, in the light of Your countenance.
>   (Psalm 89:15)

The psalmist has been singing of our blessed Lord. Those who share in His blessings know how to rejoice in His favor. Praise is an especially joyful sound; blessed are those who are familiar with its pleasant strains.

There is no hour in the day, and no day in our life, in which we may not rejoice in the name, person, and character of the Lord. We need no other reason for rejoicing. The all-sufficient Lord is our all-sufficient source of joy.

The Lord's righteous rewards for His people lift them up and encourage them, regardless of past oppression or depression they have suffered. If God were unjust or if He regarded us as being unrighteous we would be filled with misery, but since neither of these things is true, we are blessed indeed and will praise the name of the Lord.

In the Lord Jehovah we have both righteousness and strength. He is our beauty and glory when we are strong in Him as well as our comfort and food when we tremble because of conscious weakness in ourselves. Those whom the Lord makes strong are never to glory in themselves, they must ascribe all honor to the Lord alone; we have neither strength nor beauty apart from Him. Worldly people need material prosperity to lift them from despair, but believers find encouragement in the secret love of God.

Psalm 89:15–18

God's Great Guarantee

> *Today's Faith Builder:*
>   My covenant I will not break,
>   Nor alter the word that has gone out of My lips. (Psalm 89:34)

The Lord discovered David among the sheepfolds and recognized him as a man of gracious spirit, full of faith and courage, and therefore fit to be leader in Israel. Samuel anointed David to be king long before he ascended the throne.

Our Savior, Jesus, is also the Lord's Christ, or Anointed. The oil with which He is anointed is God's own oil; He is divinely endowed with the Spirit of holiness.

The almighty power of God abides permanently with Jesus in His work as Redeemer and Ruler of His people. Jesus must be among us, and then there will be no lack of power in our churches.

God was gracious and faithful to David and his descendants, and though through their sin the literal kingdom lost all its glory and the dynasty became obscure, his line remained unbroken. The former glory of David's kingdom will be more than restored by the enthroning of Him who is Prince of the kings of the earth, with whom the Lord's mercy and faithfulness remain forever. The millennial glory will reveal what the covenant holds for the once-despised Son of David, but even now faith sees Him exalted as King of kings and Lord of lords.

With Jesus the covenant is ratified both by blood and by the Word of God. It cannot be cancelled or altered but is an eternal guarantee resting on the integrity of One who cannot lie. As long as God lives, His people must live. Let those who choose to do so deny the safety of the saints; we know Christ will not forsake His own.

Psalm 89:19–34

God Keeps His Word

> *Today's Faith Builder:*

My covenant I will not break,
Nor alter the word that has gone out of My lips. (Psalm 89:34)

It is evil to be a "covenant-breaker," and such a disgraceful title will never apply to the Most High. Alterations and afterthoughts belong to shortsighted beings who meet with unexpected events which cause them to change their minds, but the Lord, who sees everything from the beginning, has no such reason for shifting His position. He is immutable in His nature and designs. He cannot change in heart and therefore not in promise.

A word once given is sacred. When a promise passes our lips, honesty forbids that we recall it unless the thing promised is impossible or wicked, neither of which can happen with the promises of God.

How comforting it is to see the Lord so steadfast! He, in the words before us, reasserts His covenant and rehearses His commitment to it. He does this at such length, and with such emphatic repetition, that it is evident He takes pleasure in His ancient and solemn contract.

God here pledges the crown of His kingdom, the excellent beauty of His person, the essence of His nature. He says if He ceases to be true to His covenant He will have forfeited His holy character. What more can He say? In what stronger language can He express His unchanging adherence to the truth of His promise?

When heaven and earth witness the Lord's promise, there remains no excuse for doubting and faith joyfully rests confidently in Him.

Psalm 89:34–52

Where Believers Live

⟩ *Today's Faith Builder:*

Lord, You have been our dwelling place in all generations.

(Psalm 90:1)

To believers, the Lord Jehovah, the self-existent God, is like their earthly homes. He shelters, comforts, protects, preserves, and cherishes each one of His own. Foxes have holes and birds have nests, but believers dwell in their God and have done so all through the ages. We do not dwell in the tabernacle or the temple but in God Himself.

We have never had to change our address. Kings' palaces have vanished beneath the crumbling hand of time, they have been burned and buried under mountains of ruins, but the imperial race of heaven has never lost its royal home. We still live where our fathers lived a hundred generations ago.

Before the mountains, those elder giants, had struggled forth from nature's womb as her great firstborn, the Lord was glorious and self-sufficient. Mountains to Him, though white with the snows of the ages, are but newborn babies, young things whose birth was only yesterday, the productions of an hour.

God was when nothing else was. He was God when the earth was only chaos, when mountains were not yet upheaved and the creation of the heavens and the earth had not begun.

In this Eternal One there is a safe home for all generations. A moment yet to come is longer than "yesterday when it is past" (Ps. 90:4), for that no longer even exists. There is barely enough time in a thousand years for the angels to change guards. God is always watching over us and a thousand years are as nothing to Him.

Psalm 90:1–11

Wisdom for Today

> *Today's Faith Builder:*
> So teach us to number our days,
> That we may gain a heart of wisdom. (Psalm 90:12)

Reflecting on the brevity of time moves people to give earnest attention to eternal things. They become humble as they look into the grave which is soon to be their bed; their passions cool in the presence of mortality; they begin to think about gaining wisdom. When the Lord is their teacher they become wise and prepare for eternity.

A short life should be spent wisely. We do not have enough time at our disposal to justify wasting even fifteen minutes. Neither are we sure of enough of time to justify procrastinating for a moment. The wise in heart will see this and seize every opportunity to serve God while they have time to do so.

When the Lord refreshes us with His presence our joy is so great that no one can take it from us. Even thoughts of approaching death are not able to distress those who enjoy assurance of salvation. Though they know the night is coming, they see nothing to fear in it. They continue to live while they live, triumphing in the present favor of God and leaving the future in His loving hands.

God's people do not want to work in vain. They know that they can do nothing without the Lord and therefore they cry to Him for help in their work, for acceptance of their efforts, and for the carrying out of their plans.

We come and go, but the Lord's work abides forever. Let us invest our lives doing things for Him that will last when we are in the grave.

Psalm 90:12–17

The One to Trust

❯ *Today's Faith Builder:*
I will say of the LORD, "He is my refuge and my fortress;
My God, in Him I will trust." (Psalm 91:2)

The blessings promised in this psalm are not for all believers, but those who live in close fellowship with God, who through the riches of His grace (Eph. 2:7) obtain continuous communion with Him. They also become possessors of rare and special benefits which are missed by those who follow afar off and grieve the Holy Spirit. Only those who know the love of God in Christ Jesus come into the secret place of the Most High. To those who dwell there, to live is Christ and to die is gain (Phil. 1:21).

Our omnipotent Lord will shield all those who dwell with Him; they will remain in His care as guests under the protection of their host. No shelter, real or imagined, can compare to the protection of Jehovah's shadow. What a shade in the day of burning heat! What a refuge in the time of deadly storm! Communion with God is safety. The closer we cling to our Almighty Father the more confident we can be.

The bird flies away to the thicket and the fox hastens to its den; every creature has its refuge for the hour of danger. Even so, let us flee to Jehovah, the Eternal Protector of His own, in every peril we face. When we are secure in the Lord, let us rejoice that our position is unassailable, for He is our fortress as well as our refuge.

We have trusted God in the past and we can trust Him still. He has never failed us, so why should we doubt His care? We ought to place our confidence in Him without hesitancy or wavering.

Psalm 91:1–2

Living Without Fear

❭ *Today's Faith Builder:*
   You shall not be afraid of the terror by night,
   Nor of the arrow that flies by day. (Psalm 91:5)

No subtle plot will succeed against one whose defense is the watchful care of God. We are foolish and weak as poor little birds and are likely to be lured to destruction by our enemies, but if we dwell near to God He will deliver us from the most skillful and dangerous deceiver.

The Holy Spirit can protect us from evil spirits; He who is mysterious can rescue us from mysterious dangers; He who is immortal can heal us from mortal sicknesses. There is a deadly epidemic of error, but we are safe from it if we dwell in communion with the God of truth. There is a fatal disease of sin, but we will not be infected by it if we cling to our Holy God.

Faith, by cheering the heart, keeps it free from the fear which in times of epidemic, kills more than the plague itself.

Close communion with God makes us immune to night fright and gives us courage in darkness. Freedom from fear is a great blessing because fear brings far more pain than real injuries. The shadow of the Almighty removes all gloom from the shadow of night.

O believer, dwell under the shadow of the Lord and none of your enemies will be able to destroy you. When Satan has emptied his quiver you will remain uninjured by his sinful strategy. His broken darts will be but trophies of the truth and power of the Lord your God who has protected you.

Psalm 91:3–8

Protection in Plagues

❭ *Today's Faith Builder:*
No evil shall befall you,
Nor shall any plague come near your dwelling. (Psalm 91:10)

In 1854, when I had been in London only twelve months, the neighborhood in which I worked was visited by Asiatic cholera and my congregation suffered from its deadly attack. Family after family called me to the bedsides of those stricken by this terrible disease and almost every day I was called to visit a grave.

With youthful enthusiasm, I threw myself into visiting the sick and was sent for by people from all parts of the area of all ranks and religions. I became weary in body and sick at heart.

My friends seemed to be falling around me one by one and I feared I was becoming sick. I felt that my burden was heavier than I could bear and I was ready to sink under it.

As God would have it, I was returning home from a funeral when my curiosity led me to read a sign in a shoemaker's window. It did not look like a trade announcement, nor was it, for it carried these words in bold handwriting:

Because you have made the Lord, who is my refuge,
Even the Most High, your dwelling place,
No evil shall befall you,
Nor shall any plague come near your dwelling.

The effect on my heart was immediate. Faith appropriated the text as her own. I felt secure, refreshed, girded with immortality. I went on visiting the dying with a calm and peaceful spirit. I felt no fear of evil and suffered no harm.

Psalm 91:9–10

Guardian Angels

> *Today's Faith Builder:*
> For He shall give His angels charge over you,
> To keep you in all your ways. (Psalm 91:11)

The Lord has promised us not one guardian angel, as some fondly dream, but protection by all the angels. These heavenly messengers make up the bodyguard of the royal princes of heaven (Heb. 1:14) and they received a commission from their Lord and ours to watch carefully over all the interests and concerns of the faithful.

The marching orders of the hosts of heaven require them to take special care of the people who dwell in God. It is not surprising that the servants are ordered to care for the comfort and protection of their Master's guests, and since they have been charged to do so by the Lord Himself we can be sure that they will carefully discharge the duty given to them. We will probably be amazed when we finally learn of the multiplied services which these unseen bodyguards have provided for us.

Christians can conquer their strongest and most deceitful enemy. Those who dwell in God live a charmed life and the evil forces of darkness become harmless before them. Their feet come into contact with the worst of foes: Satan himself nibbles at their heels, but in Christ Jesus they have the sure hope of bruising Satan under their feet shortly (Rom. 16:20).

Heirs of heaven are conscious of a special divine presence in times of severe trial. God is always near in sympathy and power to help His suffering ones. They are not preserved or rescued in a way which lowers them or makes them feel degraded. Instead, the Lord's salvation bestows honor on those it delivers.

Psalm 91:11–16

Give Thanks

> *Today's Faith Builder:*
>> It is good to give thanks to the LORD,
>> And to sing praises to Your name, O Most High. (Psalm 92:1)

Giving thanks is good ethically, for it is right; it is good emotionally, for it thrills the heart; it is good practically, for it leads others to do the same. When duty and pleasure combine, who will refuse to get involved and share in such blessings?

To give thanks to God is but a small thing for us to do since He daily loads us with benefits (Ps. 68:19). Still, the Holy Spirit calls giving thanks a good thing and we must not despise or neglect it. Devout praise is always good and is never out of season.

It is good to give thanks to the Lord in song. Nature itself teaches us to sing while expressing our gratitude to God. Do not the birds sing and brooks warble as they flow? Silent worship is sweet, but vocal worship is sweeter. Luther said, "Come, let us sing a Psalm and drive away the devil."

The day should begin with praise; no hour is too early for holy song. Lovingkindness is an appropriate theme for those dewy hours when morning is covering all the earth with drops of pearl. We should magnify the Lord eagerly and promptly.

No hour is too late for praise. The end of the day must not be the end of gratitude. When nature seems to adore its Maker in silent contemplation it is wrong for the children of God to hold back their expressions of thanksgiving. Evening is the time for reflecting on God's work in our lives. An appropriate theme for song then is God's faithfulness for another day.

Psalm 92:1–4

The Faithful Will Flourish

⟩ *Today's Faith Builder:*
The righteous shall flourish like a palm tree,
He shall grow like a cedar in Lebanon. (Psalm 92:12)

G od is both the highest and most enduring of all beings. Others rise and fall, but He is the Most High forever. Glory to His name! How great a God we worship!

The believer rejoices that he will not be permitted to perish but will be strengthened and enabled to triumph over his enemies by the power of God that is made available to him. Faith delights in foreseeing the mercy of the Lord and sings of what He will do and what He has done.

When we see a noble palm standing erect, sending all its strength upward in one bold column and growing out of the dearth and drought of the desert, we have a fine picture of the godly man. His goal in life is the glory of God and regardless of outward circumstances he is enabled by God's grace to live and thrive when all other things around him perish.

No heart has as much joy as the one which abides in the Lord Jesus. Fellowship with the stem brings fertility to the branches. If a man abides in Christ he brings forth much fruit.

Much depends on the soil in which a tree is planted; in our case, everything depends on our abiding in the Lord Jesus and deriving all our strength from Him. If we ever really grow in the courts of the Lord we will never be rooted up but will take root downward and produce fruit upward to His glory forever.

Psalm 92:5–15

Our Eternal King

> *Today's Faith Builder:*
> The LORD reigns,
> He is clothed with majesty;
> The LORD is clothed,
> He has girded Himself with strength.
> Surely the world is established, so that it cannot be moved.
> (Psalm 93:1)

Jehovah reigns! Whatever opposition may arise, His throne is unmoved; He has reigned, does reign, and will reign forever. Whatever turmoil and rebellion there may be on earth, the eternal King sits above all in supreme serenity. All things are ordered according to His eternal purposes and His will is done.

What can give greater joy to a loyal subject than seeing the king in his beauty? Let us repeat the proclamation, "The Lord reigns," whispering it in the ears of the discouraged and declaring it to our enemies.

God is clothed with majesty; not with the emblems of majesty, but with majesty itself: Everything around Him is majestic. He is not the resemblance but the reality of sovereignty. In nature, providence, and salvation the Lord is infinite in majesty. Happy are the people among whom the Lord appears in all the glory of His grace, conquering their enemies and subduing all things to Himself; then indeed He is seen to be clothed with majesty.

Strength always dwells in the Lord Jehovah, but He often hides His power until, in answer to His children's cries, He puts on strength, assumes the throne, and defends His own. It should be our constant prayer that in our day the reign of the Lord may be evident and His power displayed in and on behalf of His church.

Psalm 93

God Will Make Everything Right

> *Today's Faith Builder:*
>> For the LORD will not cast off His people,
>> Nor will He forsake His inheritance. (Psalm 94:14)

This psalm is another expression of the old question: Why do the wicked prosper? It is another instance of a good man, perplexed by the prosperity of the ungodly, cheering his heart by remembering that there is, after all, a King in heaven by whom all things will be made right. God has but to show Himself and the good cause triumphs. He comes, He sees, He conquers.

If God has proven His care for His people by a thousand acts of grace, how dare the ungodly say that He will not notice the wrongs done to them? Jacob's God led him and kept him all through his life and said concerning him and his family: "Do not touch My anointed ones, and do My prophets no harm" (Ps. 105:15).

Finally the psalmist's mind grows quiet. He no longer complains to God or argues with men, but tunes his harp to softer melodies, for his faith perceives that all is well for the most afflicted believer. Though he may not feel blessed, he is, even while being corrected by his Lord. He is precious in God's sight or the Lord would not take the trouble to correct him.

During fierce persecutions believers have sometimes thought the Lord had left His sheep and given them over to the wolf, but this has never happened, for the Lord will not withdraw His love from His own. The great Judge will come and the reign of righteousness will begin. All things will then be made right and all the godly will rejoice.

Psalm 94:1–15

Mercy for Our Times of Need

> *Today's Faith Builder:*
> If I say, "My foot slips,"
> Your mercy, O LORD, will hold me up. (Psalm 94:18)

Without the Lord's help the psalmist declares that he would have died and gone into the silent land where no more testimonies for the living God can be given. He may mean that he would not have had a word to speak against his enemies but would have been speechless and ashamed.

At such times nothing can help us but mercy; we can make no appeal to any supposed personal merit for we feel that our inbred sin makes our feet ready to slip. Our joy is that the Lord's mercy endures forever and is always at hand to rescue us from danger and hold us up when we would otherwise fall to our destruction.

This has been true for some of us ten thousand times, especially for this writer. The danger was imminent; it was upon us. We were going down; the peril was apparent; we saw it and were shocked at the sight. We were afraid and concluded it was all over for us. But then came the almighty intervention of God and we did not fall. We were held up by an unseen hand; the plans of the enemy were frustrated and we sang for joy. O faithful Keeper of our souls, be exalted forever and ever! We will bless the Lord at all times; His praise shall continually be in our mouths (Ps. 34:1).

When I am tossed to and fro with distractions, questions and fears, I will flee to my true rest. Leaving my sinful thoughts, my vain reasoning, my griefs, my cares, my conflicts, I will hurry to the Lord.

Psalm 94:16–23

Joyful Worship

> *Today's Faith Builder:*
> Oh come, let us sing to the LORD!
> Let us shout joyfully to the Rock of our salvation. (Psalm 95:1)

L et us sing to Jehovah. We love Him, we admire Him, we reverence Him; let us express our feelings about Him in song. It is good to urge others to magnify the Lord, but we must be careful to set a worthy example before them. We are not only to cry, "Come" but also to add, "let us sing," because we are singing ourselves.

Too much hymn singing is not to the Lord but to the ear of the congregation. Above all, our singing should be sincere, heartfelt, and fervently directed to the Lord alone.

With holy enthusiasm, let us sing, making a sound which will communicate our sincerity. Let us lift up our voices with abounding joy in the praise and worship of our Lord. As the children of Israel sang for joy when the smitten rock poured forth its cooling streams, let us sing joyfully to the Rock of our salvation.

It is not always easy to unite enthusiasm with reverence and frequently we destroy one of these qualities while trying to achieve the other. Perfect singing unites joy with seriousness, enthusiasm with humility, and fervency with moderation.

These attitudes are too often overlooked in ordinary worship services. People are so concerned about being serious that they put on a look of misery, forgetting that joy is as much a needed characteristic of true worship as solemnity. When we sing to the Lord, let us join the happy psalmist in singing joyfully to the Rock of our salvation.

Psalm 95:1–5

Humble Worship

❯ *Today's Faith Builder:*
Oh come, let us worship and bow down;
Let us kneel before the Lord our Maker. (Psalm 95:6)

Here the call to worship is renewed and backed with a motive which, to Israel of old and to Christians now, is especially powerful. Israel as a nation and the Israel of faith may be described as "the sheep of His pasture" (Ps. 100:3), and by both He is called "our God."

Our adoration of the Lord is to be humble. The "joyful shouting" is to be accompanied by lowliest reverence. We must come joyfully, but not proudly; familiar as children before a father, yet as reverent creatures before their Maker. Posture is not everything but it is something; prayer is heard when knees cannot bend, but it is fitting that an adoring heart should show its awe by prostrating the body and bending the knee.

If others refuse to worship, we at least will do so cheerfully. He is our God, therefore we will love Him; our Lord, therefore, we will worship Him. As He belongs to us, so we belong to Him. We are His people, whom He daily feeds and protects.

Our pastures are not ours, but His; we draw all our supplies from His storehouse. We are His as sheep belong to the shepherd. His hand is our rule, our guidance, our government, our source of supply. Israel was led through the desert and we are led through this life by "that great Shepherd of the sheep" (Heb. 13:20). The hand which opened the sea and brought water from the rock is still with us, working wonders.

Psalm 95:6–11

Sing a New Song

> *Today's Faith Builder:*
> Oh, sing to the Lord a new song!
> Sing to the Lord, all the earth. (Psalm 96:1)

The glad tidings of salvation for all people have been proclaimed, so let all who hear sing a new song. Angels announced the birth of Christ and the new dispensation with new songs; shall we not also sing?

Mourning is over and the time of singing hearts has come. The psalmist speaks as if he would lead the great choir and be the chief musician. He invites, he incites, he persuades others to worship and cries with all his heart, "O sing to Jehovah a new song."

The gospel is the clearest revelation of our Lord. Salvation outshines creation and providence, therefore let our praises overflow with this as our theme. Let us proclaim the good news and do so continually! This message is always new, always appropriate, always sure, always perfect; therefore let us declare it continually until He comes.

Each day brings a deeper experience of trusting our saving God. Each day shows us anew how much we all need His salvation; each day reveals the power of the gospel; each day the Holy Spirit works in hearts; therefore, without ceasing, let us tell the glorious message of free grace.

Let those do this who have experienced His salvation; they can tell others that there is salvation in none other and that in Him salvation for all is to be found. Let them sing and share it until the echo flies around the earth and all the armies of heaven unite to magnify the God who has demonstrated His salvation among all people.

Psalm 96:1–6

Give God the Glory

⟩ *Today's Faith Builder:*
Give to the LORD, O families of the peoples,
Give to the LORD glory and strength. (Psalm 96:7)

The first six verses of this psalm began with a triple exhortation to sing and the name of the Lord is repeated three times. Now we meet with the expression "Give to the LORD" used in the same triple manner.

The psalmist urges us to give the Lord the glory due His name. But who can completely fulfill this great obligation? Can all the nations of the earth pay this mighty debt?

All conceivable honor is due to our Creator, Preserver, Benefactor, and Redeemer, and no matter how much heartfelt honor we may offer Him, we cannot give Him more than His due. If we cannot bring the full honor He deserves, at least let us not fall short from a lack of honestly trying.

The beauty of holiness is the only beauty which God desires in our public services and nothing less can take its place. He does not regard the beauty of architecture and clothing. Moral and spiritual beauty are what delight His soul. Worship must not be rendered to Him in a careless, sinful, superficial manner; we must be reverent, sincere, earnest, and pure in heart, both in our prayers and praises.

Above and below let joy be shown. Let angels who stood amazed at the wickedness of men now rejoice over their repentance and restoration to favor. Let us all join in the song. Since the whole universe is to someday be clothed with smiles, shall we not also be glad?

Psalm 96:7–13

Who's in Charge?

❭ *Today's Faith Builder:*
The LORD reigns;
Let the earth rejoice;
Let the multitude of isles be glad! (Psalm 97:1)

J ehovah reigns" is the theme of this psalm. It is also the essence of the gospel message and the foundation of our Lord's kingdom. Jesus has come and all power is given to Him in heaven and on earth, therefore all are invited to obey Him and place their faith in Him. Believers draw comfort from these words; only rebels object to them.

Here is cause for joy! Other reigns have produced injustice, oppression, bloodshed, and terror. The reign of the infinitely gracious Jehovah is the hope of mankind and when all yield to it, the race will have its paradise restored. The entire earth should be glad that its Maker and Lord has come to His own, and the whole human race can also be glad since Jesus brings untold blessings to all who submit to Him.

Absolute power is safe in the hands of Him who cannot make a mistake or act unrighteously. When the books of God are opened, no eye will see one word that should be blotted out, one syllable of error, one line of injustice, one letter of unholiness.

The presence of Jesus in reigning power in us is as a fire to consume our lusts and melt our souls to obedience. We know that He is within us when His light shines in and fills us with holy fear, while at the same time the warmth of grace softens us to penitence, surrender, and obedience, like wax becomes soft in the presence of fire.

Psalm 97:1–6

Rejoice and Give Thanks

> *Today's Faith Builder:*
> Rejoice in the LORD, you righteous,
> And give thanks at the remembrance of His holy name.
> (Psalm 97:12)

The saints are safe: They have been saved and will be saved. Those who love the Lord will see His love revealed to them in protection from their enemies and as they keep far from evil, all evil will be kept far from them.

The full harvest of delight is not yet ours but it has been sown for us; it is springing up; it will yet fully appear. This is only for those who are right before the Lord in His righteousness, for all others darkness is reserved.

Rejoicing is not restricted to one righteous person but is for all the upright in heart. After speaking of the crown of life that will be given to him, Paul immediately added "and not to me only but also to all who have loved His appearing" (2 Tim. 4:8).

The upright ought to be glad; they have cause to be glad and they will be glad. Those who are right-hearted will also be glad-hearted. Right leads to light. In the furrows of integrity lie the seeds of happiness which develop into a harvest of joy. God has lightning for sinners and light for saints. The gospel of Jesus, wherever it goes, sows the whole earth with joy for believers.

The psalmist had called on the earth to rejoice and here he turns to the righteous of the earth and asks them to lead the song. If all others fail to praise the Lord, the godly must praise Him. Salvation from sin is the priceless gift of our holy God, therefore let us magnify Him forever.

Psalm 97:7–12

Marvelous Things

> *Today's Faith Builder:*
>   Oh, sing to the LORD a new song!
>   For He has done marvelous things;
>   His right hand and His holy arm have gained Him the victory.
>   (Psalm 98:1)

Jesus, our King, lived a marvelous life, died a marvelous death, arose by a marvelous resurrection, and ascended marvelously into heaven. By His divine power He has sent the Holy Spirit doing marvels and by that sacred energy His disciples have also done marvelous things. Idols have fallen, superstitions have withered, systems of error have fled, and empires of cruelty have perished. For all this He deserves the highest praise. His acts have proven His Deity: Jesus is Jehovah and therefore we sing to Him as the *Lord*.

Our Lord's marvelous conquests have been achieved by His unweaponed hand. Sin, death, and hell fell beneath His mighty power and the idols and errors of mankind have been overthrown and destroyed by His hand alone.

The victories of Jesus among people are more wonderful because they are not won by physical means but by moral power, the energy of goodness, justice, truth; in a word, by the power of His holy arm. His holy influence has been the sole cause of success.

The salvation which Jesus accomplished is the result of His wonderful wisdom, so it is ascribed to His right hand. It meets the requirements of justice, so the psalmist speaks of His holy arm. It is His own unaided work, so all the glory is given to Him, and it is marvelous beyond human comprehension, so it deserves a new song.

Psalm 98:1–3

Praising the Lord of All the Earth

> *Today's Faith Builder:*
> Shout joyfully to the LORD, all the earth;
> Break forth in song, rejoice, and sing praises. (Psalm 98:4)

E very tongue, aroused by a joyful heart, must vigorously applaud our Lord. We must shout like people who are welcoming a King. Loud and happy hosannas must be raised.

All should shout for joy when the Lord comes among them in the proclamation of His gospel reign. John Wesley said: "Sing lustily, and with a good courage. Beware of singing as if you are half dead or half asleep; but lift up your voice with strength. Be no more afraid of your voice now, nor more ashamed of its being heard, than when you sang the songs of Satan."

Let every form of praise be used, every kind of music pressed into service until the accumulated praise causes the skies to echo the joyful sound. There is no fear of our being too enthusiastic in magnifying the God of our salvation, but we must be sure that the song comes from the heart, otherwise the music is nothing but a noise in His ears, whether it is caused by human throats or organ pipes or loud trumpets. Let your hearts loudly ring out the honors of our conquering Savior. Let us praise the Lord with all our might because He has vanquished all our enemies and led our captivity captive (Eph. 4:8). Those who are most in love with Jesus will do this best.

The rule of Christ is the joy of nature. The hope of His coming gives this troubled earth a cause to rejoice.

Lord, my soul faints with delight at the sound of your approaching chariots and can only cry, "Come quickly" (Rev. 22:20).

Psalm 98:4–9

Our Great God

❭ *Today's Faith Builder:*
The LORD is great in Zion,
And He is high above all the peoples. (Psalm 99:2)

The Lord reigns" is one of the most joyous utterances which ever leaped from mortal lips. The overthrow of the reign of evil and the setting up of Jehovah's kingdom of goodness, justice, and truth is worthy to be praised in song again and again.

Believers tremble with devout emotion, and sinners tremble with terror when the rule of Jehovah is fully understood. The coming kingdom of Christ is not a small matter; it is a truth which, above all others, should stir the depths of our nature.

The temple's sacred hill was the center of the worship of the great King and the place where His grandeur was most clearly seen. His church is now His favored palace, where His greatness is displayed, acknowledged, and adored. There He unveils His attributes and commands the humblest respect; the ignorant forget Him, the wicked despise Him, atheists oppose Him, but among His chosen ones He is great beyond comparison. He is greatly loved and respected by those saved by His grace. He is great in Himself: great in mercy, power, wisdom, justice, and glory.

In such a God we rejoice. His greatness and high position are delightful to us; the more He is honored and exalted in hearts, the more His people are thrilled. If Israel delighted in Saul because He was head and shoulders above the people, how much more should we rejoice in our great King, who is as high above us as the heavens are above the earth. Oh, come and let us worship and bow down before Him!

Psalm 99:1–2

Exalt and Worship the Lord

> *Today's Faith Builder:*
> Exalt the LORD our God,
> And worship at His footstool—
> He is holy. (Psalm 99:5)

God is the King, the mercy seat is His throne, and the scepter He holds is holy like Himself. He never exerts His power tyrannically; He is absolute in governing His creation, but His might delights in right; His force is used only for just purposes.

Godly people in the past were sure that what the Lord did was just, and instead of questioning His actions, they humbly submitted themselves to His will, confidently rejoicing that His almighty power was devoted to promoting righteousness and justice for all.

If no one else adores the Lord, let His own people give Him their heartfelt worship. Surely we who have experienced His lovingkindness should praise Him with all our hearts. Do we need to be urged to worship Him? We ought to blush for being so backward! It should be our daily delight to magnify so good and great a God.

Holiness brings harmony of all the virtues. The Lord has not just one glorious attribute; all of His attributes are equal in Him. This is the crown of His honor and the honor of His crown. His power is not His choicest jewel, nor is His sovereignty, but His holiness.

All of God's creatures should delight in His complete moral excellence. When they do, their delight is evidence that their hearts have been renewed and they have become partakers of His holiness.

Who would not adore Jehovah, whose character is untainted purity, unswerving justice, and unbounded love?

Psalm 99:3–5

God Answers When His People Call

> *Today's Faith Builder:*
> Moses and Aaron were among His priests,
> And Samuel was among those who called upon His name;
> They called upon the LORD, and He answered them. (Psalm 99:6)

God has always had a priesthood. The three holy men mentioned here stood in His courts and saw His holiness. Moses saw the Lord in flaming fire revealing His perfect law; Aaron often watched the sacred fire devour the sin offering, and Samuel witnessed the judgment of the Lord on Eli's house because of the error of his way.

Let these men, or such as these, lead us in our worship; let us approach the Lord at the mercy seat as they did, for He is as accessible to us as He was to them. They made it their lives' work to call on Him in prayer and by doing so brought down many blessings on themselves and others.

Their prayers were not in vain. Being a holy God, He was true to His promises and answered them from the mercy seat. Here is a reason for praise: Answers to the prayers of some are proofs of God's readiness to hear others.

These three men asked for great things. They prayed for a whole nation; they stopped great plagues and turned away fiery wrath. Who would not adore so great and merciful a God? If He was not holy He would be false to His Word and refuse His people's cries; this, then, is recorded for our joy and for His glory, that holy men of old did not pray in vain.

Psalm 99:6–9

Serve the Lord with Gladness

❭ *Today's Faith Builder:*
Serve the LORD with gladness;
Come before His presence with singing. (Psalm 100:2)

Our happy God should be worshiped by a happy people. A cheerful spirit is in keeping with His nature. We should cherish His acts and be grateful for His mercies. In every land, Jehovah's goodness is seen, therefore He should be praised in every land.

The world will never be right until with one unanimous shout it adores the only God. You nations, how long will you blindly reject Him? Your golden age will never arrive until you love and honor Him with all your hearts.

"Serve the Lord with gladness." He is our Lord and therefore He is to be served; He is our gracious Lord so He is to be served with joy. The invitation to worship given here is not a melancholy one, as though adoration were a sad funeral ritual, but a cheery, glad exhortation, as though we were invited to a marriage feast.

We ought to worship and thoughtfully seek the presence of God when we approach Him. This is a serious act for every rightly instructed heart, but at the same time it must not be performed in the slavery of fear. We are not to come before Him with weeping and wailing, but with psalms and hymns.

Since singing is both a joyful and devout exercise, it should always be the way we approach God. The orderly, harmonious, hearty offering of praise by a congregation of devout people is a foretaste of the worship of heaven, where praise, absorbed in prayer, has become the only means of adoration.

Psalm 100:1–2

The Sheep of His Pasture

> *Today's Faith Builder:*
> Know that the LORD, He is God;
> It is He who has made us, and not we ourselves;
> We are His people and the sheep of His pasture. (Psalm 100:3)

Sheep gather around their shepherd and look up to him; like them, let us gather around the great Shepherd of mankind. Declaring our relationship to God is in itself praise. When we tell of His goodness we are giving our best adoration to Him.

Our public services should abound with thanksgiving; it is like the incense of the temple which filled the whole house with smoke. Sacrifices for sins are ended, but those of gratitude will never be out of date.

Thankfully, the innermost court is now open to believers, to enter into that which is within the veil. We are expected to acknowledge this high privilege by singing. Let praise be in your heart as well as on your tongue and let it all be for Him to bless His name, His character, His person. Whatever He does, be sure that you bless Him for it; bless Him when He takes away as well as when He gives; bless Him as long as you live, under all circumstances; bless Him for all His attributes.

Our hearts leap for joy as we bow before One who has never broken His word nor changed His purpose. Resting on His sure Word, we feel that joy which is commanded here and in the strength of it we now come into His presence and praise His name.

Psalm 100:3–5

The Song of the King

> *Today's Faith Builder:*
>   I will sing of mercy and justice;
>   To You, O LORD, I will sing praises. (Psalm 101:1)

This is just the kind of psalm the man after God's own heart would compose when he was about to become king in Israel. Knowing the Lord has appointed him to be king, he decides to act as becomes a ruler whom the Lord has chosen. After songs of praise, a psalm of practice provides variety and fits the occasion. We never praise the Lord better than when we do those things which are pleasing to Him.

The psalmist would praise both the love and the severity, the sweets and the bitters, which the Lord had mingled in His experience; he would admire the justice and the goodness of the Lord. Such a song would naturally lead to godly resolutions about his own conduct.

Mercy and justice would temper the kingdom of David because he had seen and loved them in the kingdom of his God. Everything God does in our lives may appropriately become the theme of a song. We ought to bless the Lord as much for the justice with which He corrects us when we sin as for the mercy with which He forgives it; there is as much love in the blows of His hand as in the kisses of His mouth (Song 1:2). Upon remembering their lives, instructed believers scarcely know which to be more grateful for—the comforts which have cheered them, or the afflictions which have cleansed them.

Our soul's sole worship must be praising the Lord. The psalmist forsakes the minor key, which was soon to rule him in Psalm 102, and resolves that, come what may, he will sing to the Lord whatever others might do.

Psalm 101

Help Needed Now!

> *Today's Faith Builder:*
> Do not hide Your face from me in the day of my trouble;
> Incline Your ear to me;
> In the day that I call, answer me speedily. (Psalm 102:2)

This psalm is a patriot's lament over his country's distress. He clothes himself in the griefs of his nation as in a garment of sackcloth, and casts her dust and ashes upon his head as signs and causes of his sorrow. He has his own private woes and personal enemies. Moreover, he is seriously ill, but the miseries of his people cause him a far more bitter anguish, and he pours this out in an earnest, sorrowful cry. However, this patriot does not mourn hopelessly. He has faith in God and looks for the resurrection of the nation through the omnipotent favor of the Lord.

It is a great relief in times of distress to acquaint others with our trouble; pains are eased when we share our problems, but the sweetest comfort of all is to have God Himself as a sympathizing listener to our complaint. He hears us. And this is no dream or fiction; we can be sure of it.

We may ask to have answers to prayer as soon as possible, but we must not complain if the Lord should think it wiser to delay. We have permission to ask and to pray repeatedly but we have no right to demand or be angry. God is as willing to grant us a favor now as tomorrow, and He is not slow to fulfill His promises. When answers come shortly after we pray they are all the more encouraging.

Psalm 102:1–11

August 16

The Enduring One

Today's Faith Builder:
> But You, O LORD, shall endure forever,
> And the remembrance of Your name to all generations.
> (Psalm 102:12)

Now the writer's mind is turned away from his personal and national troubles to the true source of all consolation, the Lord Himself, and His gracious purposes for His people. The sovereignty of God is an unfailing reason for comfort. He rules and reigns whatever happens, and therefore all is well.

What God is now He always will be; what our forefathers told us of the Lord we find to be true, and what our experience enables us to record will be confirmed by our children and their children's children. All other things are vanishing like smoke and withering like grass, but the one eternal, unchanging light shines over us all and will do so when all these shadows have disappeared.

Time impairs all things: Fashion becomes obsolete and passes away. The visible creation, which is like the garment of the invisible God, is growing old and wearing out and our great King is not so poor that He must always wear the same robes.

Before long, our Lord will fold up the worlds and put them aside as worn-out clothing. Then He will attire Himself in new clothes, making a new heaven and a new earth where righteousness dwells. How quickly this will all be done! In the restoration, Omnipotence will not be hindered!

God lives on! No decay can change or destroy Him.

What a joy this is!

O my soul, rejoice in the Lord always, since He never changes!

Psalm 102:12–28

Counting Our Blessings

❯ *Today's Faith Builder:*
Bless the LORD, O my soul;
And forget not all His benefits. (Psalm 103:2)

Music of the soul is the very soul of music. The psalmist strikes the best keynote when he begins with stirring up his inner self to magnify the Lord. He soliloquizes, holds self-communion, and exhorts himself as though he felt that dullness would soon steal over him, as indeed it will over us all, unless we watch diligently.

Jehovah is worthy of our praise in that highest style of adoration which is intended by the term *bless*. God has given all of our many faculties, emotions, and capacities to us and they ought to all join in a chorus of praise to Him.

We should not forget even one of God's blessings. They are all beneficial to us, all worthy of Himself, and all subjects for praise. Memory is very treacherous about the best things; by a strange perversity caused by the Fall, it treasures up the refuse of the past and permits priceless treasures to lie neglected. It grips grievances tenaciously and holds benefits too loosely. It needs prodding to do its duty, though that duty ought to be its delight. Observe that the psalmist calls all that is within him to remember all the Lord's benefits. God's all cannot be praised with less than our all.

The Lord has saved us with a great salvation—shall we not give Him thanks? The name of "ingrate" is one of the most shameful that one can wear; surely we cannot be content to run the risk of such a label. Let us awake, then, and with intense enthusiasm bless the Lord.

Psalm 103:1–5

Mercy Enough for Me

❯ *Today's Faith Builder:*
For as the heavens are high above the earth,
So great is His mercy toward those who fear Him. (Psalm 103:11)

Mercy pardons sin, grace bestows favor, and the Lord abounds in both of these. He can be angry and bring His righteous indignation on the guilty, but this is His unusual response. He lingers long, with loving pauses, tarrying by the way to give space for repentance and opportunity for accepting His mercy. We should learn from this to be slow to anger; if the Lord is longsuffering under our great provocations how much more ought we to endure the errors of our brothers and sisters! He is God, not man, or our sins would soon drown His love; yet above the mountains of our sins the floods of His mercy rise.

All the world tastes of His sparing mercy and those who hear the gospel receive His inviting mercy. Believers live by His saving mercy, are preserved by His upholding mercy, are cheered by His consoling mercy, and will enter heaven through His infinite and everlasting mercy. Let abounding grace be our hourly song. Let those who feel they live on it glorify the plenteous fountain from which it so spontaneously flows.

The Lord would not have His people harbor resentments and in His grace sets them a great example. In our most difficult situations, we have never suffered as we deserved to suffer; our daily lot has not been determined by what we had coming to us, but by undeserved kindness. The mercy of the Lord is limitless; like the height of heaven, it cannot be measured.

Psalm 103:6–11

Sins Gone Forever

> *Today's Faith Builder:*
> As far as the east is from the west,
> So far has He removed our transgressions from us. (Psalm 103:12)

O glorious verse! No other verse in the Bible can excel it! Sin is removed from us by a miracle of love!

What a load to move! And yet it is removed so far that the distance cannot be measured. Fly as far as the wings of imagination can bear you and if you journey through space eastward you are farther from the west with every beat of your wings. If sin is removed this far, we may be sure that the scent, the trace, the very memory of it must be entirely gone. If this is the distance of its removal, there is no shade of fear of it ever being brought back again; even Satan himself could not retrieve it.

Our sins are gone, Jesus has taken them away. As far as the place of sunrise is removed from yonder west, where the sun sinks when his day's journey is done; this far were our sins carried by our Scapegoat twenty centuries ago, and now they cannot be found.

Come now my soul, awaken thoroughly and glorify the Lord for this richest of blessings.

Hallelujah!

The Lord alone could remove sin at all and He has done it in a Godlike way, taking away all our transgressions.

Our heavenly Father never overloads us and never fails to give us strength equal to our day, because He always takes our weakness into account. Bless His holy name for His gentle care of His frail creatures!

Psalm 103:12–14

Mercy for Us and Our Children

› *Today's Faith Builder:*

But the mercy of the LORD is from everlasting to everlasting
On those who fear Him,
And His righteousness to children's children. (Psalm 103:17)

Blessed "But!" How vast the contrast between the fading flower and the everlasting God! How wonderful that His mercy should link our frailty with His eternity and make us everlasting too! The Lord has always viewed His people as objects of mercy and has chosen them to become partakers of His grace.

Jehovah does not change. His mercy is endless. Those who fear Him will find that neither their sins nor their needs have exhausted His grace. Let us sing, then, for coming generations. The past commands our praise and the future invites it. Let us sing and pray for our descendants.

Just as the sweet singer hymned the varied attributes of the Lord as seen in nature, grace, and providence, he now gathers up all his energies for one final outburst of adoration in which he would have all the subjects of the Great King unite.

He calls on the angels to speak the praises of the Lord. Dwelling nearer to God's throne than we are yet allowed to climb, they see the glory which we would adore. They are given a great intellect, voice, and mighty power which they delight to use in sacred services for Him.

The psalmist would have every servant in the Lord's palace unite with him, and all at once sing the praises of the Lord.

Psalm 103:15–22

The Garments of God

> *Today's Faith Builder:*
> Bless the LORD, O my soul!
> O LORD my God, You are very great:
> You are clothed with honor and majesty. (Psalm 104:1)

This psalm interprets the many voices of nature and sings sweetly of both creation and providence. It speaks for the whole world: Sea and land, cloud and sunlight, plant and animal, light and darkness, life and death are all proven to manifest the presence of the Lord. It begins and ends like Psalm 103, and it could not do better; when the model is perfect it deserves to exist in duplicate.

True praise begins at home. It is inconsistent to stir up others to praise if we are ungratefully silent ourselves. We should call on our hearts to awake and stir themselves, for we may become sluggish, and if this happens when we are asked to bless God we will be ashamed.

When we magnify the Lord, let us do it heartily; our best is far less than He deserves. Let us not dishonor Him by offering Him halfhearted worship. Observe also that the wonder expressed does not refer to the creation and its greatness, but to Jehovah Himself. The psalmist does not say, "The universe is very great!" but "You are very great." Many focus on the creature and become idolatrous in spirit; to praise the Creator Himself is true wisdom.

Garments both conceal and reveal a man, and the creation reveals its Creator. The Lord is seen in His works as worthy of honor for His skill, His goodness, and His power, and as claiming majesty, for He has created all things according to His sovereign will.

Psalm 104:1–6

God Provides for Us All

> *Today's Faith Builder:*
>> He causes the grass to grow for the cattle,
>> And vegetation for the service of man,
>> That he may bring forth food from the earth. (Psalm 104:14)

When the waters and vapors covered all the earth, the Lord had but to speak and they disappeared. As though they had intelligence, the waves hurried to their appointed places and left the land to itself. The mountains lifted their heads, the highlands rose, and finally the continents and islands, slopes and plains were left to form the habitable earth.

It is beautiful to see the divine system of water supply among the mountains: the rising of the fleecy vapors, the distillation of pure water, the glee with which the newborn element leaps down the crags to reach the rivers, and the eagerness with which the rivers seek the ocean and their other appointed places.

The result of this creative miracle is abundance everywhere: the soil is saturated with rain, the seed germinates, the animals drink, and the birds sing; nothing is left out of God's loving plan for their care. So too it is in the new creation; He gives more grace, He fills His people with rich blessings: "Of His fullness we have all received, and grace for grace" (John 1:16).

Grass grows as well as vegetation, for both cattle and people must be fed. Grass for cattle and corn for man are examples of food brought out of the earth, and these prove that it was God's design that the very dust beneath our feet, which seems better adapted to bury us than to sustain us, should be transformed into the staff of life. The more we think of this the more wonderful it will appear.

Psalm 104:7–18

Sweet Meditations

❯ *Today's Faith Builder:*
May my meditation be sweet to Him;
I will be glad in the LORD. (Psalm 104:34)

The Lord deserves to be praised without ceasing for what He has done. His personal being and character reveal that He would be glorious even if all the creatures were dead. The poet finds his heart gladdened by the works of the Lord and feels that the Creator Himself must have felt unspeakable delight in exercising so much wisdom, goodness, and power.

Here and hereafter the psalmist would continue to praise the Lord, for his theme is endless and remains forever fresh and new. The birds sang God's praises before people were created, but the redeemed will sing His glories when birds are no more.

Jehovah, who ever lives and gives us life, will be exalted and praised forever in the songs of the redeemed. We never sing as well as when we know that we have a part in the good things of which we sing and a relationship to the God whom we praise. I will be delighted to study His works and think of His person and He will graciously accept my notes of praise.

Meditation is the soul of religion. It is the tree of life in the middle of the garden of piety and its fruit is very refreshing to the soul that feeds on it.

As the fat of the sacrifice was the Lord's portion, so are our best meditations of the Most High due and acceptable to Him. To the meditative mind every thought of God is full of joy. Each one of our Lord's attributes is a wellspring of delight now that in Christ Jesus we are reconciled to God.

Psalm 104:19–35

Seek the Lord and Find Strength

> *Today's Faith Builder:*
>> Seek the LORD and His strength;
>> Seek His face evermore! (Psalm 105:4)

Jehovah is the author of all our benefits, therefore let Him have all our gratitude. Bring your best thoughts to Him and express them in the best language with the sweetest sounds. To worship the Lord and seek His kingdom and righteousness is the sure way to happiness; indeed there is no other. True seekers throw their hearts into the effort so their hearts receive joy.

We all need strength; let us look to the strong One for it. We need infinite power to bear us safely to our eternal resting place; let us look to the Almighty Jehovah for it.

Seek, seek, seek; we have the word three times. There must be a blessing in seeking, or we would not be repeatedly urged to do so. To seek His face is to desire and enjoy His presence, His smile, His favor.

First we seek Him, then His strength, and then His face; from personal reverence, we pass on to imparted power, and then to conscious favor. This seeking must never cease; the more we know the more we must seek to know. Finding Him, we must "our minds inflame to seek Him more and more." He seeks spiritual worshipers, and spiritual worshipers seek Him; they are therefore sure to finally meet face to face.

Blessed be His name! Jehovah condescends to be our God.

What a joy it is that our God is never absent from us! He is never a nonresident, never an absentee ruler. His justice exists everywhere we dwell.

Psalm 105:1–7

God Remembers His Promises

❯ *Today's Faith Builder:*

He remembers His covenant forever,
The word which He commanded, for a thousand generations.
(Psalm 105:8)

Here is the basis of all God's dealings with His people: He entered into a covenant with them in their father Abraham, and He remained faithful to this covenant. If the Lord has remembered His promise, surely we ought not to forget the wonderful manner in which He has kept it. It should bring the deepest joy to us that the Lord has never once forgotten His covenant, and that He will never do so.

His judgments are threatened on the third and fourth generations of those who hate Him (Exod. 20:5), but His love goes on forever, even to "a thousand generations." His promise is here said to be commanded, or vested with all the authority of a law. It is a proclamation from a sovereign whose laws will remain in effect in every jot and tittle though heaven and earth will pass away (Matt. 5:18). Therefore let us give thanks to the Lord and talk of all His works that are so wonderful for their faithfulness and truth.

The blessings promised to the seed of Abraham were not dependent on the number of his descendants or their position in this world. The smallness of a church and the poverty of its members are no barriers to God's blessing if it is sought earnestly by pleading the promise.

Were not the apostles few and the disciples feeble when the good work began? Though we are strangers and foreigners here below, as our fathers were (1 Peter 2:11), this does not increase our danger; we are like sheep among wolves, but the wolves cannot hurt us for our Shepherd is near.

Psalm 105:8–15

From Prison to the Throne

❯ *Today's Faith Builder:*

He sent a man before them—

Joseph—who was sold as a slave. (Psalm 105:17)

The presence of God, having remained with His chosen ones while they stayed in Canaan, did not desert them when they were called to go down into Egypt. They did not choose to go but went under divine direction, so the Lord prepared their way and prospered them until He chose to lead them back to the land of promise.

There is sweet comfort in knowing that the Lord has a wise plan that may even include famine: He meant for His people to go down to Egypt and the famine in Canaan was His method of leading them there.

Joseph was the advance guard and pioneer for the whole clan. His brothers sold him, but God sent him. Where the hand of the wicked is visible God's hand may be invisibly at work, overruling them.

If we were to send a man on a mission such as Joseph's we would furnish him with money—Joseph went as a pauper; we would grant him authority—Joseph went as a slave; we would give him full liberty—Joseph was a bondman. Yet money would have been of little use when corn was so scarce, authority and freedom might not have thrown Joseph into contact with Pharaoh's captain so the knowledge of his skill in interpreting dreams might not have reached Pharaoh's ear.

God's way is the right way. Our Lord's path to His mediatorial throne ran by the cross of Calvary; our road to glory runs by the rivers of grief. All the Lord's afflicted ones will one day step from their prisons to their thrones.

Psalm 105:16–23

Our Lord Delivers His People

❭ *Today's Faith Builder:*

He increased His people greatly,
And made them stronger than their enemies. (Psalm 105:24)

In Goshen, the Israelites seem to have increased rapidly from the beginning. This increased the fears of the Egyptians so they tried to slow their increase by oppression, but the Lord continued to bless them.

Finally, both in physical strength and in numbers, the Israelites threatened to become the more powerful race. Nor was this growth of the nation hindered by persecution. Instead, the reverse took place, giving an early example of what has since become a proverb in the church—"the more they oppressed them the more they multiplied." It is useless to contend with either God or His people.

God's goodness to Israel called forth the hatred of the Egyptian court. He therefore made use of this feeling to lead to the discomfort of His people and to their readiness to leave the land to which they had evidently become attached.

When the oppression was at its worst, Moses came. He who sent Joseph also sent Moses and his eloquent brother. The Lord had men ready; all He had to do was commission them and thrust them forward.

The men differed so one complemented the other and together they were able to accomplish far more than if they had been exactly alike. The main point was that they were both sent and both were clothed with divine power.

O Jehovah, You triumphed in that hour and with an outstretched arm You delivered Your people.

Psalm 105:24–38

Protection and Provision All the Way

> *Today's Faith Builder:*
> He spread a cloud for a covering,
> And fire to give light in the night. (Psalm 105:39)

Never were people so favored as those Israelites moving forward on their journey under cover of God's protective cloud. What would travelers in the desert now give for such a canopy? The sun could not scorch them with its burning ray; their whole camp was screened like a king in his pavilion.

Nothing seemed to be too good for God to give His chosen nation; their comfort was considered in every way. While cities were covered with darkness, their town of tents enjoyed illumination which modern lights cannot equal. God Himself was their sun and shield, their glory and their defense. Could they be faithless while so graciously shaded during the day, or rebellious while they walked at midnight in such a light?

The tale of their sin is as extraordinary as the story of His love, but this psalm selects the happier theme and dwells only on covenant love and faithfulness. We too have found the Lord all this to us, for He has been our sun and shield and has preserved us from the perils of joys and the evils of grief.

With Moses' rod and His own Word God split the rock in the desert, and abundant water for them to drink flowed where they had feared they would die of thirst. We know the rock pictures our Lord Jesus Christ, from whom flows a fountain of living waters which will never be exhausted until the last pilgrim has crossed the Jordan and entered Canaan.

Psalm 105:39–45

Hallelujah!

❭ *Today's Faith Builder:*
Praise the LORD!
Oh, give thanks to the LORD, for He is good!
For His mercy endures forever. (Psalm 106:1)

This psalm begins and ends with *hallelujah*—"Praise the Lord!" The space between these two expressions of praise is filled with the sad details of Israel's sin and the extraordinary patience of God. We will do well to bless the Lord at the beginning and the end of our meditations when sin and grace are the themes.

To us needy creatures, the goodness of God is the first attribute which moves us to praise Him and that praise is an expression of gratitude. We praise the Lord when we give Him thanks for what we have received from His goodness. Let us never be slow to praise the Lord; to thank Him is the least we can do; let us not neglect it.

God's goodness to sinners is seen in His mercy, so this should be a leading note in our song. Since man continues to be sinful, it is a great blessing that Jehovah continues to be merciful. From age to age the Lord deals graciously with His Church and with each individual in it. He is constant and faithful in His grace and will be forever.

We have here two arguments for praise: the Lord is good, and His mercy endures forever. These two arguments are themselves praises. The very best language of adoration is that which adoringly and plainly tells the simple truth about our Lord.

Those who praise the Lord have a subject which will never be exhausted. Throughout eternity it will be the theme of all the songs of the redeemed.

Psalm 106:1–5

No Obstacle Is Too Great for God

> *Today's Faith Builder:*
>   He rebuked the Red Sea also, and it dried up;
>   So He led them through the depths,
>   As through the wilderness. (Psalm 106:9)

Here the psalmist begins a long and detailed confession. Confession of sin is the surest way to secure an answer to the prayer of verse 4; God gives His salvation to the one who acknowledges his need of a Savior.

The Israelites saw the miraculous plagues and wondered about them; they were unable to understand their design of love, their deep moral and spiritual lessons, and their revelation of God's power and justice. Those who do not begin well can hardly be expected to finish well. Israel was not quite out of Egypt when she began to provoke the Lord by doubting His power to deliver and questioning His faithfulness to His promises. The sea was only called "Red," but their sins were really scarlet; it was known as the "sea of weeds," but weeds that were far more entangling and deadly grew in their hearts.

With a word, God rebuked the Red Sea and dried it up. The sea heard His voice and obeyed. How many rebukes of God are lost on us! Are we not more unmanageable than the ocean? The sea recognized its Master and His royal seed and opened at once.

The tribes of Israel passed over the bottom of the gulf as if it had been the dry floor of the desert. Their passage was not foolhardy, nor danger-ous, for God commanded and led them. We have also passed through many trials and afflictions under divine direction. We have been led safely through deep valleys as they were through the sea and the wilderness.

Psalm 106:6–15

When Others Turn Against Us

> *Today's Faith Builder:*
>   When they envied Moses in the camp,
>   And Aaron the saint of the LORD. (Psalm 106:16)

Though they owed everything to Moses as the Lord's chosen instrument, the Israelites were reluctant to give him the authority he needed to lead them to the land God had promised them. Some were more openly rebellious than others and became leaders of a mutiny, but a spirit of dissatisfaction was widespread, and therefore the whole nation was charged with it.

Who can hope to escape envy when the meekest of men was subject to it? How unreasonable this envy was! Of all the men in the camp, Moses worked the hardest and had the most to bear. They should have sympathized with him; to envy him was ridiculous.

Aaron was divinely set apart for holy work, and instead of thanking God that He had favored them with a high priest to intercede for them, the people rebelled at this selection and quarreled with the man who was to offer sacrifices for them. Neither church nor state was satisfactory to them; they wanted to take Moses' scepter and Aaron's miter from them. Bad men are envious of the good, and spiteful against those who would help them the most.

The earth could no longer bear the weight of these rebels and ingrates. God's patience was exhausted when they began to attack His servants, for His children are very dear to Him and he who touches them touches the apple of His eye. Moses had opened the sea for their deliverance and then as they rebelled against him the earth opened for their destruction.

Psalm 106:16–18

The Danger of Forgetting God

> *Today's Faith Builder:*
> They forgot God their Savior,
> Who had done great things in Egypt. (Psalm 106:21)

In Egypt, God had overcome all the idols, yet Israel wandered so far from Him that they compared Him to them. In the very place where they had solemnly pledged to obey the Lord they broke the second, if not the first, of His commandments: they set up the Egyptian symbol of an ox and bowed before it. The ox image is here sarcastically called "a calf." Idols are worthy of no respect; scorn is never more legitimately used than when it is poured on all attempts to make an image of the Invisible God.

Could an ox work miracles? Could a golden calf send plagues on Israel's enemies? The people were foolish to set up such a mockery of God after having seen what the true God could really do. This was enough to provoke the Lord, and it did; no tongue can tell how much He is angered every day in our own land.

The threatened destruction finally came. For the first wilderness sin, He chastened them, sending leanness into their souls; for the second He weeded out the offenders, the flame burned up the wicked; for the third He threatened to destroy them; for the fourth He lifted up His hand and almost overthrew them (v. 26); for the fifth He actually struck them and the plague broke in among them. The punishment increased with their persistence in sin.

This should serve as a warning to the one who goes on in his sins: God tries words before He comes to blows, but His words are not to be trifled with; He means them and has power to make them good.

Psalm 106:19–23

September 2

God Always Has His Person of the Hour

> *Today's Faith Builder:*
> Then Phinehas stood up and intervened,
> And the plague was stopped. (Psalm 106:30)

From unbelief to complaining is a short and natural step. Complaining is a great sin, not a mere weakness; it contains unbelief, pride, rebellion, and a whole host of other sins. It is a home sin and is generally practiced by complaints "in their tents," but it is just as evil there as in the streets, and brings just as much grief to the Lord.

Open immorality and idolatry were too serious to be overlooked. This time the offenses cried for judgment, and the judgment came at once. Twenty-four thousand persons fell before a sudden and deadly disease which threatened to run through the whole camp. Their new sins brought a disease on them that was new to their tribes. When people invent sins God will not be slow to invent punishments.

Then Phinehas stood up and intervened so the plague was stopped. God has His champions left in the worst of times, and they will stand up when the time comes for them to do battle. His honest spirit could not stand for lewdness being practiced publicly when a fast had been proclaimed.

Down to the moment when this psalm was written the house of Phinehas was still honored in Israel. His faith had performed heroically and his righteousness was declared by the Lord and honored by his family continuing in the priesthood.

The mercy of God held back His hand because of the prayer of one man. He found a reason for grace when vengeance seemed justly sure.

Psalm 106:24–31

The Multiplied Mercies of God

> *Today's Faith Builder:*
> And for their sake He remembered His covenant,
> And relented according to the multitude of His mercies.
>
> (Psalm 106:45)

I n spite of all the provoking rebellions and detestable offenses of the Israelites, the Lord still heard their prayer and pitied them. This is very wonderful, very Godlike. One would have thought that the Lord would have shut out their prayer, seeing they had shut their ears to His warnings, but He had a Father's heart and the sight of their sorrows touched His soul. The sound of their cries moved His heart, and He looked on them with compassion.

God's covenant is the sure foundation of mercy, and when outward grace is not seen in His people His love is unchanged. On this fundamental truth the Lord builds a new structure of grace. Covenant mercy is as sure as the throne of God. The Lord is so full of grace that He not only has mercy but mercies, a multitude of them, and these live in the covenant and treasure up good for the erring children of men.

The mention of the covenant encouraged the afflicted to call the Lord their God and this enabled them to pray with greater boldness for Him to intervene and rescue them.

Weaned from their idols, they desired to make mention only of Jehovah's name and attributed their mercies to His eternal faithfulness and love. The Lord had often saved them for His holy name's sake, and therefore they felt that when again restored they would give thanks and praise to Him alone.

Psalm 106:32–48

The Redeemed Should Not Be Silent

> *Today's Faith Builder:*
>   Let the redeemed of the LORD say so,
>   Whom He has redeemed from the hand of the enemy.
>   (Psalm 107:2)

This is a choice song for the redeemed of the Lord. Although it celebrates providential deliverances and therefore may be sung by anyone whose life has been preserved in times of danger, it mainly magnifies the Lord for spiritual blessings, of which temporal favors are but types and shadows. The theme is thanksgiving and the motives for it.

Whatever others may think or say, the redeemed have overwhelming reasons for declaring the goodness of the Lord. Theirs is a special redemption and they ought to render special praise for it. Their Redeemer is so glorious, the ransom price so immense, and the redemption so complete that they are under multiplied obligations to give thanks to the Lord and to exhort others to do so. Let them not only feel so, but say so: let them both sing and invite others to sing with them.

Snatched from fierce oppressions by superior power, believers, above all, have reasons to adore the Lord, their Liberator. Theirs is a divine redemption: "He has redeemed" them; no one else has done it. He needed no help to deliver them.

Should not emancipated slaves be grateful to the hand which set them free? How much gratitude is sufficient for deliverance from the power of sin, death, and hell? In heaven there is no sweeter hymn than "You . . . have redeemed us to God by Your blood" (Rev. 5:9).

With one heart and voice let the redeemed praise the Lord.

Psalm 107:1–3

Deliverance from Distress

> *Today's Faith Builder:*
> Then they cried out to the Lord in their trouble,
> And He delivered them out of their distresses. (Psalm 107:6)

Solitude greatly intensifies misery. The loneliness of a desert has a depressing influence on the one who is lost in its boundless waste. When under distress of soul, people find nothing to rest on, no comfort, and no peace; their efforts to seek salvation are many, weary, and disappointing and the discouraging solitude of their hearts fills them with dire distress.

The Israelites did not pray until they were in extreme danger, but it is merciful that they prayed then and prayed in the right manner. They cried out to the right person: to the Lord. Nothing else remained for them to do; they could not help themselves or find help in others, therefore they cried to God.

Prayers which are forced out of us by severe necessity are no less acceptable with God; indeed, they prevail even more since they are clearly sincere and make powerful appeals to the Lord's compassion. If hunger brings us to our knees it is more useful to us than feasting; if thirst drives us to the fountain it is better than the deepest drinks of worldly joy; if weakness leads to tears it is better than the strength of the mighty.

Deliverance follows prayer. The cry must have been very feeble, for they were faint and their faith was as weak as their cry; but they were heard at once. A little delay would have brought death; but there was none, for the Lord was ready to save them.

Psalm 107:4–22

God Will Calm Your Storm

⟩ *Today's Faith Builder:*
He calms the storm,
So that its waves are still. (Psalm 107:29)

Not all believers have the same deep experiences but, for wise purposes that equip them to serve Him, the Lord sends some of His children through deep trouble that there they may see the wonders of His grace more clearly than others. Sailing over the seas of inward depravity, the waters of poverty, the billows of persecution, and the rough waves of temptation, they need God above all others, and they find Him. Doubts, fears, terrors, and anxieties lift their heads like so many angry waves when the Lord allows the winds of fierce storms to beat on us.

Prayer is good in a storm. We may pray staggering and reeling and when we are at our wits' end. God will hear us amid the thunder and answer us out of the storm. He reveals His power in the sudden and marvelous changes that occur at His bidding. He commanded the storm to come and now He orders a calm: God is in all natural phenomena and we should recognize His working.

Where huge billows had been leaping high there is now scarcely a ripple to be seen. When God makes peace it is peace indeed, the peace of God which surpasses all understanding (Phil. 4:6–7). He can change the condition of a man's mind in a moment so that it will seem an absolute miracle to him that he has passed so suddenly from hurricane to calm.

Oh, that the Lord would work this way in the reader, should his heart be storm-beaten with outward troubles or inward fears. Lord, say the word and peace will come at once.

Psalm 107:23–32

September 7

Lovingkindness for Us All

<blockquote>
> Today's Faith Builder:
>   Whoever is wise will observe these things,
>   And they will understand the lovingkindness of the LORD.
>   (Psalm 107:43)
</blockquote>

None are so ready to praise God for His great mercies as those who have never before known them. Hungry souls make sweet music when the Lord fills them with His gracious gifts.

Are we hungry? Or are we satisfied with the husks of this poor, swinish world?

When the earth is watered and cultivated, cities spring up and teem with inhabitants; when grace abounds where sin formerly reigned, hearts find peace and dwell securely in God's love, like those who live in a well-fortified city. The church is built where once all was a wasteland, because the Lord has caused the broad rivers and streams of gospel grace to flow through it.

God's blessing is everything. When nations are prosperous they should recognize the gracious hand of God, for they owe their all to His blessing.

It is wise to observe what the Lord does, for He is wonderful in counsel and has given us eyes with which to see. It is foolish to close them when there is so much to see, but we must watch wisely, or we may soon confuse ourselves and others with hasty conclusions about the working of the Lord.

The lovingkindness of the Lord is shown in a thousand ways and if we will but watch carefully we will come to a better understanding of it. To understand this delightful attribute is as pleasant as it is profitable.

Psalm 107:33–43

The Power of Praise and Prayer

> *Today's Faith Builder:*
> O God, my heart is steadfast;
> I will sing and give praise, even with my glory. (Psalm 108:1)

Sometimes we must climb the ladder of prayer to praise God, and at other times we must bless Him for the past in order to be able to pray in faith for the present and the future. By the help of God's Spirit we can either pray ourselves up to praise, or praise the Lord until we get into a proper frame of mind for prayer.

We cannot resolve too often to magnify the Lord with steadfast hearts, nor need we ever hesitate to use the same words in drawing near to Him, for the Lord, who cannot endure vain repetitions, is equally weary of vain variations. Some expressions are so admirable that they ought to be used again; who would throw away a cup because he drank from it before? God should be served with the best words, and when we have found them they will surely be good enough to be used twice.

David seemed inspired to foresee that his Psalms would be sung in every land. He longed to have the whole human race listen to his joy in God and his desire has been fulfilled; no poet is so universally known as he.

He had but one theme: he sang of Jehovah alone, and his work, being made of gold, silver, and precious stones, has endured the fiery ordeal of time. It has never been more prized than it is today. Happy man. David chose to be the Lord's musician and will retain his office as the poet laureate of the kingdom of heaven until the end of time.

We long for the time when God will be universally worshiped and His glory in the gospel be made known everywhere.

Psalm 108:1–5

Victory Will Be Ours

❭ *Today's Faith Builder:*
Through God we will do valiantly,
For it is He who shall tread down our enemies. (Psalm 108:13)

Sometimes the future of a nation seems to hang on the prayers of one person. With what fervor this praying one must pour out his soul!

It is easy to pray for the Lord's people; we feel sure of a favorable answer since the Lord's heart is already set on doing them good. Still it is serious work to pray when we feel that the condition of a whole beloved nation depends on what the Lord intends to do through our prayers.

The Lord made great promises to David, and His holiness guaranteed them. David prays as if he had the blessing already and could share it among his men; this comes from having sung so heartily to the Lord his helper. He resolves to act like a man whose prayers are a part of his life and important reasons for his actions.

God's help will inspire us to help others. Faith is neither fearful nor lazy: she knows that God is with her and therefore she acts valiantly; she knows that He will tread down her enemies and therefore she rises to tread them down in His name. Where prayer and praise have preceded the battle we may expect to see heroic deeds and decisive victories. Our inward and spiritual faith proves itself by outward valorous deeds.

The church will yet praise God with all her heart and then advance with songs and hosannas to the great battle. Her foes will be overthrown and utterly crushed by the power of her God and the Lord's glory will be over all the earth.

Psalm 108:6–13

Where to Turn When Under Attack

> *Today's Faith Builder:*
> In return for my love they are my accusers,
> But I give myself to prayer. (Psalm 109:4)

If we take care of God's honor He will take care of ours. We may look to Him as the guardian of our character, if we truly seek His glory. If we live to God's praise, He will, in the long run, give us praise from others.

No one knows what will come out of lewd and lying mouths. No one can imagine the misery caused to good people by slanderous reports but the one who has been wounded by them; in all Satan's armory there are no worse weapons than deceitful tongues.

Lying tongues cannot lie still.

Bad tongues are not content to vilify bad men but choose the most gracious of saints to be the objects of their attacks. What can be worse than to be a victim of slander?

Our Lord might have emphatically used all the language of this complaint—they hated Him without a cause and returned Him hatred for love.

How it hurts the soul to be hated in proportion to the gratitude it deserves, hated by those it loved and hated because of its love! This was a cruel case and the sensitive mind of the psalmist suffered because of it.

He did nothing but pray. He became prayer as they became malice. This was his answer to his enemies: He appealed from men and their injustice to the Judge of all the earth, who must do right. True bravery can teach a man to leave his slanderers unanswered and carry his case to the Lord.

Psalm 109:1–4

God Rescues the Poor and Needy

> *Today's Faith Builder:*
> But You, O GOD the Lord,
> Deal with me for Your name's sake;
> Because Your mercy is good, deliver me. (Psalm 109:21)

Evil for good is devil-like. This is Satan's strategy and his children on earth follow it eagerly; it is cruel and wounds to the quick. The revenge which pays a man back in his own coin has a kind of natural justice in it, but what can be said of that vile attitude which returns evil for good? Our Lord endured such wicked treatment, and in His members, endures it still.

Here we see a harmless and innocent man on his knees pouring out his sorrows, but we are now to observe him rising from prayer, inspired with prophetic energy, and declaring warnings to his enemies of their coming doom. When the Judge of all threatens to punish tyrannical cruelty and treachery, virtue gives her assent and consent.

How eagerly then the psalmist turns from his enemies to his God! He compares the great Jehovah to all his adversaries and you see at once that his heart is at rest. He leaves himself in the Lord's hands, dictating nothing, but quite content as long as his God will but undertake for him. He does not plead his own merit but *The Name*. Believers have always felt this to be their most powerful plea.

The Lord has a tender regard for brokenhearted ones like the psalmist. When the adversary wounds so deeply it is time for a friend to step in. His case has become desperate without divine aid; now, therefore, is the Lord's time to rescue him.

Psalm 109:5–22

God Deserves Our Public
and Private Praise

> *Today's Faith Builder:*
I will greatly praise the LORD with my mouth;
Yes, I will praise Him among the multitude. (Psalm 109:30)

The psalmist felt as powerless in his distress as a poor insect which a child may toss up and down at its pleasure. He asks for the Lord's compassion because he had been brought to his forlorn and feeble condition by long persecution.

Laying hold of Jehovah by the appropriating word *my*, he implores His aid both to help him bear his heavy load and to enable him to rise above it. He has described his own weakness and the strength and fury of his foes and by these two arguments he presents his doubly forceful appeal.

He will loudly and enthusiastically praise the righteous Lord who redeemed him from all evil, not only in his own home or among his own family, but in the most public manner. We do not praise God to be heard by others but we do try to make our praises as public as the benefit we have received. The singer in this case is a man whose heart was broken because he had become the laughingstock of his remorseless enemies. Now he loudly praises God with a joyous spirit.

Nothing can more sweetly sustain the heart of a slandered believer than the firm conviction that God is near to all who are wronged and is sure to deliver them.

O Lord, save us from the severe trial of slander. In Your righteousness, deal with all who attack the characters of holy people and cause all who are bearing reproach to come forth unstained by their affliction like Your only begotten Son. Amen.

Psalm 109:23–31

Resting in the Victory to Come

> *Today's Faith Builder:*
> The LORD said to my Lord,
> "Sit at My right hand,
> Till I make Your enemies Your footstool." (Psalm 110:1)

David, in spirit, heard the solemn voice of Jehovah speaking to the Messiah "from of old." From this secret and intimate communion spring the covenant of grace and all its wonderful benefits.

How condescending on Jehovah's part to permit a mortal ear to hear and a human pen to record His secret conversation with His coequal Son! How greatly we should prize this revelation of His private conversation with His Son, made public here to refresh His people!

Though David was a firm believer in the unity of the Godhead, he spiritually discerns the two persons here, distinguishes between them, and perceives that in the second he has a special interest, for he calls Him "my Lord." This expresses the psalmist's reverence, obedience, faith, and joy in Christ.

Jehovah calls the Adonai, our Lord, away from the shame and suffering of His earthly life to the rest and honor of His celestial throne. His work is done, and He may sit down; it is well done, and He may sit at His right hand; it will have grand results, so He may quietly wait to see the victory which is certain to follow.

Jesus is placed in the seat of power, dominion, and dignity. Since our Lord sits in quiet expectancy, we too may sit in the attitude of peaceful assurance and await the grand outcome of all events with confidence. The sight of Jesus enthroned in His glory is the sure guarantee that all things are moving on to ultimate victory.

Psalm 110:1–2

Secure in Our Great High Priest

> *Today's Faith Builder:*
> Your people shall be volunteers
> In the day of Your power;
> In the beauties of holiness, from the womb of the morning,
> You have the dew of Your youth. (Psalm 110:3)

How truly beautiful holiness is! God Himself admires it. How wonderful also is the eternal youth of the mystical body of Christ! As the dew is new every morning, there is a constant succession of converts to give the church perpetual youth.

Since Jesus ever lives, His church will ever flourish. As His strength never fails, the vigor of His true people will be renewed day by day. As He is a Priest-King, His people are all priests and kings (Rev. 5:10), and the beauties of holiness are their priestly attire, their garments for glory and beauty.

Our Lord Jesus is a Priest-King by the ancient oath of Jehovah: He did not glorify Himself to be made a high priest but was ordained of God a high priest forever according to the order of Melchizedek (Heb. 5:5–6). It was a solemn and sure matter that led the Eternal to swear and His oath guarantees the decree forever. To make this a thousand times sure, "and will not relent" is added (Ps. 110:4).

It is done, and done forever: Jesus is sworn to be the priest of His people and He must remain so to the end because His commission is sealed by the unchanging oath of the immutable Jehovah. It is the Lord who has appointed Him a priest forever. He has done it by an oath; that oath is unchanging, is in effect now, and will stand throughout all ages. Our security in Him is then beyond all question.

Psalm 110:3–4

Our Coming King

> *Today's Faith Builder:*
>   The Lord is at Your right hand;
>   He shall execute kings in the day of His wrath. (Psalm 110:5)

The last verses of this psalm we understand to refer to the future victories of the Priest-King. He will not sit forever in waiting but will come into the fight to end the weary war by His own victorious presence. He will lead the final charge in person; His own right hand and His holy arm will bring Him the victory.

Eternal power attends the coming of the Lord and earthly power dies before it as though thrust through with a sword.

What are kings when they dare oppose the Son of God?

Our Lord will march to conquest so swiftly that He will not stop to be refreshed but drink as He hastens on His way. Like Gideon's men who lapped, He will throw His heart into the battle and shorten it in righteousness. His head will be lifted high in victory and His people, in Him, will be lifted up also.

When Jesus passed this way before, He was burdened and serious work was laid on Him, but in His second Advent He will win an easy victory. Before, He was the Man of Sorrows, but when He comes the second time, His head will be lifted in triumph. Let His people rejoice with Him. "Lift up your heads, because your redemption draws near" (Luke 21:28).

O King-Priest, we who are, in a lesser degree, king-priests too, are full of gladness because You reign now and will come before long to vindicate Your cause and establish Your kingdom forever.

Even so, come quickly. Amen.

Psalm 110:5–7

Heartfelt Praise

> *Today's Faith Builder:*
> Praise the LORD!
> I will praise the LORD with my whole heart,
> In the assembly of the upright and in the congregation. (Psalm 111:1)

Even if others refuse to sing, be sure that you always have a song for your God. Put away all doubt, questions, complaining, and rebellion and give yourselves to the praising of Jehovah, both with your lips and in your lives. The sweet singer begins the song, for his heart is all aflame; whether others will follow him or not, he will begin at once and continue long.

What we preach we should practice. The best way to make exhortation effective is to set an example, but we must see that it is an excellent one or we may lead others to do poorly. David brought nothing less than his whole heart to worship; all his love went out to God and all his zeal, his skill, and his fervor went with it.

Jehovah, the one and undivided God, cannot be acceptably praised with a divided heart, neither should we attempt to so dishonor Him, for our all is little enough for His praise. All his works are praiseworthy, and therefore we should adore Him with all our being.

Nothing is better than praising God. Praise is always timely for the church and the congregation, for the family or the community. Praising the Lord is proper and the true heart should be ready to sing hallelujah anytime and in every place.

Come, dear reader, he who pens this comment is magnifying the Lord in his heart. Will you not pause for a moment and join in this delightful duty?

Psalm 111:1

Watching God at Work

> *Today's Faith Builder:*
> The works of the LORD are great,
> Studied by all who have pleasure in them. (Psalm 111:2)

All the works of the Lord are great in design, in size, in number, and in excellence. Even the little things of God are great. From one point of view or another each of the productions of His power, or the works of His wisdom, will appear great to the wise in heart.

Those who love their Maker delight in His works. They perceive that there is more in them than appears on the surface, therefore they set out to study and understand them. The devout naturalist ransacks nature, the earnest student of history pries into hidden facts and mysterious stories of the past, and the man of God digs into the mines of Scripture, storing up each grain of its golden truth.

God's works are worthy of our research; they yield us a wonderful blend of instruction and pleasure that proves to be far greater after investigation than before. The works of mankind are noble from a distance; the works of God are great when carefully studied.

The hidden wisdom of God is the most marvelous part of His work, so those who do not look below the surface miss the best part of what He longs to teach us. Because His works are great they cannot be understood at once but must be looked into with care. It is good that all things cannot be seen at a glance, for the search into their mysteries is as useful to us as the knowledge we attain through it.

The history of the Lord's dealings with His people is a great subject for meditation by reverent minds. In them, they find sweet comfort and a never-failing source of delight.

Psalm 111:2—6

Where Wisdom Begins

⟩ *Today's Faith Builder:*
The fear of the LORD is the beginning of wisdom;
A good understanding have all those who do His commandments.
His praise endures forever. (Psalm 111:10)

To know God so as to walk rightly before Him is the greatest of all the applied sciences. Holy reverence of God leads us to praise Him and this is a wise act for any creature toward his Creator.

Obedience to God proves sound judgment. Why should He not be obeyed? Does not reason itself claim obedience for the Lord of all? Only one without understanding will justify rebellion against Him.

Practical godliness is the test of wisdom. Some may be very orthodox, very eloquent, and very profound, but the best proof of their intelligence must be found in their actually doing the will of the Lord.

The first part of this psalm taught us the doctrine of God's nature and character by describing His works; the second part supplies a practical lesson by showing that worshiping and obeying Him is the sure response of true wisdom.

The praises of God will never cease, because His works will always move us to adoration and it will always be wise to praise our glorious Lord. A word of approval from the mouth of God will be a medal of honor which will outshine all the decorations that kings and emperors can bestow.

Lord, help us to study Your works, and to breathe out hallelujahs as long as we live.

Psalm 111:7–10

Praise and Obedience Bring Rewards

> *Today's Faith Builder:*
>   Praise the LORD!
>   Blessed is the man who fears the LORD,
>   Who delights greatly in His commandments. (Psalm 112:1)

The Lord always deserves praise; we ought always to render it; we frequently forget it, and it is always good to be stirred up to it. If there is any virtue, if there is anything praiseworthy, the Lord should have all the glory for it, for we are His workmanship (Eph. 2:10).

Only cheerful obedience is acceptable; one who obeys reluctantly is disobedient at heart, but one who takes pleasure in the commands of his Lord is truly loyal.

The godly may be persecuted, but they will not be forsaken; the curses of men cannot deprive them of God's blessing, for Balaam's words are true, "He has blessed, and I cannot reverse it" (Num. 23:20).

The upright person will have days of darkness; he may be sick and sorry, poor and pining. His former riches may take wings and fly away; even his righteousness may be cruelly suspected. Clouds may lower around him, but their gloom will not last forever. The Lord will ultimately bring him light, for as surely as a good man's sun goes down it will rise again.

If his darkness is caused by depression of spirit, the Holy Spirit will comfort him. It is as natural for the righteous to be comforted as for the day to dawn. Wait for the light and it will surely come. Even if, in our last hours, our heavenly Father should put us to bed in the dark, we will find it light in the morning.

Psalm 112:1–4

Marks of a Mature Believer

❯ *Today's Faith Builder:*
He will not be afraid of evil tidings;
His heart is steadfast, trusting in the Lord. (Psalm 112:7)

One who fears the Lord and delights in His commandments will have no fear that bad news will come, and he will not be alarmed if it does come. He is neither wavering nor cowardly; when he is undecided as to what to do he is still steadfast in heart; he may change his plan but not the purpose of his soul. Faith has made him firm and steadfast and therefore, if the worst should happen to him, he would remain quiet and patient, waiting for the salvation of God.

His love to God is deep and true, his confidence in God is firm and unmoved; his courage has a firm foundation and is supported by Omnipotence. He has become settled by experience and confirmed by years. He is ready to face any adversary—a holy heart shows in a brave face. When the battle rages and the result seems doubtful, he trusts in God and is not dismayed.

What the upright man receives he distributes to those who most need it. He is God's reservoir, and from his abundance flow streams of liberality to help the needy. His generosity has flavored his righteousness, proven its reality, and secured its future.

The character of a righteous man is not spasmodic, he is not generous by fits and starts nor upright in only a few matters; his life is based on a principle, his actions flow from settled, sure, and steadfast convictions and therefore his integrity is maintained when others fail. He is not led astray by companions, nor affected by the customs of society; he is resolute, determined, and immovable.

Psalm 112:5–10

Praise the Name of the Lord

❯ *Today's Faith Builder:*

Blessed be the name of the LORD

From this time forth and forevermore! (Psalm 113:2)

This psalm is one of pure praise; a warm heart full of admiring adoration of the Most High will best comprehend this sacred hymn. Its subject is the greatness and condescending goodness of the God of Israel as shown in His lifting up the needy.

While praising God aloud, the people were also to bless Him in the silence of their hearts, wishing glory to His name, success to His cause, and triumph to His truth.

By mentioning "the Name," the psalmist teaches us to bless each of the attributes of the Most High, not quarreling with His justice or His severity, nor fearing His power, but accepting Him as we find Him revealed in the inspired Word and by His own acts, loving and praising Him for who He is.

Every time we think of the God of Scripture we should bless Him, and His majestic name should never be pronounced without joyful reverence. If we have never praised Him before, let us begin now.

Can our hearts ever cease to praise the name of the Lord? Can we imagine a period in which the praises of Israel will no more surround the throne of the Divine Majesty? Impossible. Forever, and more than forever, if more can be, let Him be magnified.

From early morning until evening our ceaseless hymn should rise to Jehovah's throne, and from east to west over the whole earth pure worship should be rendered to His glory. Above all, let us adore Him who is above all.

Psalm 113:1–4

September 22

Our Incomparable Lord

❯ *Today's Faith Builder:*

Who is like the L ord our God,

Who dwells on high? (Psalm 113:5)

None can be compared with God for an instant, Israel's God is without parallel; our own covenant God stands alone and none can be compared to Him. None of the metaphors and figures by which the Lord is described in the Scriptures can give us a complete understanding of Him. Nothing on earth or in heaven fully resembles Him. Only in Jesus is the Godhead seen, but without hesitation He declared, "He who has seen Me has seen the Father" (John 14:9).

We have a God who is high above all gods and yet is our Father, knowing what we need before we ask Him; our Shepherd, who supplies our needs. He is our Guardian, who counts the hairs of our heads; our tender and considerate Friend, who sympathizes in all our griefs. Truly the name of our condescending God should be praised wherever it is known.

Almighty arms lifted us, are still lifting us, and will lift us into the perfection of heaven. We are made kings and priests to God, and we will reign forever (Rev. 5:10).

This psalm is a circle, ending where it began, praising the Lord from its first syllable to its last. May our life-psalm be of the same character, never knowing a break or a conclusion. In an endless circle let us bless the Lord, whose mercies never cease. Let us praise Him in youth and all through our years of strength, and when we bow in the ripeness of advancing years let us still praise the Lord. Let us never forget our former condition or the grace which has rescued us. Let us praise the Lord forever.

Psalm 113:5–9

God Opens a Way for His People

> *Today's Faith Builder:*
>   The sea saw it and fled;
>   Jordan turned back. (Psalm 114:3)

The psalm begins with a burst, as if the poetic fury could not be restrained but leaped over all bounds. The soul elevated and filled with a sense of divine glory cannot wait to write a preface but springs at once into the middle of its theme. Israel came triumphantly out of Egypt, away from those among whom they had been scattered, from under the yoke of bondage and out of the personal grasp of the king who had made the people into national slaves.

The Red Sea mirrored the hosts which had come down to its shore and reflected the cloud which towered high over all as the symbol of the presence of the Lord. The sea could not endure the unusual and astounding sight, so fleeing to the right and to the left, it opened a passage for God's people.

A similar miracle happened at the end of the great march of Israel for "Jordan turned back." This was a swiftly flowing river, pouring down a steep incline, and it was not merely divided but its current was driven back so that the rapid torrent, contrary to the law of gravity, flowed up hill.

The division of the sea and the drying up of the river are placed together, though they were separated by forty years, because they are the opening and closing scenes of one great event. We may also, by faith, unite our new birth and our departure out of the world into the promised inheritance, for the God who led us out of Egypt and its bondage will also conduct us through the Jordan of death, out of our wilderness wanderings.

Psalm 114:1–3

The Presence of the Lord

❯ *Today's Faith Builder:*
Tremble, O earth, at the presence of the Lord,
At the presence of the God of Jacob. (Psalm 114:7)

Nothing is immovable but God Himself: the mountains will depart and the hills be removed, but the covenant of His grace abides forever.

The mountains of sin and the hills of trouble move when the Lord comes to lead His people to their eternal Canaan. Let us never fear, but rather let our faith say to this mountain, "Be removed and be cast into the sea," and it will be done (Mark 11:23).

This psalm calls on all nature to feel a holy awe because the Ruler of the waves is present. Let the believer feel that God is near and he will serve the Lord with fear and rejoice with trembling. Awe is not cast out by faith, rather it becomes deeper and more profound. The Lord is most reverenced where He is most loved.

See what God can do! It seemed impossible that the flinty rock would become a fountain; but He speaks, and it is done. Not only do mountains move, but rocks yield rivers when the God of Israel wills that it will be so.

"Oh, magnify the LORD with me, and let us exalt His name together" (Ps. 34:3), for He alone does such wonders as these. He supplies our temporal needs from the most unlikely sources and never allows the stream of His generosity to fail.

As for our spiritual necessities, they are all met by the water and blood which gushed from the split rock, Christ Jesus; therefore let us praise the Lord our God.

Psalm 114:4–8

Give God the Glory

> *Today's Faith Builder:*
>
> Not unto us, O LORD, not unto us,
> But to Your name give glory,
> Because of Your mercy,
> Because of Your truth. (Psalm 115:1)

This psalm was sung at the Passover and therefore it is related to the deliverance of Israel from Egypt. It seems to be a prayer that the living God, who had been so glorious at the Red Sea and at the Jordan, would again, for His name's sake, show the wonders of His power.

The repetition of the words "Not unto us" would seem to indicate a very serious desire to renounce any glory which they might at any time have proudly claimed for themselves. They loathed the idea of seeking their own glory and rejected the thought with utter disgust, disclaiming again and again any self-glorifying motive in their prayer.

In these times, when the first victories of the gospel are only remembered as histories of a dim and distant past, skeptics are liable to boast that the gospel has lost its youthful strength. They may even try to smear the name of God. We may therefore rightly pray for our Lord's intervention that the apparent blot may be removed, and that His Word may shine forth gloriously as in days of old.

We should not desire the triumph of our opinions for our own sakes but we may confidently pray for the triumph of truth that God may be honored. Let us by fervent prayer prevail on our Lord to intervene by giving His gospel such a triumphant vindication that it will silence the perverse opposition of ungodly men.

Psalm 115:1–2

God Reigns Over All

⟩ *Today's Faith Builder:*
But our God is in heaven;
He does whatever He pleases. (Psalm 115:3)

Above all opposing powers, the Lord reigns supreme on His heavenly throne. Incomprehensible in essence, He rises above the highest thoughts of the wise; absolute in will and infinite in power, He is not subject to the limitations of earth and time.

This God is our God and we are not ashamed to own Him. Though our God is neither seen nor heard, and is not to be worshiped through an image, He is nonetheless real and true, for He is where His adversaries can never be—in the heavens, from where He stretches forth His scepter and rules with limitless power.

His decrees have all been fulfilled and His eternal purposes accomplished. He has not been asleep, or out of touch with the affairs of earth. He has worked effectively and none have been able to stop or even hinder Him.

However distasteful to His enemies, the Lord has accomplished all His good pleasure without difficulty. When His adversaries have raved and raged against Him they have been compelled to carry out His great plan, even though it was against their will.

Proud Pharaoh, when most defiant of the Lord, was but as clay on the potter's wheel and the Lord's ends and designs for him were fully carried out. What God has done He will continue to do. His counsel will stand and He will do what He pleases. At the end of the great drama of human history, the omnipotence of God and His immutability and faithfulness will be more than vindicated to the eternal confusion of His adversaries.

Psalm 115:3–8

We Are Blessed

❭ *Today's Faith Builder:*
May you be blessed by the LORD,
Who made heaven and earth. (Psalm 115:15)

Whatever others do, let the elect of heaven stay true to the God who chose them. Whatever our trouble may be, and however fierce the blasphemous language of our enemies, let us not fear nor falter but confidently rest in Him who is able to vindicate His honor and protect His servants. He is a friend of His servants, both actively and passively, giving them both aid in labor and defense in danger. He is the strength and security of His servants at all times.

The Lord has many blessings, each one worthy to be remembered; He blesses and blesses and blesses again. Where He has once bestowed His favor, He continues it; His blessing delights to visit the same house often and to stay where it has once lodged. Blessing does not impoverish the Lord; He has multiplied His mercies in the past and He will pour them forth thick and tripled in the future.

So long as a man fears the Lord it doesn't matter whether he is a prince or a peasant, a patriarch or a pauper, God will surely bless him. He will not permit any of the godly to be forgotten, however small their abilities or low their position. This is a sweet medication for those who are weak in faith and consider themselves mere babies in the family of grace. The same blessing is reserved for the humblest believer as for the greatest; if anything, the small will be first; when the need is pressing, the supply will be speedy.

He who made heaven and earth can give us all things while we dwell below and bring us safely to His palace above. Happy are the people on whom such a blessing rests.

Psalm 115:9–18

Love and Prayers

❯ *Today's Faith Builder:*
I love the LORD, because He has heard
My voice and my supplications. (Psalm 116:1)

Every believer ought to be able to declare, "I love the Lord" without the slightest hesitation. It was required under the law mentioned in Deuteronomy 6:5, but it has never been produced in the heart of man except by the grace of God and on gospel principles.

It is a great thing to say, "I love the Lord," for the sweetest of all graces and the surest of all evidence of salvation is love. It is great goodness on the part of God that He condescends to be loved by such poor creatures as we are, and it is a sure proof that He has been at work in our hearts when we can say "You know all things; You know that I love You" (John 21:17).

The psalmist not only knows that he loves God, but he knows why he loves Him. When love can justify itself with a reason it is deep, strong, and abiding. They say that love is blind, but when we love God our affection has its eyes open and can sustain itself with solid reasons.

We have reasons, superabundant reasons, for loving the Lord. In this case principle and passion, reason and emotion combine to create an excellent state of mind. David's reason for his love was the love of God in hearing his prayers.

When our feeble prayers are heard and answered in the strength and greatness of God, we are strengthened in the habit of prayer. In all our days let us pray and praise the Ancient of Days. He promises that as our days our strength shall be (Deut. 33:25); let us resolve that as our days our devotion will be.

Psalm 116:1–5

God Helps Those Who Cannot Help Themselves

> *Today's Faith Builder:*
> The LORD preserves the simple;
> I was brought low, and He saved me. (Psalm 116:6)

Those who have no worldly craft and are neither clever nor crafty, but simply trust in God and do right can depend on God to take care of them. The worldly-wise, as careful as they may be, will be caught in their own trap, but those who walk in their integrity with single-minded truthfulness before God will be protected against the deceitfulness of their enemies and enabled to outlive their foes.

There are many ways in which the child of God may be brought low, but the help of God is as varied as the needs of His people: He supplies our necessities when impoverished, restores our character when maligned, raises up friends for us when deserted, comforts us when discouraged, and heals our diseases when we are sick.

There are thousands in the church of God at this time who can each say, "I was brought low, and He saved me." Whenever this can be said it should be to the praise of the glory of God's grace and for the comforting of all others who may be passing through similar problems.

Note how David, after stating that the Lord preserves the simple, proves and illustrates it from his own experience. The habit of taking a general truth and testing the power of it in our own lives brings great blessing to us and others. It is the way in which the testimony of Christ is confirmed in us so we become witnesses to the Lord our God. The Lord has dealt bountifully with us, for He has given us His Son, and in Him He has given us all things.

Psalm 116:6–13

A Servant Yet . . . Free

❭ *Today's Faith Builder:*

O Lᴏʀᴅ, truly I am Your servant;
I am Your servant, the son of Your maidservant;
You have loosed my bonds. (Psalm 116:16)

Those who are redeemed with the precious blood of Christ (1 Peter 1:18–19) are so dear to God that even their deaths are precious to Him. The deathbeds of saints are also very precious to the church; she often learns much from them. They are very precious to all believers, who delight to treasure up the last words of the departed; but they are most precious to the Lord Jehovah Himself, who views the triumphant deaths of His children with sacred delight. If we have walked before Him in the land of the living, we need not fear to die before Him when the hour of our departure is at hand.

The psalmist here rededicates himself to God; he brings himself as an offering and cries, "O Lᴏʀᴅ, truly I am Your servant," I confess that I am Yours, for You have delivered and redeemed me.

He who is set free from the bonds of sin, death, and hell should rejoice to wear the easy yoke of the great Deliverer (Matt. 11:30). Note how the sweet singer delights to dwell on his belonging to the Lord; it is evidently his glory, a thing of which he is proud, a matter which causes him intense satisfaction. If we are able to call Jesus Master and are acknowledged by Him as His servants it ought to create rapture in our souls.

God's praise is not to be confined to a closet but in the thick of the throng we should lift up heart and voice to the Lord and invite others to join us in adoring Him, saying, "Praise the Lᴏʀᴅ!"

Psalm 116:14–19

Let's All Praise the Lord

❭ *Today's Faith Builder:*
Praise the LORD, all you Gentiles!
Laud Him, all you peoples! (Psalm 117:1)

This psalm, though little in length, is large in spirit. Bursting beyond all boundaries of race or nationality, it calls on all mankind to praise the name of the Lord. It is both short and sweet and is also the shortest chapter of the Scriptures and the central portion of the whole Bible.

The nations could not be expected to join in the praise of Jehovah unless they were also to share in the benefits which Israel enjoyed, so this psalm was a reminder to Israel that the grace and mercy of their God were not to be confined to one nation but would in future happier days be extended to all people.

The Lord is kind to us as His creatures and merciful to us as sinners. His merciful kindness then extends to us as sinful creatures. This mercy has been great and powerful. The mighty grace of God has covered us like the waters of the flood covered the earth; breaking over all boundaries, it has flowed to the entire human race.

In Christ Jesus, God has shown mercy mixed with kindness to the very highest degree. We can all join in gratefully acknowledging this and in praising God for it.

God has kept His covenant promise that in the seed of Abraham all nations of the earth would be blessed and He will eternally keep every single promise of that covenant to all those who put their trust in Him. This should be a cause of constant and grateful praise, and for that reason the psalm concludes with another hallelujah, "Praise the LORD!"

Psalm 117

Our Good and Merciful God

⟩ *Today's Faith Builder:*
Oh, give thanks to the LORD, for He is good!
For His mercy endures forever. (Psalm 118:1)

Grateful hearts are eager to hear praising tongues and would like to monopolize them all for God's glory.

In the truest sense God alone is good: "No one is good but One, that is, God" (Matt. 19:17). Therefore, in all gratitude, the Lord should have first place. If others *seem* to be good, He *is* good. If others are good in a measure, He is good beyond measure. When others treat us badly, it should only stir us up to give more hearty thanks to the Lord, because He is good. And when we are conscious of how far short we fall of being good, we should reverently bless Him all the more because "He is good."

We must never doubt the goodness of the Lord, even for an instant. Whatever else may be questionable, this is absolutely certain, that Jehovah is good; His methods of carrying out His plans may vary, but His nature is always the same: always good. It is not only that He was good, and will be good, but that He *is* good, let His providence be what it may. Therefore let us, even at this present moment, though the skies be dark with clouds, give thanks to Him.

Mercy is a great part of our Lord's goodness and the one which concerns us more than any other, for we are sinners and need His mercy. The endurance of divine mercy is a special subject for song; in spite of our sins, our trials, our fears, His mercy endures forever. The best of earthly joys pass away, and even the world itself grows old and hastens to decay, but there is no change in the goodness of the Lord.

Psalm 118:1–4

No Need to Fear

❯ *Today's Faith Builder:*
The Lord is on my side;
I will not fear.
What can man do to me? (Psalm 118:6)

Prayers which come out of distress generally come out of the heart, and therefore they go to the heart of God. It is sweet to remember our prayers and often profitable to tell others of them after they are heard. Prayer may be bitter in the offering, but it will be sweet in the answering.

The man of God had called on the Lord when he was not in distress, and therefore he found it natural and easy to call on Him when he was in distress. He worshiped, he praised, he prayed, for all this is included in calling on God.

Many of us can join with the psalmist in what he said about prayer. We were in deep distress because of sin and were imprisoned under the law, but in answer to the prayer of faith we obtained the liberty of full justification by which Christ made us free, and we are "free indeed" (John 8:36). It was the Lord who set us free, and to His name we give all the glory. We had no merits, no strength, no wisdom; all we could do was call on Him, and even that was His gift, but His eternal mercy came to our rescue.

The psalmist naturally rejoiced in divine help; all had turned against him, but God was his defender and advocate, accomplishing the divine purposes of His grace. The favor of God infinitely outweighed the hatred of men, so comparing the two he felt he had no reason to be afraid. He was calm and confident, though surrounded by enemies. Let us all be calm and confident like him, for in this we honor God.

Psalm 118:5–13

Our Strength, Our Song, Our Salvation

⟩ *Today's Faith Builder:*
  The LORD is my strength and song,
  And He has become my salvation. (Psalm 118:14)

The poet-warrior knew that he was saved, and he not only ascribed that salvation to God, but he declared God Himself to be his salvation. He wanted his hearers to know that from beginning to end, in the whole and in the details of it, he owed his deliverance entirely to the Lord. Like him, all the redeemed can say, "Salvation is of the Lord."

We cannot agree with any doctrine which puts the crown upon the wrong head and defrauds the glorious King of His rightful praise. Jehovah has done it all; yes, in Christ Jesus He is all, and therefore in our praises let Him alone be exalted.

Those who can praise God equally for being their strength, their song, and their salvation are happy people. God sometimes gives a secret strength to His people and yet they question their own salvation and cannot, therefore, sing of it. Many are, no doubt, truly saved, but at times they have so little strength that they are ready to faint and therefore they cannot sing. When strength is imparted and salvation is realized the song is clear and full.

The dwelling place of saved people should be the temple of praise; it is only right that the righteous should praise the righteous God, who is their righteousness.

That hero of heroes, the conquering Savior, gives all of His people abundant reasons for unceasing song. Let none of us be silent; if we have salvation let us have joy, and if we have joy let us give it a tongue with which it may magnify the Lord.

Psalm 118:14–18

The Rejected Ones

❯ *Today's Faith Builder:*
The stone which the builders rejected
Has become the chief cornerstone. (Psalm 118:22)

David had been rejected by those in authority, but God had placed him in a position of the highest honor and the greatest usefulness, making him the chief cornerstone of the nation. The Lord has been pleased to accomplish His divine purposes in the same manner in many others who have spent their early life in conflict, but this text applies especially to the Lord Jesus Himself. He is the living stone, the tried stone, elect, precious, which God Himself appointed.

Peter said, "This is the stone which was rejected by you builders" (Acts 4:11); they considered Him to be nothing, though He is Lord of all. In raising Him from the dead God exalted Him to be the head of His church, the very pinnacle of her glory and beauty.

In all things Jesus has the preeminence, He is the cornerstone of the whole house of God. God Himself laid Him where He is and has hidden within Him all the precious things of the eternal covenant. He will forever remain the foundation of all our hopes, the glory of all our joys, the uniting bond of all our fellowship.

The exalted position of Christ in His church is not the work of man and does not depend for its continuation on any builders and ministers. God Himself has exalted our Lord Jesus.

Faith sees our great Master far above all principality and power and might and dominion and every name that is named, not only in this world, but also in that which is to come. She sees and marvels. It is indeed "marvelous in our eyes."

Psalm 118:19–23

Rejoice and Be Glad!

> *Today's Faith Builder:*
  This is the day the LORD has made;
  We will rejoice and be glad in it. (Psalm 118:24)

The day of David's enthronement was the beginning of better times for Israel, and in a far higher sense the day of the Lord's resurrection was a new day of God's own making, for it was the dawn of a blessed new era.

Having obtained so great a deliverance through our illustrious Leader and having seen the eternal mercy of God so brilliantly displayed, it would not be fitting to mourn and murmur. Rather will we exhibit double joy. We will rejoice in heart and be glad in face, rejoice in secret and be glad in public, for we have more than a double reason for being glad in the Lord.

In looking back upon our pasts we can remember many delightful occasions when with full hearts and unspeakable joy we have blessed our Savior and King. And all these memorable times are foretastes and pledges of the time when in the house of our great Father above we will forever sing, "Worthy is the Lamb who was slain" (Rev. 5:12) and with rapture bless the Redeemer's name.

Only the power of God could have brought us such light and joy as spring from the work of our Champion and King. We have received light, by which we have known the rejected stone to be the head of the corner, and this light has led us to enlist beneath the banner of the once despised Nazarene, who is now the Prince of the kings of the earth. Let us do our best to magnify the great Father of lights from whom our present blessings have come down.

Psalm 118:24–29

Blessings for Those Who Walk with the Lord

> *Today's Faith Builder:*
> Blessed are the undefiled in the way,
> Who walk in the law of the LORD! (Psalm 119:1)

This is the longest psalm. Nor is it long only, for it equally excels in breadth of thought, depth of meaning, and height of fervor. It is like the celestial city which lies foursquare and the height and breadth of it are equal (Rev. 21:16). The more one studies it the fresher it becomes. The more you look into this mirror of a gracious heart the more you will see in it.

The one theme is the Word of the Lord. The psalmist sets his subject in many lights and treats it in different ways, but he seldom fails to mention the Word of the Lord in each verse under one of the many names by which he knows it. When the name is not there the subject is still heartily pursued.

Lovers of God's holy words are blessed because they are preserved from defilement (v. 1), because they are made practically holy (vv. 2–3) and are led to follow after God sincerely and intensely (v. 2). It is seen that this holy walking must be desirable because God commands it (v. 4); therefore the dedicated soul prays for it (v. 5) and feels that its comfort and courage must depend on obtaining it (v. 6). In the prospect of answered prayer, while the prayer is being answered, the heart is full of thankfulness (v. 7) and is fixed in solemn resolve not to miss the blessing if the Lord will give enabling grace (v. 8).

The psalmist is so enraptured with the Word of God that he regards being conformed to it in his daily living as the highest ideal of blessing.

Psalm 119:1–8

How to Have Victory Over Sin

❯ *Today's Faith Builder:*
Your word I have hidden in my heart,
That I might not sin against You. (Psalm 119:11)

The psalmist is but a young man, full of passions and poor in knowledge and experience; how shall he get right and keep right? Never was there a more important question for anyone.

No nobler ambition can lie before a youth, none to which he is called by so sure a calling; but none in which greater difficulties can be found. Let him not, however, shrink from the wise goal of living a pure and gracious life; rather let him ask how all obstacles to reaching his goal may be overcome.

Young believer, the Bible must be your chart, and you must exercise great watchfulness that your way may be according to its direction. You must take heed to your daily life as well as study your Bible, and you must study your Bible that you may take heed to your daily life. With the greatest care a man will go astray if his map misleads him; but with the most accurate map he will still lose his road if he does not follow it.

Let each person, whether young or old, who desires to be holy have a holy watchfulness in his heart and keep his Holy Bible before his open eye. God's Word is the best preventive against offending God, for it tells us His mind and will and brings our spirit into conformity with the Holy Spirit.

No cure for sin in the life is equal to the Word in the heart. There is no hiding from sin unless we hide the truth in our souls. When the Word is hidden in the heart the life will be hidden from sin.

Psalm 119:9–16

A Reason to Live

❯ *Today's Faith Builder:*
   Deal bountifully with Your servant,
   That I may live and keep Your word. (Psalm 119:17)

Here the trials of the way appear to be clear to the psalmist's mind, and he prays for help to meet them. His appeal is to God alone, and his prayer is direct and personal. He speaks with the Lord as a man speaks with his friend.

Without abundant mercy we could not live. It takes great grace to keep a saint alive. Life is a gift from the Lord to all undeserving ones. Only the Lord can sustain us. His mighty grace preserves the life we have forfeited by our sin.

It is right to desire to live. It is also right to pray to live and to give credit to God for prolonging our lives because we have found favor with Him. Spiritual life, without which this natural life is mere existence, is also to be sought as one of the Lord's rich blessings, for it is the noblest work of divine grace and in it the bounty of God is gloriously experienced. The Lord's servants cannot serve Him in their own strength, for they cannot even live unless His grace abounds toward them.

Keeping God's Word should be the rule, the object, and the joy of our lives. We may not wish to live and sin; but we may pray to live and keep God's Word. There is no life in the highest sense apart from holiness. The more a person prizes holiness and the more earnestly he strives for it, the more he will be driven to God for strength.

If we give God our service it must be because He gives us grace. We work for Him because He works in us.

Psalm 119:17–24

Strength for Melting Times

❯ *Today's Faith Builder:*
   My soul melts from heaviness;
   Strengthen me according to Your word. (Psalm 119:28)

Now the troubled psalmist complains about his bondage to earthly things. His soul holds to the dust from which he was made, melts for heaviness, and cries for freedom from its spiritual prison. He was dissolving away in tears. The solid strength of his constitution was turning to liquid as if being melted by the heat of his afflictions.

Heaviness of heart is a killing thing, threatening to turn life into a long death in which one seems to experience perpetual grief. Tears are the distillation of the heart; when a man weeps his soul wastes away. Some of us know what great heaviness means, for we have been brought under its power again and again and often have felt ourselves being poured out like water and near to being like water spilled on the ground, never to be gathered up. There is one good point about this downcast state; it is better to be melted with grief than to be hardened by impenitence.

God strengthens us by pouring in His grace through His Word; the Word which creates can certainly sustain. Grace can enable us to bear the constant stress of lasting sorrow; it can repair the decay caused by the perpetual tear drip and give to the believer the garment of praise for the spirit of heaviness.

When depression comes, let us pray, for prayer is the surest and shortest way out of the depths of discouragement. In that prayer let us plead nothing but the Word of God; for there is no plea like a promise, no argument like a word from our faithful God.

Psalm 119:25–32

Longing to Live God's Way

> *Today's Faith Builder:*
>   Teach me, O LORD, the way of Your statutes,
>   And I shall keep it to the end. (Psalm 119:33)

A sense of dependence and an awareness of extreme need flow through this text, which is made up of a prayer and a plea. The former eight verses trembled with a sense of sin, quivering with a childlike feeling of weakness and folly which caused the man of God to cry out for the only help by which his soul could be kept from falling back into sin.

The psalmist longs to have the Lord for his teacher, for he feels that his heart will not grasp what he needs to know from a less-effective instructor. A sense of great slowness to learn drives us to seek a great teacher. The very desire to learn God's way is in itself an assurance that we will be taught by the Lord, for He who made us long to learn will be sure to satisfy our desire.

Those who are taught of God never forget their lessons. When divine grace sets one in the true way he will be true to it. Mere human intelligence will not have such an enduring influence; there is an end to all human perfecting, but there is no end to heavenly grace except the final fulfilling of God's purpose, which is the perfecting of holiness in the fear of the Lord.

Perseverance to the end is to be expected of those whose beginning is in God and with God and by God, but those who begin without the Lord's teaching soon forget what they learn and stray from the way of the Lord. Let us earnestly, then, drink in divine instruction so that we may keep our integrity and walk uprightly all the days of our lives.

Psalm 119:33–40

Not Ashamed to Speak for God

❭ *Today's Faith Builder:*
I will speak of Your testimonies also before kings,
And will not be ashamed. (Psalm 119:46)

What a multitude of mercies are heaped together in the salvation we have in our Lord Jesus! These include the mercies which spare us before our conversion and lead up to it. Then comes calling mercy, regenerating mercy, converting mercy, justifying mercy, pardoning mercy. Nor can we exclude from complete salvation any of those many mercies which are needed to take the believer safely to heaven. Salvation is a combination of mercies that are beyond number, priceless in value, never ceasing in application, and enduring forever. To the God of our mercies be eternal glory.

David was called to stand before kings while he was in exile, and later, when he was a king, he knew the tendency of people to sacrifice their religious convictions to pomp and ceremony, but he resolved to do nothing of the kind. He would sanctify politics and make cabinet members know that the Lord alone is Governor among the nations. As a king, he would speak to kings about the King of kings.

Diplomacy might have suggested that David's life and conduct would be enough, that it would be better not to talk about religion in the presence of royalty who worshiped other gods and claimed to be right in doing so. He had already said, "I will walk," but he does not make his righteous conduct an excuse for sinful silence, for he adds, "I will speak."

When God gives grace, cowardice soon vanishes. He who speaks for God, in God's power, will not be ashamed.

Psalm 119:41–48

Comfort in Affliction

> *Today's Faith Builder:*
>> This is my comfort in my affliction,
>> For Your word has given me life. (Psalm 119:50)

The worldly person clutches his money and says, "This is my comfort." The drunkard lifts his glass and sings, "This is my comfort." But the person whose hope comes from God feels that life-giving power of the Word of the Lord and testifies, "This is my comfort." Paul said, "I know whom I have believed" (2 Tim. 1:12).

Comfort is desirable at all times, but comfort in affliction is like a light in a dark place. Some are unable to find comfort at such times, but not believers, for their Savior has promised not to leave them comfortless (John 14:18). Some have comfort and no affliction, others have affliction and no comfort, but believers have comfort in their affliction.

Like other servants of God, David knew that he was not at home in this world, but a pilgrim passing through it seeking a better country. He did not, however, complain about this but instead sang about it. He tells us nothing about his pilgrim sighs, only of his pilgrim songs.

Even the palace where David lived was but "the house of my pilgrimage" (Ps. 119:54), the inn at which he rested. People often sing when they reach their inn, and so did this godly traveler; he sang the songs of Zion, the statutes of the great King. The commands of God were as well-known to him as the ballads of his country and they were pleasant to his taste and musical to his ears. Happy is the heart which finds its joy in the commands of God and makes obedience to them joyful recreation.

Psalm 119:49–56

Choosing God

> *Today's Faith Builder:*
> You are my portion, O LORD;
> I have said that I would keep Your words. (Psalm 119:57)

In this section the psalmist seems to take a firm hold on God; appropriating Him (v. 57), crying out to Him (v. 58), returning to Him (v. 59), comforting himself in Him (vv. 61–62), associating with His people (v. 63), and longing to experience His goodness (v. 64).

The poet is lost in wonder when he sees that the great and glorious God is all his own! How fitting! There is no possession like the Lord Himself!

David had often seen the prey divided and heard the victors shouting over it; here he rejoices as one who seizes his share of the spoil—he chooses the Lord to be his part of the treasure. Like the Levites, he took God to be his portion and left earthly possessions to those who desired them. This is a great and lasting heritage, for it includes all, and more than all, and it outlasts all.

Who that is truly wise could hesitate for a moment when the infinitely blessed God is set before him to be his choice? David seized the opportunity and the priceless blessing. With many other choices open to him, for he was a king and a man of great resources, he deliberately turns from all the treasures of the world and declares that the Lord is his portion.

We cannot always look back with satisfaction on what we have said, but in this case David has spoken wisely and well. He took God to be his Prince as well as his portion and was determined to be obedient to Him.

Psalm 119:57–64

When Trouble Is Good for Us

❯ *Today's Faith Builder:*
Before I was afflicted I went astray,
But now I keep Your word. (Psalm 119:67)

In providence and in grace, in giving prosperity and in sending adversity, Jehovah has been good to us. This kindness of the Lord is no accident: He promised to be kind and has done so according to His Word.

Often our trials act as a thorn hedge to keep us in the good pasture, but prosperity can be an opening in the hedge through which we go astray. When we remember a time in which we had no trouble, we probably recall this as a time when grace was low and temptation was strong.

Why is it that a little ease works in us such disease? Can we never rest without rusting? Never be filled without becoming fat? Never rise in one world without going down in another? What weak creatures we are to be unable to bear a little pleasure! What wicked hearts are these which turn the abundance of God's goodness into an occasion for sin (Jer. 17:9)!

Grace is in that heart which profits by chastening. Where there is no spiritual life affliction works no spiritual benefit, but when the heart is right trouble awakens the conscience, wandering is confessed, and the soul becomes again obedient to the Lord's command. Before trouble came David wandered, but his trials kept him within the hedge of God's Word and he found good pasture for his soul.

Even in affliction God is good. We believe in His goodness and honor Him by our faith; we admire that goodness and glorify Him by our love; we declare that goodness and magnify Him by our testimony.

Psalm 119:65–72

His Kindness for Our Comfort

> *Today's Faith Builder:*
   Let, I pray, Your merciful kindness be for my comfort,
   According to Your word to Your servant. (Psalm 119:76)

Hopeful people bring gladness with them. Despondent spirits spread the infection of depression, so few are glad to see them. Those whose hopes rest on God's Word carry sunshine in their faces and are welcomed by their friends.

The psalmist had been through many trials but had continued to hope in God and now says that he has been justly and wisely chastened. Because love required severity, the Lord exercised it. It was not because God was unfaithful that the psalmist found himself in difficult circumstances but for just the opposite reason: the faithfulness of God brought His chosen one under discipline. He was positive about it and spoke without a moment's hesitation. Believers are sure about the rightness of their trials even when they cannot see the purposes of them.

Having confessed the righteousness of the Lord, David now appeals to His mercy, and while he does not ask that the discipline be removed, he earnestly begs for comfort while enduring it. The words "merciful kindness" are a happy combination and express exactly what we need in affliction: mercy to forgive the sin and kindness to hold us up under the sorrow. With these we can be comfortable on the darkest day and without them we are miserable.

Blessed be the name of the Lord! In spite of our faults, we are still His servants. We serve a compassionate Master.

Psalm 119:73–80

Hope for Dark Days

> *Today's Faith Builder:*
> My soul faints for Your salvation,
> But I hope in Your word. (Psalm 119:81)

This octave is the midnight of the psalm and it describes a very dark time. Stars, however, shine through the darkness and later the psalm gives evidence of the dawn.

Nothing could satisfy the psalmist but deliverance by the hand of God. He yearned for salvation from the God of all grace and he felt he must have it or fail. Therefore he felt that salvation would come, for God cannot break His promise nor disappoint the hope which His own Word has given.

Hope sustains when desire exhausts. While the grace of desire throws us down, the grace of hope lifts us up again.

"Help, Lord" is a fitting prayer for youth and old age, for labor and suffering, for life and death. No other help is sufficient, but God's help is all-sufficient and we cast ourselves on it without fear. If we stick to God's precepts we will be rescued by His promises.

We look to the lovingkindness of God as the source of spiritual revival, and we ask the Lord to revive us, not because we deserve it but because of His grace.

What a wonderful word *lovingkindness* is! Take it apart and admire its double force of love.

We ought to admire the spiritual wisdom of the psalmist, who prays not so much for freedom from trial as for new strength that he may be supported in it. Here David seeks a revived heart; he wisely seeks what he most needs.

Psalm 119:81–88

God's Word Is Settled

❭ *Today's Faith Builder:*
Forever, O Lᴏʀᴅ,
You word is settled in heaven. (Psalm 119:89)

After tossing about on a sea of trouble the psalmist here leaps to shore and stands on a rock. Jehovah's Word is neither fickle nor uncertain; it is settled, determined, fixed, sure, immovable. Mankind's teachings change so often that there is never time for them to be settled, but the Lord's Word has always been the same and will remain unchanged forever.

Some people are never happier than when they are upsetting everything and everybody, but they do not have the mind of God. The power and the glory of heaven have confirmed each sentence which the mouth of the Lord has spoken and it must stand the same for all eternity, settled in heaven where nothing can affect it. Earlier David's soul had fainted, but here he looks out of himself and understands that his Lord is never faint or weary (Isa. 40:28), neither is there any failure in His Word.

God's purposes, promises, and precepts are all settled in His own mind and none of them will be disturbed. His promises will not be removed however unsettled the thoughts of others may become. Let us, therefore, settle it in our minds that we are safe in our Lord as long as we live.

God's Word, which established the world, is the same as that which He has given in the Scriptures. When we see the world continuing and all its laws remaining the same, we have assurance that the Lord will be faithful to His promises. If God's Word is sufficient to establish the world, surely it is sufficient to establish each believer.

Psalm 119:89—96

Loving God's Word

> *Today's Faith Builder:*
> Oh, how I love Your law!
> It is my meditation all the day. (Psalm 119:97)

The law is God's law, and therefore it is our love. We love it for its holiness and long to be holy; we love it for its wisdom and study it to be wise; we love it for its perfection and long to be perfect. Those who know the power of the gospel see an infinite loveliness in the law as they see it fulfilled and embodied in Christ Jesus.

The psalmist meditated on God's Word because he loved it, then loved it more because he meditated on it. He could not get enough of it. His morning prayer, his noonday thought, his evening song were all based on the Bible. The more of some people you know the less you admire them, but the reverse is true of God's Word. Familiarity with the Word of God leads to affection and affection seeks even greater familiarity. Those who meditate on the Bible every day find life growing holy, devout, and happy.

The Bible was the psalmist's book and God was his teacher. The letter can give us knowledge but only the Holy Spirit can make us wise. Wisdom is knowledge put to practical use. Wisdom comes to us through obedience. A holy life is the highest wisdom and the surest defense from our enemies.

Disciples who sit at the feet of Jesus are often better skilled in divine things than doctors of divinity. We may hear the wisest teachers and remain fools, but if we meditate on the sacred Word we are sure to become wise. There is more wisdom in the testimonies of the Lord than in all the teachings of the world's great libraries.

Psalm 119:97–104

A Light to My Path

❭ *Today's Faith Builder:*
Your word is a lamp to my feet
And a light to my path. (Psalm 119:105)

We all walk through this world and are often called to go out into its darkness. Let us never venture there without the light-giving Word, lest we slip and fall. We should each use the Word of God personally, practically, and continually so that we will be able to see our way and what lies ahead in it.

When darkness settles down all around us, the Word of the Lord, like a flaming torch, lights our way. This is a true picture of our path through this dark world. We would not know the way or how to walk in it if the Scriptures did not reveal it. One of the most practical benefits of the Bible is guidance in daily life; it is not sent to astound us with its brilliance but to guide us by its instruction. Happy is the one who personally appropriates God's Word and uses it daily as his comfort and counselor, a lamp to his own feet.

God's Word is a lamp by night, a light by day, and a delight at all times. David guided his own steps by it and saw the difficulties of his road by its beams. He who walks in darkness is sure, sooner or later, to stumble, but he who walks by the light of day or the lamp of night will not fall.

Whatever path might open before the psalmist, he was determined to follow only where the lamp of God's Word was shining. The Scriptures are God's judgments or verdicts on great moral questions; these are all righteous, so righteous men should resolve to keep them at all costs, since it will always be right to do right.

Psalm 119:105–112

A Place to Hide

⟩ *Today's Faith Builder:*

    You are my hiding place and my shield;
    I hope in Your word. (Psalm 119:114)

The opposite of the fixed and infallible law of God is the wavering, changing opinion of men. David had an utter contempt and abhorrence for this; all his reverence and regard went to the sure Word of testimony: the Scriptures.

When mankind thinks his best, his highest thoughts are as far below those of divine revelation as the earth is beneath the heavens. Some of our thoughts are centered on vainglory, pride, conceit, and self-trust; others are given to ambition, sinful dreaming, and confidence in man. The psalmist is not indifferent to evil thoughts but he looks upon them with a hate as true as the love that once held him close to God.

David ran to God for shelter from evil thoughts; there he hid himself from their tormenting intrusions and in solemn silence of soul he found God to be his hiding place. When he could not be alone with God as his hiding place, he could have the Lord with him as his shield by which he could ward off the attacks of wicked suggestions. He could not fight with his own thoughts or escape from them until he fled to his God and found deliverance.

Happy is the person who can truly say to God, "You are my hiding place." Sometimes when gloomy thoughts afflict us, the only thing we can do is hope. We may be ashamed of our thoughts and our words and our deeds, for they spring from within us; but we should never be ashamed of our hope, for that springs from the Lord our God. He is always faithful and we should never be ashamed of Him.

Psalm 119:113–120

A Time for God to Work

❭ *Today's Faith Builder:*
It is time for You to act, O LORD,
For they have regarded Your law as void. (Psalm 119:126)

David was a servant and therefore it was always his time to work, but being discouraged by the sight of rampant sin among his people, he feels that his Master's hand is needed and therefore appeals to Him to work against the working of evil.

People make the law of God void by denying it to be His law, by promoting doctrines in opposition to it, by replacing it with traditions, or by disregarding and scorning the authority of the Lawgiver. Then sin becomes fashionable and a holy walk is rejected as old-fashioned and puritanical.

Oh, for an hour of the King on His throne, for another Pentecost with all its wonders to reveal the power of God to the doubters and scoffers and make them see that God is alive! Man's extremity, whether because of need or sin, it God's opportunity.

When the earth was without form and void, the Holy Spirit came and moved on the face of the waters; should He not come when society is returning to a similar chaos? When the children of Israel in Egypt were at their lowest point, Moses appeared and worked mighty miracles; so too when the church is being trampled down and her message rejected we may expect to see the hand of the Lord bringing revival, defending the truth, and glorifying His name.

Let us ask the Lord to raise up new evangelists, to revive those we already have, to set His whole church on fire, and to bring the world to His feet. Our work will accomplish nothing apart from Him.

Psalm 119:121–128

Our Wonderful Source of Light

> *Today's Faith Builder:*
> The entrance of Your words gives light;
> It gives understanding to the simple. (Psalm 119:130)

God's words are full of wonderful revelations, commands, and promises. They are wonderful in their nature, as being free from all error, and bearing within them overwhelming evidence of their truth; wonderful in their effects on us: instructing, elevating, strengthening, and comforting the soul.

Jesus the eternal Word is called Wonderful, and all the words of God are wonderful. Those who know them best wonder at them most. It is wonderful that God has given His Word to sinful people and more wonderful that it is so clear, so full, so gracious, so mighty. The wonderful character of the very words of God so impressed the psalmist that he kept them in his memory; their excellence so charmed his heart that he kept them in his life.

The entrance of God's Word brings light, but merely hearing it is of little value; we must allow it to enter the chambers of the heart, scattering light all around. The Word finds no entrance into some minds because they are filled with pride or prejudice or indifference, but when full attention is given divine illumination must follow.

Those whom the world calls fools are among the truly wise if they are taught of God. Divine power clearly rests in the Word of God, since it not only bestows light but gives the ability to receive it!

Oh, that Your words, like the beams of the sun, may enter the window of my understanding and dispel the darkness of my mind!

Psalm 119:129–136

God Always Does Right

> ❭ *Today's Faith Builder:*
> Righteous are You, O LORD,
> And upright are Your judgments. (Psalm 119:137)

G od is always right and He is always actively right; He is righteous. This quality is bound up in our very idea of God. We cannot imagine an unrighteous God.

Jehovah both says and does what is right, and that alone. This is a great comfort to the soul in times of trouble, we can rest on this sure and certain fact: God is righteous and His dealings with us are righteous. We ought to sing this brave confession when all things around us appear to suggest the contrary. This is the richest form of adoration because it rises from the lips of faith when carnal reason mutters about the severity of our suffering.

What a blessing it is that we have a God who is scrupulously faithful, true to all the details of His promises, and punctual and steadfast at all times! We can risk all on His promises, which are ever faithful and sure.

The psalmist was in great distress. His griefs, like fierce dogs, had taken hold of him; he felt their teeth. He had double trouble: trouble without and anguish within, as the apostle Paul put it: "Outside were conflicts, inside were fears" (2 Cor. 7:5).

In all of his trouble, however, the psalmist found delight in the commandments of this Lord. He therefore became a riddle—troubled and yet delighted; in anguish and yet in pleasure. The child of God can understand this dilemma, for when he is discouraged by what he sees within, he is lifted up by what he sees in God's Word.

Psalm 119:137–144

Our Lord Is Near

> *Today's Faith Builder:*
> You are near, O LORD,
> And all Your commandments are truth. (Psalm 119:151)

He who has been with God in the closet will find God with him in the furnace. If we have cried we will be answered. Delayed answers may drive us to pray again and again, but we need not fear the ultimate result since God's promises are not uncertain but are eternally true.

The psalmist's hope was fixed on God's Word and this provides true security, for God is true and in no case has He ever retreated from His promise or altered what He has said. He who is diligent in prayer will never be destitute of hope. As the early bird gets the worm, so the early prayer is soon refreshed with hope.

God's methods of communicating greater vigor to our spiritual lives are very wise and it will be wise for us to receive grace, not according to our notion of how it should come to us, but according to God's method of bestowing it.

As near as the psalmist's enemy might be, God was nearer; this is a great comfort to the persecuted child of God. The Lord is always near to hear our cries and to quickly send us help. He is near enough to chase away our enemies and give us rest and peace.

If all God's commands are truth, the true believer will be glad to keep near to them, and in doing so he will find the true God near him.

God is near and God is true, therefore His people are safe.

God's presence on our side is our glory and delight.

Psalm 119:145–152

Prayer During Affliction

> *Today's Faith Builder:*
> Consider my affliction and deliver me,
> For I do not forget Your law. (Psalm 119:153)

The psalmist desired two things: first, a full consideration of his sorrow; second, deliverance. It should be the desire of each afflicted believer that the Lord would consider his need and relieve it in a way that will bring glory to God and benefit to him.

The words "my affliction" are picturesque; they seem to portion off a special spot of trouble as the writer's own inheritance, and he begs the Lord to watch over that special spot as a farmer looking over all his fields may take double care of a certain selected plot. His prayer is focused and practical, for he seeks to be delivered from his trouble and preserved from sustaining any serious damage from it.

The psalmist's affliction did not cause him to forget God's law, nor could it lead him to act contrary to the Scriptures. He forgot some of his blessings but he did not forget obedience. This is a good prayer when it is offered honestly.

If we are faithful to God's Word we may be sure that He will remain faithful to His promises. Our Lord will not forget us. He will not leave us in trouble long if our only fear in trouble is that we might wander from His way.

The psalmist so loved everything that was good and excellent that he loved all God had commanded. The principles of Scripture are all wise and holy, therefore he loved them deeply; loved to know them, to think of them, to proclaim them, and especially to practice them.

David felt like one who was half-stunned by the bitter attacks of his enemies, so he prayed for revival, restoration, and renewal.

Psalm 119:153–160

Treasuring God's Word

> *Today's Faith Builder:*
> I rejoice at Your word
> As one who finds great treasure. (Psalm 119:162)

David might have been overcome by awe of the princes who persecuted him had he not been so much in awe of God's Word. He trembled at the Word of God and yet rejoiced in it. He compares his joy to that
of one who has been in a long battle and has at last won the victory and
is dividing the spoil. This is usually the lot of princes, and though David
was not one with them in their persecutions, he had his victories, and his
spoil was equal to their greatest gains. The profits he made in searching
the Scriptures were greater than the trophies of war.

We have to fight for divine truth; every doctrine costs us a battle, but
when we gain a full understanding of it by personal struggles it becomes
doubly precious to us. May we have for our treasure a firmer hold on the
priceless Word.

Perhaps, however, the psalmist rejoiced as one who comes upon hidden treasure for which he had not fought. This reminds us of one who
while reading the Bible makes the wonderful discovery of the grace of
God, which surprises him. He had not expected to find such a prize.

Whether we discover truth as finders or as warriors fighting for it, the
heavenly treasure should be equally valuable to us. The believer should
be glad when he has discovered the promises of the Bible and is able to
enjoy them, knowing by the witness of the Holy Spirit that this treasure
belongs to him.

Psalm 119:161–168

A Prayer for Understanding

> *Today's Faith Builder:*
> Let my cry come before You, O LORD;
> Give me understanding according to Your word. (Psalm 119:169)

The psalmist is approaching the end of the psalm and his prayers gather force and fervency; he seems to break into the inner circle of divine fellowship and to come even to the feet of the Great God whose help he is requesting. This nearness to God creates a lowly view of himself and leads him to close the psalm on his face in deepest humiliation, begging to be sought out like a lost sheep.

It is sweet to one praying when he knows for sure that his prayer has gained an audience with God, when it has walked on the sea of glass before the throne and has come to the footstool of the glorious seat around which heaven and earth adore the King. It is to Jehovah that this prayer is earnestly expressed.

The psalmist is very concerned about his prayer. He longs for understanding and he resolves not to miss this priceless treasure. He desires spiritual light and understanding as it is promised in God's Word, as it proceeds from God's Word, and as it produces obedience to God's Word.

To have an understanding of spiritual things is a gift from God. To have judgment enlightened by heavenly light and conformed to divine truth is a privilege that only grace can give. Many who are thought wise in this world are fools, according to the Word of the Lord. May we be among those happy people who will all be taught of the Lord.

When the tongue speaks of God's Word it has a most fruitful subject. We should not only speak of God's works, but of His Word.

Psalm 119:169–176

Crying Out to God in Distress

> *Today's Faith Builder:*
> In my distress I cried to the LORD,
> And He heard me. (Psalm 120:1)

Suddenly we have left the continent of the vast 119th Psalm for the islands and islets of the Songs of Degrees. He who inspired the longest psalm was also the author of the shorter psalms which follow it.

Slander brings deep distress. Those who have felt the edge of a cruel tongue know that it is sharper than a sword. We could ward off the strokes of a cutlass, but we have no shield against a liar's tongue. We may not know who was the father of the falsehood, nor where it was born, nor where it has gone, nor how to follow it, nor how to stop its influence. Like the plague of flies in Egypt, it baffles opposition, and few can stand up to it. Even in such distress, however, we need not hesitate to cry out to the Lord. Silence to man and prayer to God are the best cures for slander.

It is of little use to appeal to others when slandered, for the more we stir slander the more it spreads. Appealing to the honor of slanderers will not help for they have none and demanding justice from them will only encourage them to fresh insults; one might as well plead with panthers and wolves. But when cries to man would be our weakness, cries to God will be our strength.

To whom should children cry but to their father? Does not some good come even out of slander when it drives us to our knees and to our God? Prayer to the living God is always profitable.

Jehovah hears. He will not hear the lie against us, but He will hear our prayer against the lie.

Psalm 120:1

A Prayer for Deliverance from Liars

> *Today's Faith Builder:*
> Deliver my soul, O LORD, from lying lips
> And from a deceitful tongue. (Psalm 120:2)

Lips are soft, but when they are lying lips they suck away the life of character and are as murderous as razors. Lips should never be red with the blood of honest reputations.

Some seem to lie for the sake of lying; it is their sport and spirit. Their lips deserve to be kissed with a hot iron, but the friends of Jesus are not to give people what they deserve. We need to be delivered from slander by the Lord's restraint of wicked tongues or by having our good names cleared from these lies.

Those who fawn and flatter and all the while have deceit in their hearts are miserable people; they are the seed of the devil. Better to meet wild beasts and serpents than deceivers; these are a kind of monster whose birth is from beneath and whose end lies far below. From gossips, tale-bearers, writers of anonymous letters, and all sorts of liars, good Lord deliver us!

It is better to be a victim of slander than the author of it. The coals of malice will cool, but not the fire of justice. Shun slander as you would avoid hell.

A peacemaker is a blessing, but a peace-hater is a curse. To stay with such for a night is dangerous, but to live with him is terrible. Let those who dwell with liars find comfort by remembering that both David and David's Lord endured the same trial.

Let those who have quiet and peaceful homes be grateful for such blessings. God has given this tranquility. May we never inflict on others that from which we have been spared ourselves.

Psalm 120:2–7

Help from the Lord

> *Today's Faith Builder:*
> My help comes from the LORD,
> Who made heaven and earth. (Psalm 121:2)

The psalmist now sings a choice sonnet and looks away from the slanderers by whom he was tormented to the Lord who sees all from His high places and is ready to comfort His injured servant. Help comes to believers only from above; they look elsewhere in vain. Let us lift up our eyes with hope, expectation, desire, and confidence.

Satan will try to keep our eyes on our sorrows so that we will worry and be discouraged, but we should firmly resolve that we will look out and up. Those who lift up their eyes to the eternal hills will soon have their hearts lifted up also.

The purposes of God—His attributes, the unchanging promises, the covenant, providence, predestination, and the proven faithfulness of the Lord—these are the hills to which we must lift our eyes, for from these our help must come. We are determined not to be bandaged and blindfolded, but will lift up our eyes.

What we need is help that is powerful, efficient, constant; we need a very present help in trouble (Ps. 46:1). What a blessing that we have it in our God! Our hope is in Jehovah, for our help comes from Him.

Help is on the way and will not fail to reach us in time, for He who sends it to us has never been late. Jehovah, who created all things, is equal to every emergency; heaven and earth are at His disposal, therefore let us be joyful in our all-powerful Helper.

We must look beyond heaven and earth to Him who made them. It is vain to trust the creatures; it is wise to trust the Creator.

Psalm 121:1–2

Our Keeper

❭ *Today's Faith Builder:*
    The LORD is your keeper;
    The LORD is your shade at your right hand. (Psalm 121:5)

Though the paths of life are dangerous and difficult, we will be safe, for Jehovah will not permit our feet to slide. If our feet are kept safely, we may be sure that our head and heart will be safe also.

Promised preservation should be the subject of perpetual prayer. We can pray believingly, for those who have God for their keeper will be safe from all the perils of the way.

We would not be safe for a moment if our keeper were to sleep—we need Him day and night—not a single step can be taken except under His guardian eye. God is the convoy and bodyguard of His people. When dangers are all around us we are safe, for our Preserver is awake and will not permit us to be ambushed.

No fatigue or exhaustion can cause our God to fall asleep; His watchful eyes are never closed. He will never permit the house to be broken up by a silent thief; He is ever watching and sees every intruder. He keeps us as a rich man keeps his treasures, as a captain keeps a city with men under his command, as a royal guard keeps his king from danger and death.

God is as near us as our shadow, and we are as safe as angels. How different this is from the experience of the ungodly, who have Satan standing at their right hand.

Happy are the pilgrims to whom this psalm guarantees safe conduct. They may journey all the way to the celestial city without fear.

Psalm 121:3–6

God Preserves His People

> *Today's Faith Builder:*
>   The LORD shall preserve you from all evil;
>   He shall preserve your soul. (Psalm 121:7)

God not only keeps His own in all evil times but from all evil influences and operations. This is a far-reaching promise; it includes everything and excludes nothing. The wings of Jehovah amply guard His own from evils great and small, temporary and eternal.

Soul-keeping is the soul of keeping. If the soul is kept, all is kept. God is the sole keeper of the soul. Our soul is kept from the dominion of sin, the infection of error, the crush of depression, the puffing up of pride. We are kept from the world, the flesh, and the devil; kept for holier and greater things; kept in the love of God; kept for the eternal kingdom and glory. What can harm the one who is kept by the Lord?

When we go out in the morning to work and come home in the evening to rest, Jehovah will keep us. When we go out in youth to begin life and come in at the end to die, He will keep us. Our entrances and our exits are under His protection.

The Lord's keeping is eternal, continuing from this time forth, even forevermore. The whole church is assured of everlasting security; the final perseverance of the saints is declared and the glorious immortality of believers is guaranteed.

None are so safe as those whom God keeps; none so much in danger as those who feel safe in themselves. Jehovah will keep the door when it opens and closes and He will continue to do so as long as there is a single person left who trusts in Him, as long as a danger survives; in fact, as long as time endures.

Psalm 121:7–8

What Makes Us Glad?

> *Today's Faith Builder:*
> I was glad when they said to me,
> "Let us go into the house of the LORD." (Psalm 122:1)

Good children are pleased to go home and glad to hear their brothers and sisters call them to return to their house. David loved the worship of God and he was delighted others invited him to go where his desires had already gone.

The word from these calling to David was not "go" but "Let us go," so he found double joy in it. He was glad for the sake of others; glad that they wished to go themselves, glad that they had the courage and concern to invite others. He knew this would do them good; nothing better can happen to people and their friends than to love the place where God is honored. What a great day it will be when many people will say,

Come, and let us go up to the mountain of the LORD,
To the house of the God of Jacob;
He will teach us His ways,
And we shall walk in His paths. (Micah 4:2)

David was glad also for his own sake; he loved the invitation to the holy place, he delighted in being called to go to worship. Some might have said, "Mind your own business," but not King David. He was not teased but pleased by being pressed to attend holy services. He was glad to go into the house of the Lord, glad to go in holy company, glad to find good men and women willing to fellowship with him. He may have been sad before but this invitation made him glad. He was pleased at the very mention of his Father's house. Are we like him?

Psalm 122:1–5

Praying for Peace

> *Today's Faith Builder:*
> Pray for the peace of Jerusalem:
> "May they prosper who love you." (Psalm 122:6)

Peace in a church is to be desired, expected, promoted, and enjoyed. If we may not say "peace at any price" we may certainly cry "peace at the highest price."

Those who are upset daily by alarming experiences are happy to find peace in a holy fellowship. In a church one of the main ingredients of success is internal peace: strife, suspicion, party-spirit, and divisions are deadly things. Those who break the peace of a church deserve to suffer and those who sustain it receive a great blessing.

Peace in the church should be our daily prayer and in so praying we will bring peace to ourselves, for the psalmist goes on to say, "May they prosper who love you." Whether this statement is regarded as a promise or a prayer does not matter, for prayer pleads the promise and the promise is the ground of prayer.

Prosperity of soul is already enjoyed by those who take a deep interest in the church and the work of God. They are people of peace and find peace in holy service; God's people pray for them and God delights in them.

We wish the church rest from internal dissension and external assault. It is to the advantage of all Israel that there should be peace in Jerusalem. It is for the good of every Christian, yes, of every person, that there should be peace and prosperity in the church. By a flourishing church our children, our neighbors, and our fellow countrymen are likely to be blessed.

Psalm 122:6–9

Looking Up

❯ *Today's Faith Builder:*
Unto You I lift up my eyes,
O You who dwell in the heavens. (Psalm 123:1)

We are climbing. The first step (Ps. 120) saw us lamenting our troublesome surroundings and the next saw us lifting our eyes to the hills and finding rest. From this we rose to delight in the house of the Lord; but here we look to the Lord Himself, the highest of all.

It is good to have someone to look up to. The psalmist looked so high that he could look no higher; he looked not to the hills but to the God of the hills.

Uplifted eyes naturally and instinctively represent the heart which fixes desire, hope, confidence, and expectation on the Lord. When we cannot look to any helper on our level it is wise to look above us; in fact, if we have a thousand helpers, our eyes should still be toward the Lord.

The higher the Lord, the better it is for our faith since that height represents power, glory, and excellence and these will all be important to us in our rescue from trouble. We ought to be thankful for spiritual eyes and we must resolve to lift them for they will not naturally turn upward but are inclined to look downward or inward or anywhere but to the Lord. Let us keep looking heavenward.

When we are looking to the Lord in hope it is well to tell Him so in prayer; the psalmist used his voice as well as his eyes. This is helpful to the heart.

We can always lift up our eyes to the Lord. He is always at home. We must not limit our Lord's love by thinking He is not always available to us. No night is too dark for us to look to Him.

Psalm 123:1–2

In Need of Mercy

> *Today's Faith Builder:*
> Have mercy on us, O LORD, have mercy on us!
> For we are exceedingly filled with contempt. (Psalm 123:3)

The psalmist prays earnestly for mercy; the very word seems to capture him and he focuses on it. We can pray about everything and turn everything into prayer, especially when we are reminded of a great need.

His consecutive prayers for mercy show the eagerness of the psalmist's spirit and his urgent need; what he needed speedily he prays for repeatedly. All believers need mercy, and they shall all have it, so we pray, "Have mercy on us." Our enemies will have no mercy on us. Let us not ask it then from them, but turn to the God of mercy and seek His aid alone.

Contempt is bitterness; those who feel it directed toward them may well cry for the mercy of God. This contempt had monopolized their minds and had become the sorrow of their hearts. Oh, to be filled with communion with Christ—then contempt will run off from us and never be able to fill us with its biting vinegar.

Great hearts have been broken and brave spirits have withered beneath the power of slanderous lies and the blight of contempt. We can remember that our Lord was despised and rejected of men, yet He did not cease His perfect service until His mission was accomplished.

Let us firmly believe that the contempt of the ungodly will turn to our honor in the world to come. Even now it serves as a reminder that we are not of the world, for if we were of the world the world would love us as its own (John 15:19).

Psalm 123:3–4

The Lord Is on Our Side

> *Today's Faith Builder:*
> Blessed be the LORD,
> Who has not given us as prey to their teeth. (Psalm 124:6)

The blessed Lord became our ally; He took our part and entered into a treaty with us. If Jehovah had not been our protector, where would we be? Nothing but His power and wisdom could have guarded us from the malicious plans of our adversaries; therefore let all His people say so and openly honor Him for His protection.

Here are two "ifs" (vv. 1 and 2), and yet there is no "if" in the matter. The Lord was on our side and is still our defender and will be forever. Let us praise Him with holy confidence for His faithfulness to us! Let us sing to the Lord!

This cruel world would destroy us if it were not that Jehovah stops them. When the Lord appears, cruel throats cannot swallow and the consuming fires cannot destroy. It is only because the Lord lives that His people are alive.

In floods of persecution and affliction, who can help but Jehovah? But for Him, where would we be? We have experienced times when the combined forces of earth and hell would have made an end of us had not omnipotent grace rescued us.

The Lord has refused permission to any foe to destroy us; praise His name! The more imminent the danger the more eminent the mercy which would not permit us to perish in it. Let us praise God forever for His protection, for restraining the fury of the foe, and for saving His own. He has given us to His Son Jesus and He will never give us to our enemies.

Psalm 124:1–6

The Great Escape

> *Today's Faith Builder:*

Our soul has escaped as a bird from the snare of the fowlers;

The snare is broken, and we have escaped. (Psalm 124:7)

Our soul is like a bird for many reasons, but in this case the likeness is weakness and the ease with which it is enticed into a snare. Fowlers have many methods of trapping small birds and Satan has many methods of trapping souls. Some are decoyed by evil companions, others are enticed by the love of pleasure; fear causes some to fly into the net.

Happy is the bird that has a strong deliverer, ready to rescue in the moment of peril; happier still is the soul over which the Lord watches day and night to pluck it out of Satan's net. How the rescued one sings and soars and soars and sings again!

Our hope for the future, our ground of confidence in all trials present and to come is the name of the Lord. Jehovah's revealed character is the foundation of our faith; He is our sure source of strength. Our Creator is our preserver. He is great in His creating work; all heaven and the whole round earth are the works of His hands.

When we worship the Creator let us increase our trust in our Comforter. Did He create all that we see, and can He not preserve us from evils which we cannot see? He who has formed us will watch over us; He is our help and our shield. He made heaven for us, and He will keep us for heaven; He made the earth and He will nourish us on it until the hour comes for our departure. Every work of His hand tells of the duty and delight of trusting Him.

Psalm 124:7–8

Surrounded

> *Today's Faith Builder:*
> As the mountains surround Jerusalem,
> So the LORD surrounds His people
> From this time forth and forever. (Psalm 125:2)

In this psalm, another step is taken toward higher ground, another station on the journey is reached. Faith has praised Jehovah for past deliverance and here she rises to a confident joy in the present and future safety of believers. She asserts that they who trust themselves with the Lord will be secure forever.

What a privilege it is to be allowed to rest in God! To trust in the living God is sanctified common sense. There is no conceivable reason why we should not trust in Jehovah and there is every possible argument for doing so, but apart from all arguments, the future will prove the wisdom of our faith.

The result of faith is not occasional and accidental; its blessing comes not to some who trust but to all who trust the Lord. Trusters in Jehovah will be as fixed, firm, and stable as the mountain where David lived and the ark was kept. As the Lord sits King forever, so do His people sit enthroned in perfect peace when their trust in Him is firm. We trust in the eternal God and our safety will be eternal.

The mountains surrounding Jerusalem are emblems of the all-surrounding presence of the Lord. Jehovah encircles His people; look as far as you please and you will see that His protection extends forever. Note it is not said that Jehovah's power or wisdom defends believers, but that He Himself is round about them; they have His personality for their protection, His Godhead for their guard.

Psalm 125:1–2

A Prayer for the Righteous

> *Today's Faith Builder:*
> Do good, O LORD, to those who are good,
> And to those who are upright in their hearts. (Psalm 125:4)

The people of God are not to expect immunity from trials because the Lord surrounds them, for they may feel the power and persecution of the ungodly. Unbelievers often are in power and are likely to oppress those who belong to the Lord.

Egypt's rod was heavy on Israel but the time came for it to be broken. God has set a limit to the woes of His people. The saints abide forever, but their troubles are temporary.

Even the righteous may fall into sin when passing through trials, but it is not God's will for them to yield to the stress of the times in order to escape from suffering. Godly people must not see trouble as an excuse to sin; they must resist with all their might until it pleases God to stop the violence of their persecutors and give His children rest.

To be good, one must be good at heart. Those who trust in the Lord are good, for faith is the root of righteousness and produces it in our lives. Faith in God is a good and upright thing and its influence makes the believer live righteously. To these God will do good; the prayer here is but another form of a promise.

When God is punishing the unfaithful not a blow will fall on the faithful. The chosen of the Lord will have peace. He who has peace with God can enjoy peace concerning all things. Link the first and last verses of this psalm together: Israel trusts in the Lord (v. 1), and Israel has peace (v. 5).

Psalm 125:3–5

Great Things

❯ *Today's Faith Builder:*
The LORD has done great things for us,
And we are glad. (Psalm 126:3)

What captives we have been! At conversion, what freedom we experienced! Never will that hour be forgotten. Joy! Joy! Joy!

Since then we have been set free from many troubles: from depression of spirit, from miserable backsliding, from nagging doubts, and we are not able to describe the joy which followed each release.

Let our hearts gratefully remember the lovingkindnesses of the Lord; we were sadly low, sorely distressed, and completely past hope, but when Jehovah appeared He did not merely lift us out of depression, He raised us into wonderful happiness. The Lord does nothing by halves; those whom He saves from hell He brings to heaven. He turns exile into ecstasy and banishment into bliss.

The emancipated people remembered this flood of joy for years and here the record of it turned into a song. Note the when and then: God's when is our then. When He fills us with grace, then we are filled with gratitude.

We should not be ashamed of our joy in the Lord. There is so little happiness around that if we possess a full share of it we should not hide our light under a bushel but let it shine on all who are in the house (Matt. 5:15–16).

None are so happy as those who are newly turned and returned from captivity; none can more promptly give a reason for the gladness that is in them. The Lord Himself has blessed us greatly, blessed us individually, blessed us assuredly, and because of this we sing to His name. God has done great things for us and we cannot help but sing.

Psalm 126:1–3

Joyful Reaping

❭ *Today's Faith Builder:*
 Those who sow in tears
 Shall reap in joy. (Psalm 126:5)

Present distress must not be viewed as if it would last forever; it is not the end, by any means, but only a means to an end. Sorrow is our sowing, rejoicing will be our reaping. If there were no sowing in tears there would be no reaping in joy. If we were never captives we could never learn to appreciate freedom. Our mouths would never have been filled with holy laughter if they had not first been filled with the bitterness of grief.

We may have to sow in the wet weather of sorrow, but we will reap in the bright summer season of joy. Let us keep to the work of this present sowing time and find strength in this positive promise of joyful reaping in the future.

When a person's heart is so stirred that he weeps over the sins of others, he is chosen for usefulness. Winners of souls are first weepers for souls. As there is no birth without travail, so there is no spiritual harvest without painful plowing. When our own hearts are broken with grief at the sins of others we will break other men's hearts; tears of sincerity bring tears of repentance.

It is interesting to find this promise of fruitfulness in close contact with the return from captivity, yet this is also true in our own experience, for when our own soul is revived the souls of others are blessed by our labors. If any of us, having once been lonesome captives, have now returned home and have become longing and laboring sowers, may the Lord soon transform us into glad-hearted reapers. And to Him will be praise forever and ever. Amen.

Psalm 126:4–6

The Master Builder

> *Today's Faith Builder:*
> Unless the LORD builds the house,
> They labor in vain who build it;
> Unless the LORD guards the city,
> The watchman stays awake in vain. (Psalm 127:1)

God's blessing on His people is their greatest necessity and privilege. We are here taught that builders of houses and cities, systems and fortunes, empires and churches all labor in vain without the Lord; but under His divine favor they enjoy perfect rest. This is the builder's psalm: "For every house is built by someone, but He who built all things is God" (Heb. 3:4), so to God be praise.

The word *vain* is the key here, and we hear it ring out clearly three times in the psalm. Those desiring to build know that they must labor, so they use all their skill and strength, but let them remember that if Jehovah is not with them their plans will fail.

When Solomon resolved to build a house for the Lord all things in his great undertaking were under divine direction. God also blessed and led him in building his own palace, for this verse refers to all sorts of house building.

Without God we are nothing. Great houses have been constructed by ambitious people, but like weak fabric they have passed away and scarcely a stone remains to tell where they once stood. Trowel and hammer, saw and plane are worthless unless the Lord is the Master builder.

Much can be done by man; he can both labor and watch, but without the Lord he has accomplished nothing, and His staying awake has not warded off evil.

Psalm 127:1

Stop Worrying and Sleep

> *Today's Faith Builder:*
> It is vain for you to rise up early,
> To sit up late,
> To eat the bread of sorrows;
> For so He gives His beloved sleep. (Psalm 127:2)

Some deny themselves needed rest; the morning sees them rise before they are rested, the evening sees them working long after a reasonable quitting time. They threaten to bring themselves into the sleep of death by neglecting the sleep which refreshes life. Nor is sleeplessness the only evidence of their continual worrying; they deprive themselves of meals. They eat the poorest food and the smallest possible quantity of it, and what they do swallow is washed down with the salty tears of grief.

This is not the way the Lord wants His children to live. He would have them lead happy and restful lives, taking proper amounts of rest and food for their health. True believers will never be lazy or extravagant but neither will they be worried and miserly. Faith brings calm with it that overcomes the obstacles to rest and sleep.

Through faith, the Lord gives His chosen ones rest; they are happy and free from care. Those whom the Lord loves are delivered from the fret and fume of life, and they rest sweetly in Him. He restores and blesses them.

God is sure to give His best to those He loves and here we see that He gives them sleep. Remember how Jesus slept during the storm at sea. He knew that He was in His Father's hands and therefore He was so quiet in spirit that the waves rocked Him to sleep.

Psalm 127:2

Children Are Our Heritage

⟩ *Today's Faith Builder:*
Behold, children are a heritage from the LORD,
The fruit of the womb is a reward. (Psalm 127:3)

Another way of building a house is by leaving descendants to keep our name and family alive on the earth. Without children, what is the purpose in accumulating wealth? Why build a house if there are no heirs to receive it? Yet in this a man is powerless without the Lord. Many wealthy people would give half of their estates if they could hear the cry of a child of their own. Children are a heritage which Jehovah Himself must give.

God gives children as blessings, not burdens; they are to be received as rewards from the Lord, without regret. Children are our inheritance. Our best possessions are our own dear children, for whom we thank God every day.

Children born to us when we are young, by God's blessing become the comfort of our riper years. Let the Lord favor us with loyal, obedient, affectionate children and we will find them to be our best helpers. Of course, a large number of children means a large number of trials, but when these are met by faith in the Lord it also means a lot of love and many joys.

He who is the father of many spiritual children is also happy and blessed. He can answer all who speak against him by pointing to souls who have been saved by his efforts. Converts are certainly the heritage of the Lord and the reward of deep and prayerful concern over the lost. By these, through the power of the Holy Spirit, the church is built up and the Lord receives the glory.

Psalm 127:3–5

The Way of Blessing

> *Today's Faith Builder:*
> Blessed is every one who fears the LORD,
> Who walks in His ways. (Psalm 128:1)

The last psalm ended with a blessing, for the word there translated "happy" is the same as the one here rendered "blessed." The two psalms are bound by a blessing.

The fear of God is the cornerstone of all blessings. We must reverence God before we can be blessed by Him.

The God-fearing person has both present and future blessings. He is happy now, for he is the child of the happy God, the ever-living Jehovah. He is a joint heir with Jesus Christ (Rom. 8:17), whose heritage is not misery, but joy.

Let us cultivate that holy, loving fear of God which is the essence of the Christian life. The fear of God is reverence, a dread to offend, an anxiety to please; it involves total submission and obedience. The fear of the Lord is the fountain of holy living; we look in vain for holiness apart from it. Only those who fear the Lord will ever walk in His ways.

God's ways will be our ways if we have a sincere reverence for Him; if the heart is joined to God the feet will follow after Him. The heart can be seen in the walk and blessings will come where heart and walk are both with God.

Heaped up happinesses belong to the one who fears the Lord. If we fear God we can dismiss all other fears. In walking in God's ways we will be under His protection, provision, and approval. Danger and destruction will be far from us; all things will work for our good, filling our lives with blessings (Rom. 8:28).

Psalm 128:1–2

Blessings for Life

> *Today's Faith Builder:*
> The LORD bless you out of Zion,
> And may you see the good of Jerusalem
> All the days of your life. (Psalm 128:5)

A man is happiest when he is not alone. A wife was needed in Paradise and she is just as important now. "He who finds a wife finds a good thing" (Prov. 18:22); she will share in his blessings and increase them.

To complete blessings in a home, children are sent. They come as the lawful fruit of a marriage and must not be seen as burdens, but as blessings.

Good wives are also fruitful in kindness, thrift, helpfulness, and affection; if they bear no children they are by no means barren if they bear us clusters of comfort. Blessed is the man whose wife is fruitful in good works that enrich their marriage.

Our children gather around our table to be fed and this involves expenses, but this is better than to see them on beds of sickness, unable to come for their meals! What a blessing to have sufficient to put on the table! Let us give praise for the bounty of the Lord.

A spiritual blessing will be received by those who trust in the Lord. The blessing of the house of God will be on their houses. They will experience the priestly benediction recorded in Numbers 6:24–26:

> The LORD bless you and keep you;
> The LORD make His face shine upon you,
> And be gracious to you;
> The LORD lift up His countenance upon you,
> And give you peace.

Psalm 128:3–6

Surviving Attacks of Our Enemies

> *Today's Faith Builder:*
> Many a time they have afflicted me from my youth;
> Yet they have not prevailed against me. (Psalm 129:2)

I n her present hour of trial, Israel can remember her former afflictions
and speak of them for her comfort, drawing assurance from them that
He who has been with her for so long will not desert her in the end.

The trials of the church have also been repeated again and again; the
same afflictions are fulfilled in us as in our fathers. Jacob of old found his
days full of trouble. Israel as a whole has proceeded from tribulation to
tribulation.

Persecution is the heritage of the church and the mark of the elect.
Israel was different from other nations and this difference brought many
foes against her. When in Canaan, at first the chosen people were often
severely tested; in Egypt they were heavily oppressed; in the wilderness
they were fiercely attacked, and in the promised land they were often
surrounded by deadly enemies. It was a miracle that this afflicted nation
survived to say, "Many times have they afflicted me." The earliest years of
Israel and of the church were spent in trials.

When the psalmist says, "Yet they have not prevailed against me," we
seem to hear the beat of timbrels and the clash of cymbals: The foe is
defeated; his malice has failed. Israel has wrestled and has overcome in
the struggle. The enemy has had his opportunity and his advantage, but
not once has he gained the victory.

Psalm 129:1–3

The Righteous Conqueror

> *Today's Faith Builder:*
>   The LORD is righteous;
>   He has cut in pieces the cords of the wicked. (Psalm 129:4)

Whatever others may be, Jehovah remains just and will therefore keep His covenant with His people and dispense justice to their oppressors. The Lord bears with the long furrows of the wicked, but He will surely make them stop their plowing before He is through with them. The rope which binds the oxen to the plow will be cut; the cord which binds the victim will be broken; the bond holding the enemies of the righteous in cruel unity will be snapped.

Sooner or later our righteous God will interrupt the persecutors of His people and when He does, His action will be extremely effective. He will not unfasten, but cut in two, the harness which the ungodly use in their labor of hate.

God hates those who hurt His people even though He permits their hate to triumph temporarily for His own purpose. The shortest route to ruin is to meddle with God's people; the Bible warns, "He who touches you touches the apple of His eye" (Zech. 2:8).

It is but justice that those who hate, harass, and hurt the good should be brought to nothing. Those who confound right and wrong ought to be confounded. This present age is so confused that one who loves the Savior is called a fanatic and one who hates the powers of evil is called a prude.

Lord, number me with Your saints. Let me share their grief that I may share their glory. I will magnify Your name because Your afflicted ones are not destroyed and Your persecuted ones are not forsaken.

Psalm 129:4–8

A Cry for God to Hear

> *Today's Faith Builder:*
> Lord, hear my voice!
> Let Your ears be attentive
> To the voice of my supplications. (Psalm 130:2)

The psalmist never ceased to pray even when brought low through severe trials. The depths usually silence all they engulf, but they could not close the mouth of this servant of the Lord. Beneath the floods, prayer lived and struggled; above the roar of the billows rose the cry of faith.

It matters little where we are if we can pray, but prayer is never more real and acceptable than when it rises out of the worst places. Deep places develop deep devotion. Depths of earnestness are stirred by depths of tribulation. Diamonds sparkle most in the darkness.

The more distressed we are, the more excellent is the faith which trusts bravely in the Lord and therefore appeals to Him and to Him alone. Good people may be in deep temporal and spiritual trouble but in such cases look only to their God; they are then more earnest in prayer than at other times. The depth of their distress moves the depths of their being and from the bottom of their hearts a great and bitter cry rises to the living God. He who cries out of the depths will soon sing in the heights.

The psalmist spoke aloud in prayer; this is not necessary, but it is very helpful, for speaking assists our thoughts. Still, there is a voice in silent supplication, a voice in our weeping, a voice in sorrow; that voice the Lord will hear, for it is meant for His ear.

Psalm 130:1–2

Forgiveness and the Fear of the Lord

> *Today's Faith Builder:*
> But there is forgiveness with You,
> That You may be feared. (Psalm 130:4)

If we were to be judged only for our works, who among us could hope to be accepted? Convicted of his sins, the psalmist comes confessing he is a sinner. He admits that he cannot stand before the great King in his own righteousness, and he is so struck by a sense of the holiness of God and the perfection demanded by the law that, contemplating judgment, he cries, "O Lord, who could stand?" None could do so: "There is none who does good, no, not one" (Rom. 3:12).

Were it not for the Lord Jesus, could we hope to stand? Dare we meet Him on the basis of law and justice when we give an account of ourselves to Him? What a mercy it is that we need not do so, for there is another way of acceptance to which we flee.

Free, full, sovereign pardon is in the hand of the great King; it is His right to forgive and He delights to exercise it. Because His nature is mercy and because He has provided a sacrifice for sin, He offers forgiveness to all who come to Him confessing their sins. The power of pardon permanently resides with God; He has forgiveness in His hand at this moment.

None fear the Lord like those who have experienced His forgiving love. Gratitude for pardon produces far more fear and reverence of God than the dread of punishment. If the Lord were to execute justice on all, there would be none left to fear Him; if all were continually apprehensive of God's deserved wrath, despair would harden them against Him. Grace leads the way to a holy regard for God and a fear of grieving Him.

Psalm 130:3–4

Hopeful Waiting

> *Today's Faith Builder:*
> I wait for the LORD, my soul waits,
> And in His word I do hope. (Psalm 130:5)

Expecting my Lord to come to me in love, I quietly wait for His appearing. I wait on Him in service and for Him in faith. I wait for God and for Him only; if He will show Himself I will have to wait no longer, but until He appears for my help I must wait on in hope, even in difficult times.

If the Lord makes us wait, let us do so with whole hearts, for blessed are all who wait for Him. He is worth the wait.

Waiting on God is beneficial to us: It tests faith, exercises patience, teaches submission, and makes the blessing more wonderful when it comes. Believers have always been waiting people; they waited for the first Advent and now they wait for the second. They waited for a sense of pardon and now they wait for perfect sanctification. They waited when they were in dark valleys and are not weary now waiting in happier circumstances. Probably their past praying sustains their present patience.

God's Word is our sweet source of strength while waiting. Those who do not hope cannot wait; but if we hope for what we do not see we wait patiently for it. God's Word is true, but at times it tarries; if our faith is true it will await the Lord's time.

A word from the Lord is as bread to the soul of a believer and refreshed by it, he holds out through the night of sorrow expecting the dawn of deliverance and delight. Waiting, we study the Word, believe the Word, hope in the Word, and live on the Word. God's Word is firm ground on which to wait and rest.

Psalm 130:5–8

A Humble Prayer

> *Today's Faith Builder:*
>   LORD, my heart is not haughty,
>   Nor my eyes lofty.
>   Neither do I concern myself with great matters,
>   Nor with things too profound for me. (Psalm 131:1)

Comparing all the Psalms to gems, we should think of this one as a pearl. It is one of the shortest Psalms to read, but one of the longest to learn. It speaks of a young child, but contains the experience of one who is mature in Christ.

Lowliness and humility here relate to a sanctified heart, a will subdued to the mind of God, and a hope looking to the Lord alone. Happy is the one who can use these words as his own; he is like his Lord, who said, "I am gentle and lowly in heart" (Matt. 11:29).

The psalmist appeals to the Lord, who alone knows the heart. He begins with his heart, for that is the center of our nature, and if pride is there it defiles everything, just as mud in the spring causes mud in all the streams. This holy man did not seek some high position where he might gratify pride, nor look down on others as being inferior to him. When the heart is right, and the eyes are right, the whole man is on the road to a healthy and happy condition.

Through longing to be great, many have failed to be good. They were not content to serve in the lowly places the Lord had appointed them so they have sought prestige and power and have found destruction instead of honor.

Lord, keep us humble. Make this verse our truthful prayer.

Psalm 131:1

Hope for Today and Forever

❯ *Today's Faith Builder:*
O Israel, hope in the LORD
From this time forth and forever. (Psalm 131:3)

The psalmist has been on his best behavior and has smoothed down the roughness of his self-will; by holy effort he has mastered his own spirit so that he is not rebellious to God nor arrogant to people.

It is easier to calm the sea or rule the wind or tame a tiger than to have a quiet spirit. We are, by nature, angry, uneasy, and irritable; nothing but grace can make us quiet when we are facing trouble and disappointments. The psalmist has become as subdued and content as a well-fed child.

Spiritual infancy is over when we no longer demand the childish joys that once seemed so important to us and find our comfort in Him who denies them to us; then we act like mature believers. If the Lord removes our dearest delight we bow to His will without complaining; in fact, we find a delight in giving up our delight. This is no spontaneous fruit of human nature but a product of God's grace; it grows out of humility and lowliness and is the stem on which peace blooms as a beautiful flower.

See how lovingly a man who is free from selfishness thinks of others! David thinks of his people and loses himself in his care for them. He has given up the things which are seen and therefore he values the treasures which are not seen except by the eyes of hope.

How David prizes the grace of hope! There is room for the greatest hope when self is gone, ground for eternal hope when transient things no longer hold the mastery of our spirits.

Psalm 131:2–3

God Remembers

> *Today's Faith Builder:*
>   LORD, remember David
>   And all his afflictions. (Psalm 132:1)

Jehovah, who does not change, will never forget one of His servants or fail to keep His promises to them. We know that He remembered Noah and ended the flood; He remembered Abraham and sent Lot out of Sodom; He remembered Rachel and Hannah and gave them children; He remembered Israel and mercifully delivered His people.

Here God is urged to bless the family of David for their father's sake; how much stronger is our argument in prayer that God will bless us for Jesus' sake! David had no personal merit — the plea is based on the covenant graciously made with him. But Jesus has boundless merits of His own which we can claim in prayer without hesitation.

The afflictions of David were those which came upon him as a godly man in his efforts to maintain the worship of Jehovah, to provide for its decent and suitable celebration. There were always ungodly people in the nation who were quick to slander and try to hinder and harm this servant of the Lord.

Whatever were David's faults, he kept true to the one, only, living, and true God. Since he zealously delighted in the worship of his Lord, he was despised and ridiculed by those who could not understand his enthusiasm.

God will never forget what His people suffer for His sake. Under the New Testament dispensation, as well as the Old, there is a full reward for the righteous. That reward frequently comes to their descendants rather than to themselves; they sow service to God and their children reap blessings.

Psalm 132:1–7

Righteousness and Joy

> *Today's Faith Builder:*
> Let Your priests be clothed with righteousness,
> And let Your saints shout for joy. (Psalm 132:9)

No garment is as beautiful as a holy character. Whoever looks at the servants of God should see holiness. Now this holiness is requested for those who serve in the presence of the Lord; this teaches us that holiness is only to be found among those who commune with God. God will dwell among a holy people; and, on the other hand, where God is the people become holy.

Holiness and happiness go together; where one is found the other ought never to be far away. Holy people have a right to great and enthusiastic joy; they may shout because of it. O Lord, You have made it their duty to rejoice and to let others know of their joy. Believers are commanded to rejoice in the Lord (Phil. 3:1). Where righteousness is their clothing, people will be occupied with joy. What a happy religion that makes it our duty to be glad!

If we are anointed of the Spirit, the Lord will look on us with favor. This is especially true of Him who represents us and is on our side: Christ—the truly anointed of the Lord.

Jesus is both our David and God's anointed; in Him is found the fullness of the Spirit. For His sake all those who are anointed in Him are accepted. God blessed Solomon and succeeding kings for David's sake, and He will bless us for Jesus' sake.

How humble the Son of the Highest was to take on Himself the form of a servant, to be anointed for us and to go in before the mercy seat to plead for us—to meet our deepest need!

Psalm 132:8–10

The Everlasting Kingdom

> *Today's Faith Builder:*
>> The LORD has sworn in truth to David;
>> He will not turn from it:
>> "I will set upon your throne the fruit of your body." (Psalm 132:11)

Here we come to a great example of the kind of covenant praying that always prevails with God. He never changes, nor turns from His purpose, much less from His promises solemnly guaranteed by His Word. What a rock they stand on who have an unchanging promise of God for their foundation!

We know that this covenant of an everlasting kingdom was really made with Christ, the spiritual seed of David, for Peter quotes it at Pentecost, saying,

> Men and brethren, let me speak freely to you of the patriarch David, that he is both dead and buried, and his tomb is with us to this day. Therefore, being a prophet, and knowing that God had sworn with an oath to him that of the fruit of his body, according to the flesh, He would raise up Christ to sit on his throne, he, foreseeing this, spoke concerning the resurrection of the Christ. (Acts 2:29–31)

Christ therefore sits on a sure throne forever.

Jesus came from the line of David, as the New Testament writers are careful to record; He was "of the house and lineage of David" (Luke 2:4). He is the King of the Jews, and the Lord has also given Him the nations for His inheritance (Ps. 2). He must reign, and of His kingdom there shall be no end. God Himself has set Him on the throne and no rebellion of men or devils can shake His dominion. The honor of Jehovah is at stake in His reign, and therefore it is never in danger, for the Lord will not permit His promise to fail.

Psalm 132:11–14

God's Abundant Provision for Us All

❭ *Today's Faith Builder:*
I will abundantly bless her provision;
I will satisfy her poor with bread. (Psalm 132:15)

How can we be without blessings when the Lord is among us? We live on His Word, we are clothed by His love, we are armed by His power. All sorts of provisions are in Him; we are abundantly blessed.

Daily provision, royal provision, satisfying provision, over-flowingly joyful provision will all be received by the Church. We will receive this provision by faith, feed on it by experience, grow on it by sanctification, be strengthened by it to labor, cheered by it to patience, and built up by it to perfection.

The Lord's poor will have food that will please their tastes, remove their hunger, fill their desires, build up their bodies, and perfect their growth. The bread of earth perishes, but the bread of God endures to eternal life.

The saints will shout for joy. They will be so abundantly blessed, so satisfied, and so clothed that they can do nothing else than shout to show their astonishment, their triumph, their gratitude, their enthusiasm, and their joy in the Lord.

If the morning stars sang together when the earth and the heavens were made, how much more will all the children of God shout for joy when the new heaven and the new earth are finished and the New Jerusalem comes down out of heaven from God, prepared as a bride for her husband (Rev. 21:2)! Meanwhile, even now the dwelling of the Lord among us is a perennial fountain of sparkling delight to holy minds. God says they will shout aloud, and depend on it, they will!

Psalm 132:15–18

Pleasant Fellowship

> *Today's Faith Builder:*
>> Behold, how good and how pleasant it is
>> For brethren to dwell together in unity! (Psalm 133:1)

Brothers united in love is a wonder seldom seen, therefore behold it! It can be seen, for it is the characteristic of real saints, therefore do not fail to observe it! It is well worthy of admiration; pause and ponder it! You will be moved to imitate it, therefore note it well! God looks on it with approval, therefore give it full attention.

No one can describe the excellence of unity, so the psalmist does not attempt to measure either the good or the pleasure of it but invites us to see for ourselves. We all love pleasant things and yet frequently pleasure is evil; here the condition is as good as it is pleasant and as pleasant as it is good.

Brothers in spirit ought to dwell together in church fellowship and in that fellowship unity is essential. If we possess unity, we have oneness of life, truth, and way; oneness in Christ Jesus; oneness of object and spirit. These we must have or our services will be gatherings of contention rather than churches of Christ.

The closer the unity we experience the better, for this means we have more of the good and pleasant things of the Christian life. Since we are imperfect, some evil and unpleasant things are sure to intrude into our lives, but these can quickly be neutralized and ejected by the true love of believers for each other. A church united in earnest service of the Lord is a well of goodness and joy to all who live around it.

Psalm 133

Praising God at Night

> *Today's Faith Builder:*
> Behold, bless the LORD,
> All you servants of the LORD,
> Who by night stand in the house of the LORD! (Psalm 134:1)

This psalm teaches us to pray for those who are continually ministering before the Lord and it invites all ministers to pronounce benedictions on their loving and prayerful people.

Those on night watch at the temple are called to look around and find reasons to praise the Lord. Let them look above them at night and magnify Him who made heaven and earth and lighted the one with stars and the others with His love. Let their hallelujahs never end.

Think well of Jehovah and speak well of Him. Adore Him with reverence, draw near to Him with love, delight in Him, and exalt Him. Do not be content with praise such as all His works render to Him, but as His people see that you bless Him. He blesses you, therefore, zealously bless Him.

Oh, to abound in blessing! May *blessed* and *blessing* be the two words which describe our lives. Let others flatter their friends or bless their stars or praise themselves; as for us, we will bless Jehovah, from whom all blessings flow.

It is your responsibility to bless God; take care that you lead in this. Servants should speak well of their masters. No one should serve God because he is compelled to do so, but all should bless Him while serving Him. Bless Him also for permitting you to serve Him, fitting you to serve Him, and accepting your service. To be a servant of the Lord is a great honor, a blessing beyond imagination.

Psalm 134

Pleasant Praises

❭ *Today's Faith Builder:*
Praise the LORD, for the LORD is good;
Sing praises to His name, for it is pleasant. (Psalm 135:3)

This psalm is mainly made up of selections from other Scriptures. It has been called a mosaic. While it is a compound of many choice texts, it has all the continuity and freshness of an original poem. The Holy Spirit occasionally repeats Himself, not because He has any lack of thoughts or words, but because sometimes we are enriched by hearing the same things in the same form. When our great Teacher uses repetition, it is usually with instructive variations which deserve our careful attention.

Let those who are full of holy praise influence others to exalt the Lord with them. Let us call in all our friends and neighbors, and if they have been lacking in praise, lovingly encourage them to join us. Let the character of the Lord be praised and let all that He has revealed concerning Himself be the subject of our song.

We ought to always be at it, obeying this command: praise, praise, praise. Let the Three-in-One have the praises of our spirit, soul, and body. For the past, the present, and the future, let us sing threefold hallelujahs.

Pleasant here can apply to singing praises and to the Lord's name. They are both pleasant. Pleasure is to be found in the joyful worship of Jehovah; all joys are contained in His sacred name as perfumes lie slumbering in a garden of flowers. The whole being is filled with delight when we are singing the praises of our Father, Redeemer, and Comforter.

Psalm 135:1–3

Praise Our Great God

❯ *Today's Faith Builder:*
  For I know that the LORD is great,
  And our Lord is above all gods. (Psalm 135:5)

The greatness of God is as much a reason for adoration as His goodness. We learn this when we are reconciled to Him. God is positively great, comparatively great, and supremely great: "above all gods." The psalmist was absolutely sure of this: "I know," he said, and all should long for this kind of assurance.

God's will is carried out throughout all space. The King's authority reaches to every part of the universe. He rules over all. He works His will; what He pleases to do, He does. No region is too high, no abyss too deep, no land too distant, no sea too wide for His omnipotence. His divine pleasure travels over all the realm of nature and His commands are obeyed.

As a king is the master of his own treasure, so is our God the Lord of tempests and hurricanes. As princes do not spend their treasure without considering where it is going, so the Lord does not permit even the wind to be wasted or squandered without fulfilling His purposes.

Everything in the world is under the immediate direction and control of the Lord of all the earth. He is at work everywhere; His power is supreme. Let us praise Jehovah for the power and wisdom with which He rules clouds and lightning, winds and all other mighty and mysterious agencies of His creation.

God's name is eternal and will never be changed. His character is immutable; His fame and honor will remain for all eternity. There will always be life and sweetness and comfort in the name of Jesus.

Psalm 135:4–13

The Lord and His People

> *Today's Faith Builder:*
>   For the LORD will judge His people,
>   And He will have compassion on His servants. (Psalm 135:14)

The Lord will exercise personal discipline over His people but will not allow their enemies to mistreat them beyond limits which He has established. When the correction is ended He will arise and avenge them of their oppressors. He may, at times, seem to forget His people, but He will lovingly take up their cause and deliver them.

The judges of Israel were also their deliverers and so is the Lord. When He has chastened them and they lie low before Him, He will pity them as a father pities his children (Ps. 103:13), for He does not willingly afflict them.

God's heart is moved to see His loved ones oppressed by their enemies, even though they may deserve all they suffer. He cannot see them hurt without feeling pangs of love and compassion.

Israel, the chosen nation, is here called "His people" and then "His servants." As His people He judges them, as His servants He finds comfort in them. He is most tender to them when He sees their service.

Should not the servants of God praise Him? He plagued Pharaoh's servants but has mercy on His own and returns to them in love after He has chastened them for their sins. "Praise Him, O you servants of the LORD!"

God remains among His people: He is their dwelling place and they are His dwelling place. Let this intimate communion bring intense gratitude on the part of His chosen ones. "Praise the LORD!"

Psalm 135:14–21

Thanksgiving for Enduring Mercy

❯ *Today's Faith Builder:*
Oh, give thanks to the LORD, for He is good!
For His mercy endures forever. (Psalm 136:1)

This psalm contains nothing but praise. It can only be fully enjoyed by a devoutly grateful heart.

We thank our parents, let us praise our heavenly Father; we are grateful to those who give to us, let us give thanks to the Giver of all good. God is goodness itself; all that He does is good. Let us thank Him that we have seen, tasted, and proven that He is good.

God is good beyond all others; He alone is good in the highest sense. He is the source of good, the sustainer of good, the perfecter of good, and the rewarder of good. For this He deserves the constant gratitude of His people.

"For His mercy endures forever" is repeated in every verse of this song, but not once too often. It is the sweetest song we can sing. What joy that there is mercy with Jehovah, enduring mercy, mercy enduring forever! We are ever needing it, trying it, praying for it, receiving it; therefore let us ever sing of it.

There are many earthly lords, but Jehovah is the Lord of them all. He makes and administers law; He rules and governs mind and matter; He possesses in Himself all sovereignty and power.

Our Lord mingles mercy with His justice and reigns for the benefit of us all. He pities the sorrowful, protects the helpless, provides for the needy, and pardons the guilty; and He does this from generation to generation, never wearying of His grace. Let us rise up and praise our glorious Lord! Let His grace be reason enough for three thanksgivings, or for three thousand!

Psalm 136:1–3

The God of Life and Light

> *Today's Faith Builder:*
>   To Him who by wisdom made the heavens,
>   For His mercy endures forever. (Psalm 136:5)

God wisely designed and created an atmosphere for the earth that would be suitable for human life. What wisdom lies in this one creative act! The discoveries of our most learned scientists have not yet revealed all the evidences of design which are found in the universe.

The lives of plants, animals, and people are dependent on the atmosphere; had the air we breathe been anything other than what it is we would not be here to praise God. Divine foresight planned the atmosphere to accommodate the human race.

God's mercy began in the heavens and gradually descended to "our lowly state" (v. 23). This is really an ascent, for mercy becomes greater as its objects become less worthy. Mercy is far-reaching, long-enduring, all-encompassing. Nothing is too high for its reach, and nothing is too low for it to stoop and save.

The creation of the great lights above is also a miracle worthy of our heartfelt thanks. What would we do without light? Let thanks be given to the Lord who has not left us in darkness. Mercy gleams in every ray of light and is most clearly seen in the way it shines down on us from the sun and the moon.

The benefits of the sun are too many to mention but they come to all. The sun rules because God rules. We should not worship the sun as some have done, but the Creator of the sun. Every sunbeam is a mercy, for it falls on undeserving sinners who otherwise would sit in dismal darkness and find earth a hell.

Psalm 136:4–9

December 6

The One Who Divided the Sea

> *Today's Faith Builder:*
> To Him who divided the Red Sea in two,
> For His mercy endures forever. (Psalm 136:13)

We have heard of the glory of the world's creation and now we are to praise the Lord for the creation of His favored nation by their Exodus from Egypt. The unfailing mercy of the Lord is seen in His separation of His people from the world. He brings out His redeemed and they praise His name.

In the Exodus the great power and glory of the Lord were seen. He made a road across the bottom of the sea, causing the divided waters to stand like walls on either side. People may deny miracles but once one believes there is a God, it is easy to believe in miracles.

Since rejecting miracles would require me to become an atheist, I prefer the smaller difficulty of believing in the infinite power of God. He who causes the waters of the sea to remain as one mass can just as easily divide them. He who can throw a stone in one direction can with the same force throw it another way. The Lord can do precisely what He wills, and He wills to do anything necessary to deliver His people.

God's mercy endures through the sea as well as over the dry land. He will do new things to keep His old promises. His way is in the sea and He will make a way for His people through it, leading them down into the deep and safely up on the other shore.

By faith we also give up all reliance on works and choose to walk in a way which we have not known before: the way of faith in His atoning blood.

Hallelujah! His mercy endures forever!

Psalm 136:10–15

The God of Heaven

❭ *Today's Faith Builder:*
Oh, give thanks to the God of heaven!
For His mercy endures forever. (Psalm 136:26)

For the Lord even to think of us reveals how rich He is in mercy. Our state was so low that we were at hell's mouth. We have been low in poverty, bereavement, depression, sickness, and sorrow. Our fears reveal that we are sinfully low in faith and love and every other grace; yet our Lord has tenderly remembered us.

We thought ourselves too small and too worthless for God to be concerned about us, yet He remembered us. He remembered us in our low condition; in our highest joys we will exalt His name since we are sure He will never leave nor forsake us (Heb. 13:5).

Israel's enemies brought them low, but the Lord rescued them, redeemed them. In our case, the redemption which is in Christ Jesus is a great reason for giving thanks to the Lord. Sin is our enemy and we are redeemed from it by the atoning blood of Christ; Satan is our enemy and we are redeemed from him by our Redeemer's power; the world is our enemy and we are redeemed from it by the Holy Spirit. We have been ransomed, let us enjoy our liberty; Christ has redeemed us, let us praise His name.

The title "the God of heaven" is full of honor. The Lord is God in the highest realms and among celestial beings. His throne is in glory, above all, out of the reach of His enemies, where He oversees the universe. He who feeds ravens and sparrows is the glorious God of heaven. Angels consider it their privilege to proclaim His glory on heaven's streets. Let us, with all our powers of heart and tongue, give thanks to the Lord for ever and ever!

Psalm 136:16–26

When It's Difficult to Sing

> *Today's Faith Builder:*
> How shall we sing the LORD's song
> In a foreign land? (Psalm 137:4)

Water was abundant in Babylon; it was a place of broad rivers and streams. Glad to be away from the noisy streets, the captives gather along the river where the flow of the waters seem to be in sympathy with their tears. It is some comfort to be out of the crowd and to have a little breathing room, so they sit down in small groups, mingling their memories with their tears.

Everything reminded the Israelites of their banishment from the holy city, their slavery, their helplessness under a cruel enemy, and therefore they sat down by the river in sorrow. The strong men and the sweet singers wept. They did not weep when they remembered the cruelties of Babylon, but when their beloved city came to their minds they could not refrain from floods of tears.

Better to be unable to speak than to please an enemy with forced song. What cruelty to make a people sigh and then require them to sing! Shall people be carried away from their homes and all that is dear to them and yet sing merrily for the pleasure of their unfeeling captors? Nothing would please the Babylonian mockers but one of Israel's psalms, which in happier days the people had sung to the Lord, whose mercy endures forever.

With one voice the Israelites refuse, but the refusal is humbly worded by being put in the form of a question: "How shall we sing the LORD's song in a foreign land?" There are many things which the ungodly can do and think nothing of doing it, while those who belong to the Lord must refuse to do.

Psalm 137

Strength for the Soul

> *Today's Faith Builder:*
> In the day when I cried out, You answered me,
> And made me bold with strength in my soul. (Psalm 138:3)

The psalmist is determined to praise the Lord with his whole heart. He will not restrain his praise because of the opinions of others, but in the presence of the enemies of the living God he will be as hearty in worship as if all about him were friends who would cheerfully join him. If others do not praise the Lord, this is a good reason for us to enthusiastically do so.

The Hallelujah Legion will win the day. Praising and singing are our armor against depression caused by insolent attacks on the truth and our weapons for defending the gospel. Faith, when displayed in cheerful courage, is contagious. Others learn to believe in the Most High when they are His servants confident of victory.

No proof is so convincing as experience. No one doubts the power of prayer who has received answers from the Lord. The true and living God hears the pleadings of His people and answers them.

Praying strengthened the psalmist's soul and this was a true answer to his prayer. If the burden was not removed, strength was given to bear it. It may not be best for us that a trial end; it may be far more to our advantage that by its pressure we learn patience. Sweet are the uses of adversity and our wise Father in heaven will not deprive us of these benefits.

Strength imparted to the soul is a great blessing, bringing courage, assurance, and heroism. By His Word and Spirit the Lord makes tremblers brave. When God strengthens, none can make us weak.

Psalm 138:1–3

Revival in Troubled Times

❯ *Today's Faith Builder:*
  Though I walk in the midst of trouble, You will revive me;
  You will stretch out Your hand
  Against the wrath of my enemies. (Psalm 138:7)

When walking through trouble we have no cause for fear, for God is with us to revive us. Even when we are walking through intense darkness, we have the best of company, for God is with us to refresh us with new life. He has promised to be with us in trying times: "When you pass through the waters, I will be with you" (Isa. 43:2).

How often our Lord has revived us by our sorrows! Are they not His most effective means of bringing the holy life within us to full strength? If we receive reviving, we need not regret affliction. When God revives us, trouble will never harm us.

Our foes fall when the Lord comes to deal with them; He makes short work of the enemies of His people. His wrath soon quenches their wrath; His hand halts their hand. Adversaries may be many and malicious and mighty, but our glorious Defender has only to stretch out His arm and their forces flee.

The sweet singer rehearses his assurance of salvation and sings of it to the Lord in confident words: He will be saved; he has no doubt about it. God will defend His own elect.

God is concerned with all that concerns His servants. He will see to it that none of their valuable experiences are wasted: their lives, their strength, their hopes, their graces. Jehovah Himself will see to this. Such confidence does not cause us to live without prayer but encourages us to pray all the more.

Psalm 138:4–8

God Knows All About Us

❭ *Today's Faith Builder:*
O Lord, You have searched me and known me. (Psalm 139:1)

The true God, Jehovah, understands us and is intimately acquainted with our nature and character. How good it is to know the God who knows us!

God's knowledge of us is both thorough and searching; it is as if He had searched us as the police search a man for contraband goods or as thieves ransack a house for valuables. This infallible knowledge has always existed and it continues to this day, since God cannot forget what He has once known. There never was a time when we were unknown to God and there never will be a moment in which we will be beyond His observation.

The Lord judges our active life and our quiet life; He considers our actions and our rest and sees what is good and what is evil. This should fill us with awe so that we do not sin, with courage so that we do not fear, with delight so that we do not mourn.

God has placed us where we are and surrounds us with His presence. He is behind us recording our sins or in grace blotting them out; He is before us knowing all that we will do and providing for all our needs. We cannot turn back and escape Him, for He is behind us; we cannot go forward and outmarch Him, for He is before us. God is very near and we are in His care. Our heavenly Father has folded His arms around us and caresses us with His hand.

We should not be surprised that God's knowledge is higher than any we can achieve. Even standing on tiptoe, we cannot reach the lowest step of His throne.

Psalm 139:1–6

We Cannot Hide from God

❭ *Today's Faith Builder:*
   Where can I go from Your Spirit?
   Or where can I flee from Your presence? (Psalm 139:7)

Here God's omnipresence is the theme. Not that the psalmist wishes to get away from God or to avoid the power of the Holy Spirit in his life, but he asks these questions to show that no one can escape from the Lord.

We must be, whether we like it or not, as near to God as the soul is to the body. This makes sin very serious, for when we sin we offend the Almighty to His face and commit acts of treason at the very foot of His throne. We cannot flee from Him nor quietly withdraw from Him. His Spirit is over our spirit; we are ever in His presence.

Dense darkness cannot hide us from God. Some foolishly choose night and darkness for sinful living, but it is impossible for any act to be hidden from the Lord; one might just as well transgress in broad daylight. A good person will not wish to be hidden by the darkness and a wise one will not expect it.

God is in all places at all times and nothing can be kept from His all-observing, all-comprehending mind. The Lord understands all time and space and yet is infinitely greater than these or anything else He has made.

The Lord owns all of our parts and passions; He not only dwells within His people but possesses them as His own. Before we had any cares, God cared for us. Before we saw the light of day, the Light of the World was with us; before we were born we were under the care and guardianship of God.

Psalm 139:7–13

Praising God for Creating Us

> *Today's Faith Builder:*
> I will praise You, for I am fearfully and wonderfully made;
> Marvelous are Your works,
> And that my soul knows very well. (Psalm 139:14)

Those who wish to praise God have many reasons to do so. We too often forget the wonder of our creation and the skill and kindness of God revealed in it, but the sweet singer of Israel has been taught to remember his origin and therefore he prepares a song about his creation for the chief musician.

We cannot begin too soon to bless our Maker, who began so soon to bless us. Even in the act of creation, there are many reasons for praising His name. Who can gaze on a model of our anatomy without wonder and awe? Who can consider the human body without marveling at its complexity and trembling at its frailty?

The psalmist had little knowledge of the nerves, sinews, and blood vessels of his body, but he had seen enough to arouse his admiration of its creation and his reverence for the Creator. We need not go to the ends of the earth for marvels, nor even leave our homes; they abound in our own bodies.

The Lord is a master-worker, performing great wonders in accomplishing His kind designs. If we are marvelous works of God even before we are born, what shall we say of the Lord's work in us after we leave His secret workshop and He directs our pathway through the pilgrimage of life? The new birth is even more mysterious than our natural birth and exhibits more of the love and wisdom of the Lord.

Psalm 139:14–24

Deliver Us from Evil People

> *Today's Faith Builder:*
> Deliver me, O LORD, from evil men;
> Preserve me from violent men. (Psalm 140:1)

This psalm is the cry of a hunted soul, the prayer of a believer who is continually persecuted and surrounded by enemies who hunger for his destruction. David was hunted like a partridge on the mountains and seldom enjoyed a moment's rest. This is his moving appeal to the Lord for protection, an appeal which gradually intensifies into a denunciation of his bitter foes.

With this sacrifice of prayer David offers the salt of faith, for he clearly expresses his personal confidence in the Lord as protector of the oppressed and as his own God and defender. Few short psalms are so rich in expressions of faith.

The persecuted psalmist turns to God in prayer. How wise! Who can meet evil people and defeat them except Jehovah, whose infinite goodness is more than a match for all the evil in the universe?

We cannot battle the enemy in our own strength, but the Lord knows how to deliver His people. He can keep us out of the enemy's reach; He can sustain us by His power; He can rescue us when our doom seems sure; He can give us victory when our defeat seems certain.

Evil is an angry thing when it manifests itself, so evil people soon become violent. What watchfulness, strength, and valor can preserve the child of God from deceit and violence? There is but One who can rescue us and it is wise to hide under the shadow of His wings. We cannot pass through the world without enemies, but we can be rescued out of their hands. The psalmist seeks this blessing by prayer and expects it by faith.

Psalm 140:1–5

God Cares for Poor and Suffering People

> *Today's Faith Builder:*
> I know that the LORD will maintain
> The cause of the afflicted,
> And justice for the poor. (Psalm 140:12)

The prayers of believers are heard in heaven even though they may not be eloquent. The Lord can understand our cries of sorrow and will respond to them. Because He is God, He can hear us; because He is our God, He *will* hear us. The more we consider His greatness and our insignificance, His wisdom and our foolishness, the more we will be filled with God's praise when He hears and answers our prayers.

All through the psalm the writer is bravely confident and speaks with full assurance. This slandered one knew of Jehovah's care for suffering people because he had experienced it.

God cares about the rights of the poor. The prosperous and wealthy can stand up for their own rights, but God helps those who cannot help themselves.

As surely as God will destroy the wicked, He will save the oppressed and fill their hearts and mouths with praise. The righteous may suffer but finally they will magnify the Lord for His delivering grace. On earth before long, and in heaven forever, the pure in heart will sing praises to the Lord. The songs of the redeemed will be loud and sweet in the millennium, when the meek will inherit the earth and delight themselves in the abundance of peace (Ps. 37:11).

How high we have climbed in this psalm! We began being hunted by evil enemies and end living in the presence of our righteous Lord! Faith raises us from the lowest depths to heights of peaceful rest.

Psalm 140:6–13

December 16

Praying in Emergencies

> *Today's Faith Builder:*
> LORD, I cry out to You;
> Make haste to me!
> Give ear to my voice when I cry out to You. (Psalm 141:1)

David saw prayer as his last resort and he believed God would not fail him. His prayer was painful and feeble, worthy only to be called a cry; still it was a cry to God and this was not the first time he had cried out to the Lord in a desperate situation. He could have said, "I have cried to You, I still cry to You, and I intend to always keep crying to You." Where else could he go? Who but God would listen?

The weapon of prayer is one which we can always carry with us to use in every time of need. David's situation was urgent so he prayed with urgency, asking God to answer him quickly. He longed to be heard at once. If help came late, it might be too late, so his cry for an immediate answer to his prayer was understandable.

Sometimes prayer is presented without words by the very motions of our bodies; bended knees and lifted hands are evidences of earnest, expectant prayer. Whatever form David's prayer might take, his desire was that it would be accepted by God.

Now David makes a bold request: He wants his humble cries and prayers to be regarded as highly by the Lord as the morning and evening sacrifices of the holy place. But this prayer is not too bold, for the Lord values spiritual things higher than ceremonial things; the offerings of our lips are more acceptable sacrifices than the offerings of the stall.

Psalm 141:1–2

Guard My Mouth

❯ *Today's Faith Builder:*
    Set a guard, O LORD, over my mouth;
    Keep watch over the door of my lips. (Psalm 141:3)

David's mouth had been used in prayer so it would be sad to have it defiled with lies, pride, or anger. Still, that would likely happen unless it was carefully watched, for these intruders are always eager to enter our lives and take control. David feels that, in spite of his own watchfulness, he may fall into sin, so he begs the Lord to keep him from it.

When Jehovah keeps watch the city is well-guarded; when the Lord guards the mouth the whole person is well-protected. God has made the lips the door of the mouth, but we cannot sufficiently guard that door ourselves, so we ask the Lord to guard it for us.

Oh, that the Lord would both open and shut our lips, for we can do neither right without His guidance and power! In times of persecution, we are especially liable to be too quick to speak or too evasive in speaking, therefore we should ask to be protected by the Lord from this and every form of sin.

How gracious the Lord is! We are honored by being doorkeepers for Him, and yet He is willing to be a doorkeeper for us.

The psalmist is careful of his heart. He who holds the heart is in control of the whole person, but if the tongue and the heart are both in God's care, all is well.

The way the heart inclines, the life soon leans. Unless the fountain of life is kept pure, the streams that flow from it will soon be polluted.

Psalm 141:3–10

Telling God About Our Troubles

> *Today's Faith Builder:*
> I pour out my complaint before Him;
> I declare before Him my trouble. (Psalm 142:2)

This psalm is a prayer offered by David while he was in a cave, one of his many hiding places where he could conceal himself from Saul and his bloodhounds. Had David prayed as much in his palace as he did in his cave, he might never have fallen into the sin which brought such misery to him later.

In the loneliness of the cave he could talk as much as he pleased, so he made its gloomy walls echo with his appeals to heaven. When there was no one in the cave seeking his blood, David, with all his soul, was seeking God.

David dwells on the fact that he spoke aloud in prayer. This was evidently so impressed on his memory that he repeats it. It is good when we find such pleasure in our prayers that we enjoy looking back on them. He who is cheered by the memory of his prayers will pray again.

Consider how this prayer of David grew in scope and depth as he continued speaking. Praying people pray better as they proceed. We do not tell our troubles to the Lord that He may see *them*, but that *we* may see *Him*. It is for our relief, not for His information, that we speak plainly to Him concerning our problems.

We will be helped if we name our troubles in prayer, for this will cause many of them to disappear like ghosts which cannot stand the light of day. Pour out your thoughts before the Lord; tell Him all of your troubles; then, in comparison to His great love for you, they will seem as nothing.

Psalm 142:1–2

A Place to Hide

❯ *Today's Faith Builder:*
> I cried out to You, O LORD:
> I said, "You are my refuge,
> My portion in the land of the living." (Psalm 142:5)

David was a hero but he was feeling weak. He could knock a giant down but he could not keep himself up. Then he looked away from himself and his troubles to God, who is always watching over us and who knows everything, and was comforted in remembering that all was known to his heavenly Friend.

It is good to know that God knows what we do not know. We may lose our heads but God never closes His eyes; our thinking may be clouded but His mind is always clear.

Looking back, the psalmist rejoiced that he had so gracious a Guardian who kept him from unseen dangers. Nothing is hidden from God; no secret snare can harm the one who dwells in the place of the Most High, for he shall abide under the shadow of the Almighty (Ps. 91:1).

Since people would not help David, he was driven to his God. Was not this a gain made out of a loss? Anything that causes us to cry to God is a blessing.

David spoke to God and of God when he said, "You are my refuge." He fled to God alone, hiding himself beneath the wings of the Eternal. He not only believed this, but said it and practiced it. For David to say these things when he was in distress was a great victory. It is easy to boast bravely when all is going well but to speak with confidence when we are afflicted is quite another matter.

Psalm 142:3–7

God Is Faithful and Righteous

> *Today's Faith Builder:*
>   Hear my prayer, O LORD,
>   Give ear to my supplications!
>   In your faithfulness answer me,
>   And in Your righteousness. (Psalm 143:1)

This psalm is like a box of ointment containing different ingredients: sweet and bitter, pungent and precious. It is the cry of an overwhelmed spirit, struggling to rise to full potential.

David called on God to hear his prayer, however feeble and poorly stated it might be. Believers desire to be answered as well as heard; they long to find the Lord faithful to His promise and righteous in defending the cause of justice.

We can be grateful that our safety and our best interests in all things are in the care of our righteous Lord. Since God is faithful and righteous, we are protected from danger on all sides. These are active attributes of God and assure the answering of any prayer which it would be right to answer. Requests which do not appeal to either God's faithfulness or righteousness would not be for the glory of God to answer, for they would contain desires for things unpromised and unrighteous.

David had prayed for an audience at the mercy seat, not at the judgment seat. Though without guilt before men, he could not claim innocence before God. Even though he knew he was the Lord's servant, he did not claim perfection or plead his own merit, for even as a servant of God he considered himself unprofitable (Luke 17:10). If this is the prayer of a humble servant of the Lord, what should the pleading of a sinner be?

Psalm 143:1–4

December 21

Remembering Better Days

> *Today's Faith Builder:*
> I remember the days of old;
> I meditate on all Your works;
> I muse on the work of Your hands. (Psalm 143:5)

When we see nothing new to cheer us, let us remember old blessings. Once we had happy days of deliverance and joy and thanksgiving; why not again? Jehovah rescued His people in the past, why should He not do so again? We have a rich past to look back on; we have sunny memories, sacred memories, satisfactory memories, and these are flowers for the bees of faith to visit to make honey for present use.

When my own works reproach me, God's works refresh me. We ought to take a wide view of all the works of God, for they work together for good and are worthy of prayerful study (Rom. 8:28).

Creation had been the book in which the psalmist had read of the wisdom and goodness of the Lord. He repeats his study of the page of nature and finds it a balm for his wounds, a prescription for solving his problems. He chases away gloom from his soul by holy communion with God.

David was eager for fellowship with God. His thoughts of God kindled burning desires in him and these led to fervent expressions of his inward longings. As the soil cracks and yawns, opening its mouth in silent pleadings, so did David's soul thirst after God.

No heavenly shower had refreshed him. His soul felt parched and dry; nothing would make him content but the presence of his God. If he could but feel the presence of His Lord, his thirst would be replaced with peace and joy.

Psalm 143:5–12

Why Does God Care About Us?

> *Today's Faith Builder:*
> Lord, what is man, that You take knowledge of him?
> Or the son of man, that you are mindful of him? (Psalm 144:3)

With all his strength David blesses the God of his strength. Not only does the Lord give strength to His people, but He is their strength. Strength is theirs because God is theirs. God is full of power and He becomes the power of those who trust Him.

What a contrast there is between our Lord and us. This thought moves the psalmist to compare the glorious sufficiency of God to the insignificance of man and cries, "Lord, what is man?"

What is man in the presence of the infinite God? To what can we compare him? Certainly he is not fit to be the rock of our confidence; he is too feeble and too fickle to rely on. The psalmist wonders why God would stoop to know him.

God knows His people intimately, always watching over them carefully. He foreknew them in love and He will continue to know and accept them forever.

Why is this? What has man done to deserve such love and care? This is an unanswerable question. Only infinite, condescending love can account for God stooping to be the friend of man, making him the child of eternal love, His own next of kin.

How is it that the eternal God should care so much for mortal man, who begins to die as soon as he begins to live? David trusts in God and finds Him everything; then he wonders how the great God takes notice of him.

Psalm 144:1–4

Songs and Prayers

> *Today's Faith Builder:*

I will sing a new song to You, O God;
On a harp of ten strings I will sing praises to You. (Psalm 144:9)

Fired with fresh enthusiasm, David decided to compose a new song that would be unlike any other; it would be all and altogether for his Lord. He would tune his best instruments and sing his best songs. His hand would unite with his tongue in truthful praise.

In his many battles, David would have perished had not God preserved him. He escaped death because of the delivering hand of God. Because of God's faithfulness in sparing his life, David expects the blessings of God to continue and prays for them to fall on all the families of Israel.

Where there are happy households there must be bountiful provision for them, for famine brings misery even when love abounds. When God answers our prayers and our provision is plentiful, we ought to be joyfully giving thanks and worshiping our Provider.

These verses may also be applied to a prospering church, where the converts are growing and spiritual increase brings joy to the entire congregation. There, minister and workers serve with holy vigor and the people are happy and united. May the Lord make it so in all of our churches.

The heart and soul of happiness lies in people being right with God. Those who worship the happy God become happy people, then even if they do not have temporal blessings they have something better; those who do not have the silver of earth may have the gold of heaven, which is much more valuable.

Psalm 144:5–15

Great Praise for Our Great God!

❯ *Today's Faith Builder:*

Great is the LORD, and greatly to be praised;
And His greatness is unsearchable. (Psalm 145:3)

David had blessed God many times in other psalms, but he regarded this one as his crown jewel of praise. We cannot offer David's praise to God, for only David could do that, but we may take this psalm as a model. Let each Christian present his own praise to the Lord. What a rich variety of praise will then be presented to Him!

David as God's king adores God as his King. It is good when the Lord's royalty arouses our loyalty and our spirit is moved to magnify His majesty.

To bless God is to praise Him with a personal affection for Him. David declares that he will offer every form of praise and that his praise will never end. Our praise of God will be as eternal as the God we praise.

Worship should be like its object: great praise for our great God. There is no part of Jehovah's greatness that is not worthy of great praise. No chorus is too loud, no orchestra too large, no psalm too lofty for praising the Lord of Hosts.

All the great minds of the centuries would not be enough to search out the unsearchable riches of God. He is past finding out and deserves more praise than we can offer to Him.

Let us praise God before our children and never cause them to think that serving God makes life unhappy. Praising the Lord enlarges the heart and as it grows our minds grow with it. Let us all delight to speak lovingly of our Lord.

Psalm 145:1–10

God Lifts Up Those Who Are Down

> *Today's Faith Builder:*
>> The LORD upholds all who fall,
>> And raises up all who are bowed down. (Psalm 145:14)

He who reigns in glorious majesty lifts up and holds up those who fall. He is always doing this; He is Jehovah upholding.

God chooses the fallen and the falling as objects of His gracious help. The fallen may be shunned by us but the Lord looks tenderly on those who are the least regarded by others.

The falling ones among us are too liable to be pushed down by the strong; their timidity and dependence makes them the victims of the proud and domineering. To them also the Lord gives His upholding help. Our Lord loves to reverse things: He puts down the lofty and lifts up the lowly.

Many are depressed and cannot lift up their heads with courage or their hearts with comfort, but God cheers them. He strengthens those who are bent low with their daily load.

Think of the Infinite One bowing to lift up the bowed and His stooping to be leaned on by those who are ready to fall. The Lord is kind to all who are afflicted.

As children look to a father for all they need, the creatures of earth look to God, the all-sufficient Provider. They wait and God gives. Like a flock of sheep the creatures stand around the Lord as their great Shepherd; all eyes are to His hand expecting to receive their food, and they are not disappointed. If we wait on the Lord for pardon, renewing, or whatever else we need, we will not wait in vain. The hand of grace is never closed to seeking sinners.

Psalm 145:11–21

December 26

Lifelong Praise

> *Today's Faith Builder:*
> While I live I will praise the LORD;
> I will sing praises to my God while I have my being. (Psalm 146:2)

We are now among the Hallelujah Psalms. The rest of our journey lies through the Delectable Mountains. All is praise to the close of the book. The key is high-pitched; the music is on the high-sounding cymbals. Oh, for a heart full of joyful gratitude that we may run and leap and glorify God, even as these psalms do!

With holy awe let us pronounce the word "Hallelujah" and think of it as a call to ourselves and all others to adore the God of the whole earth. Let us all immediately unite in holy praise!

The psalmist declares he will practice what he has preached. He will be the leader of the choir he has assembled. It is poor business to exhort others to praise and then not set the example in praising God ourselves. Come heart, mind, and thought! Come my whole being, my soul, my all, be all aflame with joyful adoration! Lift up the song! Praise the Lord!

I will not live here forever. This mortal life will end in death; but while it lasts I will praise the Lord my God. I cannot tell how long or short my life will be, but every hour of it will be given to the praises of my God. While I live I'll love and while I breathe I'll bless.

When I reach heaven I will not only praise, but sing praises. Here I have to sigh and praise, but there I will only sing and praise. We cannot be too firm in our holy resolve to praise God, for the chief end of living is to glorify God and enjoy Him forever.

Psalm 146

The Healer of Broken Hearts

> *Today's Faith Builder:*
>> He heals the brokenhearted
>> And binds up their wounds. (Psalm 147:3)

This is an especially remarkable song; it celebrates the greatness and goodness of God. The God of Israel is praised for caring for the sorrowing, the insignificant, and forgotten. The psalmist finds great joy in praising One who is so gracious.

The Lord is not only a builder but a healer; He restores broken hearts as well as broken walls. He cares for the sick, the sorrowful, the wretched, and the wounded! He walks the hospitals as the good Physician! His deep sympathy with mourners reveals His goodness.

Few seek fellowship with those who are depressed, but Jehovah chooses their company and stays with them to heal and comfort them. He heals broken hearts by applying the ointment of grace and soft bandages of love; He binds up the bleeding wounds of those convicted of sin. This is our compassionate God.

The Lord is always healing and binding, and this is not new work for Him; He has been doing it through the ages and is not tired of His work of love. Come, broken hearts; come to the Physician who never fails to heal; uncover your wounds to Him who so tenderly treats them.

From worlds to wounds is a distance which only infinite compassion can bridge. He who is a surgeon for wounded hearts commands the heavenly host and reads the roll call of suns and stars and planets.

O Lord, it is good to praise You as ruling the stars, but it is also pleasant to adore You as the healer of broken hearts!

Psalm 147:1–10

December 28

The People Who Please God

> *Today's Faith Builder:*
The Lord takes pleasure in those who fear Him,
In those who hope in His mercy. (Psalm 147:11)

While the Lord takes no pleasure in physical prowess, spiritual qualities in His people bring the Lord delight. The fear which He approves is reverential trust in Him, and the hope which He accepts is hope in His mercy. It is a striking thought that God is not only at peace with those who trust in Him but that He even finds comfort and joy in their company.

Who are these favored people in whom Jehovah takes pleasure? Some of them are the least in His family, who have never risen beyond hoping and fearing. Others of them are more fully developed in faith, but still blend both fear and hope; they fear God with holy awe and loving reverence and they also hope for forgiveness and the blessings of God because of His mercy.

As a father takes pleasure in His children, the Lord takes pleasure in those who have been born again and who evidence it by fear and hope. They fear, for they are sinners; they hope because God is merciful. They fear Him, for He is great; they hope in Him, for He is good. Their fear sobers their hope, their hope brightens their fear; God takes pleasure in them both in their trembling and in their rejoicing.

There is a rich cause for praise in this special feature of the Lord's character. As people are known by the nature of the things which give them pleasure, the Lord is known by the fact that He takes pleasure in the righteous, even though that righteousness may yet be only in its initial, infant stage of fear and hope.

Psalm 147:11–20

High Praise

❯ *Today's Faith Builder:*
Praise the Lord!
Praise the Lord from the heavens;
Praise Him in the heights! (Psalm 148:1)

Here is a song of nature and grace. As a flash of lightning flames through space and clothes both heaven and earth in glory, the adoration of the Lord in this psalm lights up all the universe and causes it to glow with the radiance of praise. Understanding it requires a heart on fire with reverent love for the Lord.

No place is too high for the praises of the most High. Heavens and heights become higher and more heavenly as they resound with the praises of Jehovah. Is He not worthy of all possible praise? Pour it out in full volume before Him.

The sun and moon, as joint rulers of day and night, are paired in praise. They are closely associated in the universal call to worship. The sun has its special way of glorifying the Great Father of lights, and the moon has its own unique method of reflecting His brightness. There is perpetual adoration of the Lord in the skies; it varies with night and day but will continue while the sun and moon endure.

There are so many stars that no one can count them, yet not one of them refuses to praise its Maker. If we cannot be the sun or moon let us be one of the "stars of light" and our every twinkling be to the honor of our Lord.

As the highest of the highest, so the best of the best are to praise the Lord. If we could climb as high above the heavens as the heavens are above the earth, we would cry: "Praise the Lord!"

Psalm 148

A New Song for New People

> *Today's Faith Builder:*
> Praise the LORD!
> Sing to the LORD a new song,
> And His praise in the assembly of saints. (Psalm 149:1)

This is "a new song," evidently intended for the new creation and people who are of new heart. It is the kind of song that we may sing at the coming of the Lord, when the new dispensation will bring an overthrow of the wicked and honor to all the saints.

Praise the Lord, you chosen people, whom the Lord has made His saints! You have praised Him before, praise Him again; praise Him forever! Lift up your song to the Lord with new zeal and fresh delight.

Sing, for it is the most natural way to express reverent praise. Sing a newly composed hymn, for you now have a new knowledge of God. His mercies are new every morning (Lam. 3:23), His deliverances are new in every night of sorrow; let your gratitude and thanksgivings be new also.

Our singing should be to the Lord. The songs we sing should be of Him and to Him, "for of Him and through Him and to Him are all things" (Rom. 11:36). New songs will add variety to our expressions of praise. Sadly, many are more fond of making new complaints than new psalms.

Our new songs should be composed in Jehovah's honor; our newest thoughts should be of Him. Joy and rejoicing are to be the special characteristics of the new song. God is the source of our joy. And we ought to always be glad in Him.

Psalm 149

Praise the Lord!

❯ *Today's Faith Builder:*
Let everything that has breath praise the LORD.
Praise the LORD! (Psalm 150:6)

We have now reached the last summit of the mountain chain of Psalms. It rises high into the clear blue and its brow is bathed in the sunlight of heavenly worship. The poet-prophet is full of inspiration and enthusiasm and cries with burning words, "Praise Him, Praise the Lord!"

The call here is to all in earth and heaven to praise the Lord. Should we not all declare the glory of Him for whose glory we are and were created?

Jehovah, the one true God, should be the one object of our adoration. To give the least particle of His honor to another is shameful treason; to refuse to give praise to Him is heartless robbery.

Praise begins at home. In God's own house pronounce His praise. In His church below and in His courts above hallelujahs should be continually presented. Whenever we gather for holy purposes, we should praise the Lord our God.

Let all who have breath praise the Lord! He gave them breath, let them breathe His praise. All breath comes from Him, therefore let it be used for Him! What a day it will be when all things in all places unite to glorify the one only living and true God! This will be the final triumph of His church!

This psalm and the book of Psalms ends with a glowing word of adoration. Let us pause and worship the Lord our God. Hallelujah!

Psalm 150